D0031910

THE COMPLETE PEMBROKE WELSH CORGI

Ch. Leonine Leprechaun head-study painted by Marjorie Walker, one of this country's earliest Pembroke breeders.
Courtesy of C. Kruger, DVM

Ch. Redclyffe's Tonic of Trafran, whelped December 5, 1973, owner: Mary Ann Parker. Breeder: Travis Shackelford and Joan Maskie. A Best in Show winning double grandson of Ch. Rozavel Field Marshall, son of Eng. Ch. Kaytop Marshall. Puppies are by Field Marshall out of a Kaytop Marshall daughter.

THE COMPLETE

Pembroke Welsh Corgi

*by Mary Gay Sargent
and Deborah S. Harper*

First Edition

**HOWELL
BOOK HOUSE**
New York

Howell Book House
Macmillan Publishing Company
866 Third Avenue, New York, NY 10022

Collier Macmillan Canada, Inc.
1200 Eglinton Avenue East, Suite 200
Don Mills, Ontario M3C 3N1

Library of Congress Cataloging in Publication Data

Sargent, Mary Gay.
    The complete Pembroke Welsh corgi.

    Bibliography: p. 285
    1. Pembroke Welsh corgi.   I. Harper, Deborah S.,
joint author.   II. Title.
SF429.P33S27   636.7′3   79-18573
ISBN 0-87605-224-3

Macmillan books are available at special discounts for bulk purchases for sales promotions, premiums, fund-raising, or educational use. For details, contact:

Special Sales Director
Macmillan Publishing Company
866 Third Avenue
New York, NY 10022

10

Printed in the United States of America

Contents

Ch. Penrick Flewellyn, CDX, a double Symphony granddaughter, and the dam of six champions. *Ludwig*

Ch. Rupertbear of Wey (Bryherdene Black Prince of Wey ex Dollychick of Wey), whelped March 3, 1971, breeder: Mrs. K. Butler, owner: Mrs. Herman Bohr, Jr. He is a BIS and multiple Group winner, and was BB at the 1976 PWCCA Specialty show.   *Booth*

Ch. Tindervale Startrek (Eng. Ch. Penmoel Minstrel ex Tindervale Lees Cameilla), whelped March 17, 1976, breeder: Mrs. B. Snelling, owner: Mrs. William B. Long. Best of Breed at the 1977 PWCCA Specialty, he is a well-known Eastern Group and BIS winner.

Mary Gay Sargent with Gaygarth Piped Aboard

Deborah S. Harper with Walborah's Leaf Frolic

About the Authors

MARY GAY SARGENT first met the Pembroke Welsh Corgi in 1949 when she worked for Mrs. Van Beynum's Willow Farm Kennels. In 1952 she acquired her first Pembroke, Willow Farm Bundle, and became totally captivated by the breed's innate charm.

Miss Sargent's association with Willow Farm continued until 1960. Here she developed an intense knowledge of the breed, its background and unique personality.

In 1963 she began work as a kennel assistant for the world-renowned Cote de Neige Kennels of the late Marjorie Butcher. Although she only worked eight months at Cote de Neige, she remained closely associated with Mrs. Butcher until the latter's death in 1973. Under Mrs. Butcher's guidance, Miss Sargent gained a wealth of additional invaluable experience with every facet of keeping, breeding and showing the Pembroke. Today she is one of the world's most respected Pembroke authorities.

The knowledge gained at Willow Farm, Cote de Neige and from her own Gaygarth Pembrokes has proven an asset to the entire breed. Miss Sargent's contributions to the fancy are numerous, her accomplishments admirable and her energies amazingly prolific.

A member of the Pembroke Welsh Corgi Club of America since 1961 and a Board member since 1967, she became Second Vice-President in 1975 and is currently First Vice-President. She writes the bimonthly Pembroke column in AKC's *Pure-Bred Dogs—American Kennel Gazette* and once wrote a regular obedience column for the *Pembroke Welsh Corgi Newsletter,* a quarterly publication of the PWCCA.

Mary Gay Sargent was among those who prepared *An Illustrated Study of the Pembroke Welsh Corgi Standard.* This book, published by the PWCCA is considered one of the finest works of its kind. Miss Sargent's judging debut came in 1965 when she did the Sweepstakes at the PWCCA Specialty. Since 1973 she has been regularly approved and has judged at some of America's most important shows: Westminster, Trenton, Philadelphia, Golden Gate PWCF and PWCC of Southern California.

In addition to her achievements in the conformation sphere, she has done well with Pembrokes in obedience. Her second dog, Willow Farm Beaver, CDX, was an enthusiastic worker that was trained for Utility and certified for Tracking.

The author joined the Port Chester Obedience Training Club in 1961 and held several offices in the course of her membership. In 1968 and 1969 she was editor of the Club's newsletter *Sit 'N' Stay.*

Miss Sargent is a graduate of Mount Holyoke College, class of 1960, with a B.A. in Zoology and is a senior research technician with Sloan-Kettering Institute for Cancer Research.

Scientist, administrator, breeder, exhibitor, trainer, judge—Mary Gay Sargent brings all these excellent qualifications to the effort on the pages that follow.

DEBORAH S. HARPER acquired her first Pembroke Welsh Corgi in 1960. The first time she showed him, at the 1963 PWCCA Specialty, he was one of the main winners. The bug bit deep that day and Deborah Harper is thriving in the after-effects.

Mrs. Harper is the current Secretary of the PWCCA, a position she has held since 1970.

A busy wife and mother, Deborah Harper limits the number of dogs she keeps to four adults at a time. Even with this restriction, five of the seven Corgis she has owned have become champions. Four of these were homebreds and three came from one litter! To her greater credit, Mrs. Harper handles her dogs herself.

She has judged a number of Specialty matches and in 1978 had the honor of judging Sweepstakes at the Lakeshore Pembroke Welsh Corgi Club Specialty.

The authors first met in 1960 and have been good friends ever since. How well their knowledge and talents are blended into this masterful work is proven by the reading.

12

Preface

Mrs. MARJORIE BUTCHER, owner of the Cote de Neige Kennels and breeder of some of the world's finest Pembroke Welsh Corgis, died before ever getting to a project she had always wanted to do someday. That was to write a book about the Pembroke Welsh Corgi in America.

Several years before Marjorie's death in September 1973, Howell Book House contacted her about writing *The Complete Pembroke Welsh Corgi*. Marjorie was extremely interested and asked me if I would collaborate with her in the writing of such a book.

In that Marjorie and I, with other members of the Pembroke Welsh Corgi Club of America Standard Visualization Committee were in the process of starting work on the much needed *Illustrated Study of the Pembroke Welsh Corgi Standard*, the idea of writing the book was set aside for the time being.

Unfortunately for all concerned, Marjorie died before the work on the illustrated Standard could be completed and before the book could be written, a book the depth of which very few authors writing on the breed in this country, other than Marjorie, would be able to approach.

Some while after Marjorie's death, I was asked by Howell Book House if I would consider undertaking the project of writing *The Complete Pembroke Welsh Corgi*. To help Marjorie with the work had been a fine idea. But the thought of doing it by myself without the aid of Marjorie's vast experience and her knack of making it all come alive on paper was overwhelming. I was afraid to say "yes" but I felt somehow I would be letting Marjorie down to do otherwise.

I was concerned at the onset that my lack of available time in which to work on the book would present problems, and it did, indeed, prove to be an insurmountable obstacle. Fortunately, Mrs. Wallace Harper, Jr. kindly came to my rescue and agreed to help me finish the work on the manuscript. Debbie has made vast contributions to every aspect of the work, and *The Complete Pembroke Welsh Corgi* is considerably richer for her efforts.

MARY GAY SARGENT

Eng. Ch. Barngremlin of Braxentra was a line-bred Zephyr grandson, breeder-owner: Miss V. Palmer-Cummings. He was the all-time top British BIS-winning Pembroke and Pembroke Welsh Corgi of the Year in 1963 and 1964. *C.M. Cooke & Son*

Foreword

THE PEMBROKE WELSH CORGI has captured the hearts of many people all over the world for its neat compact build, gay affectionate temperament and great intelligence. Having judged Corgis in the United States several times during the last twenty years, I have found it interesting to see how they have spread over the country. Starting in the East in the 1930s, Corgi popularity grew and the breed travelled quickly to the West Coast and the Midwest. Now the Corgi is to be found in nearly every part of the United States, which speaks well for the charm and character of our favourite breed. While the Corgi has gained steadily in popularity, it has never reached the top of the poll. I consider this a very good thing, as nothing ruins a breed more quickly than to become too popular. Overpopularity leads to indiscriminate breeding by people who do not have the good of the breed at heart.

Mary Gay Sargent and Debbie Harper are two of the most dedicated Pembroke Corgi enthusiasts I know, and we are lucky to have such knowledgeable authors for this new book on our breed. Mary Gay and Debbie have served on the Board and committees of the Pembroke Welsh Corgi Club of America in various capacities for many years, and they have both raised and shown Corgis with success. Mary Gay is a very well-respected breed judge.

In 1972 the PWCCA drew up a new and very explicit Standard for the breed. Following the revision, work was started on an *Illustrated Study of the Pembroke Welsh Corgi Standard*. Mary Gay and the rest of the committee completed this project begun by the late Marjorie Butcher of the famous Cote de Neige Kennels. The Standard with some material from the illustrated booklet

15

will be found in *The Complete Pembroke Welsh Corgi*, a book that is a "must" for all Corgi lovers, be they serious breeders and exhibitors or pet owners.

The Complete Pembroke Welsh Corgi is a most welcome addition to all "Corgi libraries." It is so comprehensive, covering all aspects, from the Corgi's early history to management of breeding stock, puppy rearing and training, care of the dogs in old age, and coverage of the Corgi for obedience and its original job of herding cattle. Much of interest is to be found in the pedigrees. The abundance of excellent illustrations, picturing some of the very early Corgis and others right up to the present day champions, shows us how the breed has become standardized for type and size over the years.

I feel sure *The Complete Pembroke Welsh Corgi*, researched with such care and accuracy by Mary Gay and Debbie, will find its way to pride of place on many Corgi owners' bookshelves.

PAT L. CURTIES

(The authors and publisher are deeply honored to have this Foreword written by Miss Pat L. Curties of the world-renowned Lees Kennels of Horsham, Sussex, England. Miss Curties has bred many of the world's finest Pembrokes and is one of the leading authorities on the breed. A championship show judge, she has influenced the Pembroke's fortunes for many years. Her opinion as a judge has been as eagerly sought around the world as has the cream of her breeding program. She is, in every regard, a peerless authority on the Pembroke and one of its staunchest friends.)

Ch. Cormanby Cavalier, a home-bred son of Ch. Cormanby Commotion. Owner: Mrs. Barbara Hedberg.   *Tauskey*

16

Acknowledgements

THE WRITING OF THIS BOOK would not have been possible without the wholehearted assistance we have received from numerous people, regretfully too many to thank individually here.

We are specially grateful to Phyl Young for providing the photo series on puppies and numerous other photographs which appear throughout the book. Barbara Spengler, too, has been tremendously helpful in taking photographs for the book and in preparing copies of photos for us when the originals had to be returned immediately. We thank Mrs. Gladys Orlowski for making Mr. Orlowski's collection of Corgi scrapbooks available to us in our search for information and photographs. We are indebted to the Welsh Corgi League for their permission to draw on material presented in their League Handbooks and to the Pembroke Welsh Corgi Club of America for permission to use material from the *Pembroke Welsh Corgi Newsletter,* the *Pembroke Welsh Corgis in America* Handbooks and *An Illustrated Study of the Pembroke Welsh Corgi Standard.* Mrs. Barbara Ludowici has been helpful in sending information on Corgis in Australia, and Mrs. Lilian Timmins kindly prepared an album on the Corgi in Canada for our use. Tasha Tudor's charming drawing of a Corgi's special grooming session will be treasured forever. We also wish to acknowledge the permission granted by the Lisa Studios, Ltd., for the inclusion of the two photographs of members of the British royal family with their Corgis.

As is inherent in any book of this nature, many people and many important dogs, unfortunately, have had to go unmentioned. As Corgi fanciers, we all are deeply indebted to those whose industrious efforts have advanced breed type while maintaining the century-old character of the breed. They have preserved for us one of the most satisfying companions known to man, the Pembroke Welsh Corgi.

SCOTLAND

Lancaster

York

Leeds

Manchester

Chester

WALES

ENGLAND

Cardigan

Carmarthen

Cirencester

Pembroke

Cardiff

London

Reading

Wiltshire

Winchester

This diagrammatic map of England and Wales is correlated with the early history of the Welsh Corgi. Note the distance of Lancaster, the area where the Lancashire Heeler has existed for many years, from Pembrokeshire and Cardiganshire. Also of interest is the great distance travelled by Welsh farmers and their Corgis when they drove cattle to London.

1

Origins of the

Pembroke Welsh Corgi

JUST HOW or when the Pembroke Welsh Corgi and his northern cousin, the Cardigan Welsh Corgi, came to be no one knows. The Welsh people will tell you the sturdy, little Corgi has been a familiar sight watching over the cattle and guarding the homestead in Wales for many, many centuries.

With the Corgi seeming to have been in existence in Wales forever, it is not surprising that many legends and fireside stories about Corgis were passed from one generation of Welshmen to the next.

One such legend provides a charming tale for the curious of how the Corgi came to live in the hills of southwest Wales. According to the legend, two young children out tending the family's cattle on the king's land found a pair of puppies which they thought were little foxes. When the children took the puppies home, they were told by the menfolk that the little dogs were a gift from the fairies. The "wee folk" of Welsh legend used the small dogs either to pull their carriages or as fairy steeds. As the fox-like puppies grew, they learned to help their human companions watch over the cattle, a task which was to be the duty of their Corgi descendants for many centuries to come. Should anyone doubt the truth of the legend, the present-day Welsh Corgi still bears the marks over his shoulders of the little saddle used by his fairy riders.

Possible Origin

Numerous breeds have, at one time or another, had their ancestry traced back to the dogs of ancient Egypt and the Corgi is no exception. It has been claimed by the occasional zealous writer that dogs portrayed in the mural decorations of Egyptian tombs are clearly of Welsh Corgi type. And though most breed authorities have dismissed the theory as grasping at straws, it has been written that the small, short-coated dogs with prick ears and pointed muzzles depicted on the famous statue of Anubis, the Egyptian God of the Setting Sun, were direct ancestors of the Welsh Corgi.

What has been considered to be more plausible evidence of the Corgi's antiquity is found in the Laws of Hywel Dda, or Howell the Good, King of South Wales. The laws were codified in about 920 A.D. from earlier, unwritten Welsh law. Among the ancient laws was one which placed a value on the various types of dogs according to the work they performed. No, not for taxation yet, but rather for purposes of redress should an animal be killed or stolen. The shepherd's or herdsman's cur was said to be of the same value as an ox, providing it was proven to be a genuine herder or drover, making it of more value than either the watch cur or the house cur.

Whether or not the herdsman's cur and the Corgi were one and the same is open to speculation. Those who contend that the Corgi was, indeed, the herdsman's cur base their conclusion on the belief that the Corgi is the only breed of cattle dog to have been established in Wales.

The tenth century homesteader in the unyielding Welsh hills had to struggle to secure what at best would be a meager existence for his family. Most likely the poorer farmers could not afford to maintain a number of dogs, each with a specialized function. Whatever dog the farmer kept, whether bred primarily as a bird dog, a ratter or a cattle dog, had to be a jack-of-all-trades.

Demonstrating the frugality of the Welsh farmers even in modern times are the dogs of the various sporting breeds which have been pressed into use as general purpose farm dogs in Wales. Reports are not uncommon of the Welsh Springer Spaniel, a breed noted for its excellence in the field, and of the fine terrier breeds developed in Wales, successfully working livestock.

While it is entirely possible that the early ancestors of the Welsh Corgi were included in the classification of herdsman's cur, the term itself most likely referred to any dog who proved to be a useful cattle dog, regardless of type or heritage. Tempting though it may be, we cannot look to the Laws of Hywel Dda for valid evidence of the antiquity of the Corgi breeds.

Lloyd-Thomas' Theory of Separate Origin

Popular opinion would have us believe the Pembroke and Cardigan Welsh Corgi originated as two entirely separate and unrelated breeds; the Pembroke being a member of the large Spitz family and the Cardigan evolving from the Dachshund or Tekel class. Members of the Spitz family, such as the Schipperke, the Pomeranian, the Keeshond and the Samoyed, are characterized by prick ears, a pointed muzzle and a curly tail. The Tekel group, which includes the Dachshund and the Basset Hound, are essentially long-bodied, deep-chested, short-legged dogs, heavier in muzzle than typical Spitz types.

The probable source of the separate origin theory seems to be a series of articles written by W. Lloyd-Thomas on the Cardigan Welsh Corgi, which appeared in issues of *Pure-Bred Dogs—American Kennel Gazette* in the Fall of 1935. Lloyd-Thomas, a native of Cardiganshire, South Wales and a recognized authority on Welsh farm dogs, put forth the theory that ancestors of the Cardigan Corgi were brought into Wales from central Europe by invading Celtic tribes about 1200 B.C.

Satisfied that the early Pembroke Corgi possessed none of the identifying Tekel characteristics of the Cardigan Corgi, but, instead, strongly resembled the members of the Spitz family, Lloyd-Thomas concurred with what he termed the "tradition" that the Pembroke Corgi was introduced into Wales by Flemish weavers in 1107 A.D.

Eventually a striking similarity in appearance between the two Corgi breeds developed. Lloyd-Thomas attributed the development of stockier, lower-to-ground, heavier-headed Pembroke strains to occasional crossings of the Pembroke with the "original" Corgi, as he preferred to call the Corgi from Cardiganshire. We are told in his account that Corgi puppies brought down by enterprising young lads from Bronant, a district in the heart of the Cardiganshire hills, were sold for pocket money to the farmers in South Wales. And it was the influence of these dogs that brought about the change in Pembroke type.

Lloyd-Thomas stoutly maintained that the Corgi traffic never went in reverse. That is, the early Pembrokeshire Corgis were never seen in the Cardiganshire hills. In fact, we are told no dog other than the original Corgi was known in the Bronant district until at least the late 1850s.

The Cardigan Corgi's gradual refinement and somewhat diminished size from that of the original Corgi, along with a change of ear carriage from a drooping ear to an erect, slightly hooded ear, plus changes in coat quality, all supposedly were brought about by the influence of breeds other than the Pembroke Corgi, breeds which began to appear on Cardiganshire farms during the last quarter of the nineteenth century.

Until about 1875, Welsh farmers grazed their cattle on unfenced Crown or common land. Over the years, families came to regard certain areas of the common grazing land as being theirs, and other farmers' cattle on the particular parcel of land were trespassers. Mr. Lloyd-Thomas was of the opinion that the original Corgi was not a herding dog but rather was a "courser" used to chase trespassing cattle out of a claimed grazing area. Anyone who has watched a modern Corgi on a dead-run chase after a squirrel trespassing at the bird feeder will be able to picture exactly how a coursing

This Swedish Vallhund bitch, Litton of Duncliffe of Ormareon, a current winner in the English show ring, illustrates the similarity between the Vallhund and Pembroke Corgi as modeled by Ch. Larklain's Firebright.

Ch. Larklain's Firebright, whelped March 13, 1961 (Ch. Red Envoy of Brome ex Larklains Token). Breeder: Mrs. E. Swinney Erganbright. Owner: Robert Hurst.   *Bennett Associates*

Corgi set off about his task. The original Corgi's failure to adapt as a herding dog was said to be his undoing, for once the grazing land was fenced, the Welsh farmer needed a dog to take the cattle to and from pasture, not a dog whose only talent was to scare off trespassing stock.

Farmers in the Cardiganshire hills soon looked to Collies and Herders to help them manage their cattle. And it was through subsequent crossings of the original Corgi with herding dogs, such as the Red Herder, the Brindle Herder, the Scotch Collie and the early Pomeranian that the Corgi, of which Lloyd-Thomas writes, changed in appearance. Thus the breed came to resemble more closely the Corgi of southwest Wales, the Pembroke Corgi.

Unfortunately, what could only be theory about the separate origins of the two Welsh Corgi breeds has become accepted as established fact, especially here in America. While Lloyd-Thomas wrote convincingly about the history of the Corgi, it should be noted that his observations were based on his own memories and on the recollections of the aged Cardiganshire hillmen with whom he conversed. At no point in his *Gazette* articles, did he substantiate his claims with references to earlier source material. At best, his theory was based on actual observation of the Corgi breeds over an eighty year period with stories and descriptions passed on from another generation or so of the Bronant crofters. The time span involved covered but a very short period of the Corgi's history, if the original Corgi was introduced into Wales in 1200 B.C.

The many unanswered questions and unresolved discrepancies raised by the separate origin theory make its acceptance difficult, if not impossible, for many Corgi enthusiasts.

Hubbard's Theory of Scandinavian and Flemish Influence

Clifford Hubbard, well-known for his in-depth study of the two Corgi breeds, proposed a rather different theory of origin for the Pembroke Corgi. He dates the beginnings of the breed back to the ninth and tenth centuries when Scandinavian Vikings invaded coastal regions of Wales from Anglesey to the south of Pembrokeshire. According to Hubbard's theory, the Vikings, who eventually settled in South Wales, brought with them a Swedish cattle dog known as the *Vallhund* or *Vastergotland Spitz*. The Vallhund, remarkably similar in appearance to the Pembroke Corgi, was very likely crossed with the native Welsh herd dog, the Corgi. It was perhaps at this point in time that two distinctly different Corgi types began to develop: the original short-legged, long-bodied, deep-chested dog with droopy ears remained as the Cardigan-shire Corgi, while the Corgi of the Pembrokeshire region took on many of the Spitz-like characteristics of the Vallhund.

Hubbard further postulated that the Spitz characteristics seen in the Pembroke Corgi as a result of the Vallhund influence were subsequently accentuated by crosses with dogs thought to be either Schipperkes or early Pomeranians. These came to South Wales with Flemish weavers when they were settled in Pembrokeshire in about 1107 A.D. during the reign of Henry I.

Although they came to Pembrokeshire as craftsmen, the Flemish weavers were agrarian by nature and set about establishing small farms patterned after those left behind in their homeland. It is not unreasonable to assume that farm dogs accompanied the livestock known to have been brought into Wales by the Flemish immigrants.

The Flemish dogs probably descended from small Spitz dogs developed during the Stone Age by Neolithic dwellers in the lake settlements of Switzerland, Hungary and parts of Russia. The northern Spitz breeds were noted for being clever, capable herding dogs. If the Pembrokeshire farmers found the offspring of outcrosses between native Corgis and the newly introduced Flemish dogs to be proficient cattle dogs as well as bright, attractive companions with their foxy faces and erect ears, it is not surprising that the new strain was purposely continued.

Mr. Hubbard, himself, recognized the difficulties involved in the theory of the influence of the Vallhund on the development of the Pembroke Corgi. Not the least of which is the fact that the present-day Vallhund, commonly found in the southwestern provinces of Sweden, is virtually unknown in Norway or Denmark where the invading Norsemen originated.

Another point referred to by Hubbard is that of color. The Vallhund is typically wolf-gray, a color which is found in other Spitz breeds such as the Keeshond and the Norwegian Elkhound but is not seen in the Corgi. While claiming the dominant red or sable colors of the Flemish dogs obliterated the Vallhund coloring in the Pembroke Corgi, Mr. Hubbard overlooked the matter of color when he used the Lancashire Heeler as another example of a Spitz-like heeling dog which he considered closely related to the Swedish Vallhund.

The Lancashire Heeler, a small black and tan cattle dog, quite similar in appearance to the Corgi, has existed for centuries in northern England. It is said to still persist in the Ormskirk district of Lancashire. The late Miss Eve Forsyth-Forrest, whose Corgis carried the well-known Helarian prefix, believed the existence of the Lancashire Heeler substantiated her theory that the Corgi was the original native dog of Britain. Accordingly, at the time of the Saxon invasions some Britons fled into the depths of the Forest of Elmet, and it was there a pocket of their Corgi-like Lancashire Heelers survived the passing centuries. The suggestion that the early Corgis, both Pembroke and Cardigan, were commonly black and tan in color strengthens the theory of a probable link between the Corgi breeds and the Lancashire Heeler.

The pronounced similarity in appearance, as well as in the instinctive guarding and herding capabilities shared by the Pembroke Corgi and the Swedish Vallhund leaves little doubt that their paths have crossed. Just when and where will most likely remain another matter of conjecture.

Derivation of the Name

What knowledge of the Pembroke Welsh Corgi's earliest history that time, itself, has not buried, the very name "Corgi" has. Not only is the true meaning of the word "corgi' unknown, but it is often impossible to discern, even in present-day writings, whether the references being made are to Pembroke or Cardigan Corgis. The ambiguity makes any effort to trace the history of either breed just that much more frustrating.

Some breed historians believe the term "corgi" is derived from the word "cur" meaning "to watch over." This definition is certainly appropriate for a little dog whose duty for centuries was to watch over the livestock on Welsh homesteads. Others believe that "corgi" was the Celtic word for "dog" and at the time of the Norman Conquest, "corgi" or "curgi" took on the connotation of "cur" or mongrel, as the Normans disdainfully considered all local dogs to be mongrels. In Wales, the name evolved to mean simply any small cattle dog.

In an attempt to uncover the anglicized meaning of "corgi," Clifford Hubbard's own laborious search through sources made available to him at the National Library of Wales and the Dictionary Department of the Board of Celtic Studies led him to agree that the word "corgi" actually meant "cur" or "cur dog." Hubbard found this meaning for *Korgi ne gostoc* in one of the earliest dictionaries, Wyllam Salesbury's *A Dictionary in Englyshe and Welshe,* London, 1574 and a similar definition of "cur" in Spurrell's *Geiriadur Cynaniaethol Seisoneg A Chymraeg,* Caerfyrddin, 1872.

The three types of curs referred to in the ancient Welsh laws, the watch cur, the house cur and the shepherd's or herdsman's cur, suggest that while "corgi" can be interpreted as meaning "cur dog," the term "cur" was not used explicitly to designate the Corgi.

Though the "cur dog" meaning of the word "corgi" seems to be most widely accepted, other possible meanings have been proposed. One such popular interpretation is that "cor" is Welsh for "dwarf," and "gi" is a form of the Welsh word "ci" meaning "dog." Freeman Lloyd, a well-known breed authority and an honorary president of the Welsh Corgi Club of America in the Club's formative years, made good use of the "dwarf dog" theory. He postulated that the Corgi is a miniature of the Welsh Sheepdog, common to the mountainous parts of Wales; or if of mixed descent, the Corgi evolved from a cross of Welsh Sheepdogs and some kind of terrier.

25

Turning the "dwarf dog" interpretation around slightly, others have suggested perhaps it is just as the Welsh legends tell it, and that "corgi" means "dog of the dwarfs."

In the south of Wales, a common endearment, *Y Corgi Bach,* means "you little rascal." Knowing how the Corgi delights in being a lovable, little rascal, it is not surprising that "corgi" and "rascal" came to be colloquial synonyms.

The English name "Heeler," which was applied to both the Cardigan and the Pembroke Corgi, originated from the Corgi's habit of hurrying cattle to and from pasture by nipping at their heels. The Welsh verb meaning "to heel" is *sodli,* and the Welsh farmers frequently referred to the Pembrokeshire Corgi as *Ci Sodli* or in northern Wales, *Ci Sodlu.*

Just when the term "corgi" came into widespread use is not clear. Despite the references to Corgis in early literature, the name "corgi" was supposedly known to very few people even as late as the 1800s. The familiar, short-legged, long-backed cattle dog was known as the "Welsh Cur," and it was under the classification of *Cwn Sodli* (Plural of Ci Sodli), Curs or Heelers that the Corgi was first exhibited at agricultural shows in Wales at the close of the nineteenth century.

Through common usage "corgis" has now become the accepted plural of "corgi," though what is thought by many to be the proper plural form, *corgwyn,* is still seen occasionally. As it is claimed by some Welsh people that the singular and plural forms are one and the same, "corgi," it is possible the use of the different plural forms varied with the district in Wales. The plural spelled with an "e," "corgies," is simply a misspelling and has never been considered to be a correct plural form. The "shire" has been dropped from the names of both Corgi breeds, and in many Corgi circles today we hear the breeds referred to as Pems and Cardis.

Although uncertainties about the derivation and use of the name "corgi" are unlikely to be resolved, perhaps future archaelogical findings, such as the discovery of a complete dog skeleton and skeletal remains of other dogs unearthed during excavations of the Windmill Hill neolithic site in Wiltshire, England, will reveal the true origin of the Pembroke Welsh Corgi. Maybe then we will learn of the actual relationship between the two Corgi types and, in turn, their connection with the seemingly related Vallhund of Sweden and the Lancashire Heeler of northern England.

Until such a time, the incorrigible romantic is at liberty to believe the Welsh Corgi came as a gift from the "wee folk"—a gift of loving sagacity, rich with the sparkle of humor.

2

Early Recorded History

BY THE NINETEENTH CENTURY, with working Welsh farm dogs being tax-exempt, the popularity of the Corgi burgeoned. Scores of Corgis, or Welsh Curs, as they were commonly called, were seen at market places and livestock fairs, especially in the Maenclochog, Pembrokeshire district of South Wales. There were said to be one or two Corgis on every farm in the district at the turn of the century.

Despite the popularity which the Pembroke Welsh Corgi enjoyed in his native locale, he was unknown to the outside world until the early part of this century. The advent of classes for Cwn Sodli, Heelers or Curs at early shows combined with the interest taken in the breed by a number of dedicated dog fanciers in the Pembrokeshire area was the beginning of a new era for the breed. It was an era in which successful efforts would be made to standardize Pembroke type; and the little Corgis would leave their homeland to take up residence at Buckingham Palace and in new homes around the world.

First Shows

In a diligent search through Welsh journals and newspapers dating back to the 1890s, Clifford Hubbard uncovered what appears to be the earliest record of classes offered for Curs at an agricultural show. The show was held by the Bancyfelin Horticultural and Agricultural Society at Bancyfelin, Carmathenshire, in 1892. Mr. Hubbard listed the prize winners as being "first - Mr. J. Thomas, Cwmcoch; second - Mr. J. Thomas, Castellwaun; commended - Mr. D. Davies." Since the prizes were awarded in the name of

27

Left to right: Eng. Ch. Rozavel Golden Girl, unknown, Eng. Ch. Bowhit Bisco, Eng. Ch. Crymmych President and Eng. Ch. Shan Fach, the first English Pembroke champion.

the exhibitor, we do not know the names of the first Corgis to win in show competition.

It was not until the Royal Welsh agricultural show held at Carmarthen in August of 1925 that Corgi classes were held under official Kennel Club rules. Some of the Corgis that were prominent in early Pembroke pedigrees appeared at this important show. Buller, sire of the famous Caleb, won the open dog class with Ted, the sire of Caleb's dam, taking second place. A Cardigan won the open bitch class, while Rose, the first Corgi to be registered with the Kennel Club, settled for third place.

The Corgi Club

In December 1925, a giant step forward was taken when the Corgi Club was formed in Carmarthen. The majority of the members of the newly formed club resided in the Pembrokeshire area. It was not surprising that it was to the Pembroke type to which they gave their allegiance.

To counteract the spreading influence of the Pembroke fanciers, in 1926 Cardigan supporters formed their own society, eventually named the Cardigan Welsh Corgi Association.

The original officers and eighteen-member committee of the Corgi Club included such early pillars of the breed as Captain Jack Howell, his brother Adrian, Mr. John John, Mr. D. T. Davies and Mr. W. Merchan Phillips. Captain Howell presided at the first annual meeting held at the Castle Hotel in Haverfordwest. Captain Williams served as Honorary Secretary.

In 1926, in order to comply with a Kennel Club directive, the name of the club was changed to include ''Welsh'' and the Welsh Corgi Club was officially registered with the Kennel Club.

Still an active club in Wales, members of the Welsh Corgi Club celebrated its Golden Jubilee in 1975, marking a half century devoted to furthering the interests of the Pembroke Welsh Corgi.

In 1928, the labors of the Corgi's earliest supporters finally reaped deserved rewards. The Welsh Corgi was removed from the Kennel Club register of ''Any Other Variety not Classified,'' and the breed was assigned to the Non-Sporting Group. Official recognition brought with it the granting of coveted Challenge Certificates for the Welsh Corgi, a tremendous encouragement for the breeders engaged in an uphill struggle to establish the Corgi as a worthy show dog.

Shan Fach, a red Pembroke bitch, whelped in 1928, was the first Corgi, either Pembroke or Cardigan, to become a champion. Her first two Challenge Certificates were won while she was owned by Mrs. G. Gwyn Jones. She gained her crowning C.C. in the ownership of Mr. Oliver Jones, of the Pantyblaidd prefix under judge Mr. Sid Bowler of Bowhit fame.

Eng. Ch. Bowhit Pepper (Caleb ex Glandofan Fury), whelped 1926.

Eng. Ch. Crymmych President (Newman Chatter ex Crymmych Beauty), whelped 1929, sired 11 English champions including Ch. Rozavel Red Dragon. *Fall*

30

The first dog champion, also a Pembroke Corgi, was Bonny Gyp, bred by Mr. Bennett and owned by Mr. F. C. Davies.

It was the breed's good fortune to have numbered among its staunchest supporters in Pembrokeshire several experienced breeders of Sealyham Terriers. These Sealyham breeders who turned their attentions to the Pembrokeshire Corgi included Captain Jack Howell, master of the Pembrokeshire Fox Hounds and charter member of the Welsh Corgi Club. Also in this group were Captain Checkland Williams, another soldier and sportsman, breeder of the "Wern" Pembrokes and specialist judge; Mr. and Mrs. Sid Bowler, whose Bowhit Pembrokes had such an impact upon the breed it would be virtually impossible to find a Pembroke today that did not have some Bowhit blood many generations back; and Mrs. Victor Higgon, some of whose "of Sealy" Pembrokes were among the first of the breed to be exported to various parts of the world.

In spite of the advances made by the breeders of the 1920s, the Corgi scene remained just short of ruinous chaos for several years following the granting of championship status. Cardigans and Pembrokes were classified together as a single breed in the Kennel Club registry, and the two Corgi types, shown together, were judged by a single Standard.

Mongrelly-looking dogs of every description—heavy set, long and low, fine boned and terrier like, straight fronted or crooked fronted, with or without tails—all appeared in the Corgi ring. The ancestry of the dogs being shown was an equally jumbled-up affair. Some dogs were of unknown and perhaps questionable ancestry, some of indeterminant mixture of Corgi types and some of properly pure Pembroke or Cardigan blood.

Chronic hard feelings between Cardigan and the Pembroke fanciers erupted into open animosity, reaching the point where the supporters of one Corgi type would not exhibit their dogs under a judge who was even suspected of favoring the other type. The dispute probably originated when exhibitors showing the Cardigan type in the classes for Heelers at the early agricultural shows were indignant that the Pembrokeshire Corgi should also be allowed to compete as a Heeler.

As unpleasant as the situation was, it most likely prevented the development of one far worse, the merging of the two Corgi types into one and the loss of two valued separate breed types. While there was sporadic interbreeding of the Pembroke and Cardigan types, the disdain followers of one type held for dogs of the other type prevented the practice from becoming widespread.

The Kennel Club ruling in 1934, giving the Pembroke and Cardigan Corgis separate breed status, brought the disruptive controversy to an end. With the air cleared and the fences mended, breeders could settle down to the business at hand of building lines which would conform with a Standard specific for each breed. An additional Kennel Club ruling made in 1934 which made tail docking permissible aided breeders in their efforts to establish greater uniformity of appearance among Pembrokes.

When a new name in Pembrokes, Rozavel, first appeared in 1930 the spotlight on the breed's advancement began to shift from Southern Wales to England where the Pembroke was to meet with skyrocketing success. While her Rozavel Pembrokes were making an indelible impact upon the breed, Mrs. Thelma Gray (then Miss Thelma Evans) was dedicating her seemingly endless energies to the promotion of the breed both in England and abroad. Pembroke fanciers are greatly indebted to Mrs. Gray, not only for the contributions made by the Rozavel Corgis, but also for the detailed records of the early producers and show dogs provided in her books on the Welsh Corgi breeds.

Through Mrs. Gray's efforts, the Welsh Corgi League was founded in England in 1938. Over the years the League has remained a prominent force in the breed and currently enjoys a membership of approximately 1400 home and overseas members.

Foundation Stock

In the late 1920s and early 1930s, three dogs emerged as the foundation on which many lines were subsequently built. The first of the triad was Ch. Bowhit Pepper, a rich red dog sired by Caleb out of Glandofan Fury. Pepper was the sire of six Pembroke champions, including the breed's first champion, Shan Fach.

Pepper was one of the few dogs of note who appeared in both Pembroke and Cardigan pedigrees. Apparently Pepper, himself, was from a litter of both Corgi types, for it is reported that at an early Cardiff show, Pepper won as a Pembroke while his litter sister, Jill, won at the same show, listed as a Cardigan.

Mated to Fancy, a daughter of Ch. Bonny Gyp, Pepper sired his seventh champion, the well known Cardigan, Ch. My Rockin Mawer. Ch. My Rockin Mawer, in turn, was to make his mark on the Pembroke breed by siring Defiant Girl of Merriedip, the Best of Breed Winner at the Pembroke Welsh Corgi Club of America's first Specialty show.

Pepper was a dog of intensely good type for his time, and proved to be a prepotent stud. His offspring were especially noted for their charm and keen intelligence. In fact, Pepper was used so extensively that where to go with heavily-bred Pepper stock became a very real problem.

An answer to the dilemma appeared in 1929 with the arrival on the scene of an outcross dog, Ch. Crymmych President, a son of Newman Chatter out of Crymmych Beauty. After President was purchased by the Rozavel

Eng. Ch. Rozavel Red Dragon (Eng. Ch. Crymmych President ex Felcourt Flame), whelped 1932. Winner of 12 Challenge Certificates and sire of 11 English champions, he exerted a profound influence on the breed.

Petronella of Lees, a Red Dragon daughter, is pictured at four months. Petronella was the foundation bitch of Miss Pat Curties' world-famous Lees Kennels.

Kennels from his breeder, Mr. Oliver Jones, he quickly gained his title and proved himself a noteworthy sire with seven of his offspring becoming champions. Despite the consistent quality he sired, President is chiefly remembered as the sire of a dog whom many consider to be the great progenitor of the breed, Ch. Rozavel Red Dragon.

Ch. Rozavel Red Dragon, bred by Mr. G. Jones in 1932, was purchased at six weeks of age by the Rozavel Kennels. The sire of eleven English champions and numerous other champions around the world, Dragon also made his mark as a spectacular show dog. Of the twelve Challenge Certificates won by Dragon, eleven were won under different specialist judges and the last nine were taken in succession with Dragon being undefeated in the breed each time. His last C.C. was won at the Welsh Corgi League show in May, 1940, under Miss Pat Curties, owner of the world-famous Lees Kennels—Dragon's last show and the last Corgi Specialty show held in England until after the war.

At the time of his death, Mrs. Barbara Douglas-Redding wrote in the 1950 *Welsh Corgi League Handbook* of Red Dragon:

> As a youngster, from the word "go" he was obviously a "character" and a bit of a "card." He picked his friends carefully with the air of a connoisseur, and although he acknowledged them like the great gentleman he always was, one felt that he had conferred an honour on one as he answered a greeting remark. He was reserved without being in the least shy and kept his entire allegiance and great integrity for his owner and his adored guardians Mr. and Mrs. Sonley with whom he always lived. He was their first consideration and pride, and they were so obviously his in return. "Buster" shared their whole life. He was an honoured and welcome patron at the cinema when they went, and travelled about the countryside with joy and poise on the back of Mr. Sonley's motorcycle. He was never left out of anything.
>
> Mrs. Sonley always had his favorite dinner of spaghetti with cheese and tomato sauce ready for him on his return from the shows, and it was she who knitted him those beautifully-fitting emerald green coats that became his colouring so well when he went off to shows in cold weather.
>
> He was never off colour or dull. Always on his toes whether in the ring or out of it. He loved to play ball and would retrieve and work seriously as well. A more brilliant vital personality in the canine world either as a showman or a stud force it would be hard to find. He went "all out" in the ring. A dynamic small figure right on its toes. Rich flaming red and white; impossible to overlook; he won literally everywhere under everybody. They just couldn't do anything else.

Dragon died at the remarkable age of 17 years and five months with his type and stamina, as well as the intelligence and personality of a glorious dog, thoroughly ingrained in the breed for generations to come.

3

New Beginnings in America

It WAS IN LONDON'S PADDINGTON STATION in 1933 that Mrs. Lewis Roesler (later Mrs. Edward Renner) first saw and fell in love with Little Madam. Little Madam, a Bowhit Pepper daughter, was on her way to a show with her owner, Mrs. Lewis of Fishguard, Wales. Captivated by Little Madam's charm, Mrs. Roesler purchased her on the spot for a total of twelve pounds.

First Recorded Imports

Before returning home to her Merriedip Kennels, Mrs. Roesler visited a number of Corgi kennels in Wales, and a Pembroke named Captain William Lewis after one of Mrs. Roesler's own Welsh ancestors was selected to accompany Little Madam on her journey to America in the spring of 1934.

The Merriedip Kennels, then located in the Berkshire Hills of Massachusetts, were already well established as a leading force in Old English Sheepdogs when the new Corgi immigrants arrived. Mrs. Roesler attributed the success of her Merriedip Old English line to its strong foundation consisting of the best imports Mrs. Roesler could locate during her numerous trips abroad. Intent upon achieving a similar success with her Corgis, Mrs. Roesler continued over the years to seek out the best available Pembroke stock to build a broad base of bloodlines from which she could establish her own strain.

When the Welsh Corgi received official recognition as a breed in the United States, Little Madam of Merriedip became the first Corgi to be

Ch. Little Madam of Merriedip, a Bowhit Pepper daughter, the first Pembroke Welsh Corgi to be registered with the American Kennel Club in 1934.

Eng. Am. Can. Ch. Sierra Bowhit Pivot (Eng. Ch. Crymmych President ex Chalcot Saucebox), whelped in 1933, the first American Pembroke champion. *Ladin*

registered with the American Kennel Club, and Captain William Lewis, the second registered. Their names appear in the August 1934 *Stud Book* under the listing, Welsh Corgis, for then as in England, Pembroke and Cardigan Corgis were not yet recognized as separate breeds.

Early records suggest that though Pembrokes were the first of the two Corgi types to be registered with the American Kennel Club, a pair of Cardigans were actually the first known Corgi imports to America. Born in the Bronant district of Wales, Cassie and a six-months-old companion, Cadno, arrived in Boston in June 1931. Sired by Mon, the last of the original Corgis of Bronant, Cassie is claimed by some to be the true ancestress of the Cardigan breed, for she heads nearly every successful strain in existence today.

The Merriedip imports are the first Pembrokes of which we have official record in the United States. There is, however, reason to believe others were brought to the country prior to the arrival of Little Madam and Captain William Lewis.

Mrs. Helen Bole Jones, a prominent Cardigan fancier, believes that her grandmother, Mrs. Patterson Bole, imported Pembrokes before 1934. Mrs. Jones' belief is substantiated by a column in the March 1935 issue of *Pure-Bred Dogs–American Kennel Gazette* in which Mrs. Harriet Price wrote that Mrs. Bole had been breeding both Corgi types since 1932, though her preference was for the Cardigans.

Early West Coast Activity

Early Corgi activity in this country was by no means restricted to the East Coast. Pembroke history was rapidly in the making in California as well.

The prominent figure behind the record-setting California Pembroke Corgis was Mr. E. M. Tidd of Oakland. The first Pembroke to be registered by Mr. Tidd was Toots, a bitch of Rozavel breeding. Toots was purchased from Ralph Gardener, the pioneer breeder of Pembrokes in Canada and was in whelp to Rozavel Gaiters when she arrived in the States. Her litter, whelped August 15, 1934, became the first Pembroke litter to be registered with the American Kennel Club. Puppies from this Canadian-bred litter were registered under the prefix Sierra.

Early in 1935, Mr. Tidd had the good fortune to buy Bowhit Pivot, an exciting young dog from the Bowhit Kennels in Wales. The late Sid Bowler had purchased Pivot for his wife at the Crufts show where the dog had been shown under the name of Vipont Scamp by his breeder, Lord Hothfield.

Pivot is described as a dark red, nice fronted, low-to-ground dog with a good head and intelligent expression. He completed his English championship in three straight shows, all in good company. Having already picked off the plum of being the first Pembroke Welsh Corgi to win Best in Show at a British all-breed Open show with his spectacular win at Carmarthen in May 1934, Bowhit Pivot continued to make Corgi history after arriving in California. The honor of being the first American Pembroke champion as well as being the first imported English champion fell to Pivot. He also had the distinction of being the first Pembroke to win a Group placing in this country.

Pivot started off his American show career by winning the breed's first major. This three-point win came under judge W. H. Pym at California's Golden Gate show in March 1935. It was followed by another three-point win and a Working Group fourth at the Berkeley show the following June. Pivot's wins continued, as he took majors and was Best of Breed at Del Monte and Santa Cruz in June and July of 1935, respectively. On September 8, 1935, Pivot finished with another three points and Best of Breed at the Oakland show. He thus became America's first Pembroke champion just one month before Little Madam was to complete her championship and become the country's first champion Pembroke bitch.

Bowhit Pivot's offspring followed in the history-making footsteps of their illustrious father. Before leaving England, Pivot sired Robin Hood of Down East, who was imported for the Down East Kennels in Blue Hill, Maine, by the well-known professional handler and, later, all-breed judge Percy Roberts. Robin Hood of Down East was a consistent winner for his owner, Elizabeth Anderson, and made his mark in canine history by being the first Corgi to win a Group placing at the Westminster show. Robin Hood's celebrated Westminster win was at the 1936 show. The same show marked the official beginnings of the Pembroke Welsh Corgi Club of America.

As he was by Crymmych President out of Chalcot Saucebox, a double Bowhit Pepper granddaughter, Pivot carried the Pepper-President combination breeders in both England and America were finding so successful.

Mr. Tidd's Canadian bitch, Toots, was sired by a double Pepper grandson, Rozavel Pimpernel. Her dam was a half-sister to President, both being out of Crymmych Beauty. Thus the mating of Toots to Bowhit Pivot concentrated still more the Pepper-President combination in a litter whelped August 10, 1935, the first American-bred Pembroke litter on record.

Out of the first Pivot-Toots litter came Sierra Bruin. Purchased by Mr. C. B. Owen of Minneapolis, Bruin won a number of Bests of Breed and several Group placings, ultimately distinguishing himself by becoming the first American-Bred Pembroke dog champion.

A repeat of the Pivot-Toots breeding produced the country's first American-bred Pembroke bitch champion, Sierra Vixen. Both Vixen and her older brother, Bruin, completed their championships early in the summer of 1937.

Derek Rayne, one of America's foremost all-breed judges and long-time Pembroke fancier, purchased Ch. Sierra Bruin from Mr. Owen in 1937. At that time, Mr. Rayne already owned three Pembrokes: a Merriedip bitch, a Waseeka bitch and the imported Ch. Helarian Reta. The following year, the illustrious Bowhit Pivot was purchased from Mr. Tidd, and he joined his son, Bruin, in Mr. Rayne's Pemwelgi Kennels.

During this time, Mr. Rayne was the trainer at the Obedience Club of California, so it was only natural that Bruin soon entered obedience competition. In short order, Bruin was not only the first American-bred Pembroke champion on record, but he also was the first American-bred Pembroke champion with a CD obedience title.

Eng. Am. Ch. Sierra Bowhit Pivot continued to enjoy show ring successes in Mr. Rayne's ownership. At the close of his remarkable career Pivot had won Best of Breed at least forty times and sired five champions. Demonstrating the staying power of the breed, Pivot won the Working Group under Mrs. Beatrice Godsol at San Diego at the age of 7½ years and went on to enjoy yet another ten years of good health.

The Show Scene in the 1930s

Corgi competition in the East did not build up as quickly as it did on the West Coast. Championship points were awarded to Eastern Pembrokes for the first time at the Kennel Club of Philadelphia show, November 16 and 17, 1934. Four Cardigans and two Pembrokes were shown together for a total entry of three dogs and three bitches. Little Madam, enroute to Best of Breed, was Winners Bitch for her first two points. Mrs. Bole's Cardigan bitch, Megan, was Reserve. In dogs, Tip, another Cardigan owned by Mrs. Bole, took the dog points, and Mrs. Roesler's Captain William Lewis was Reserve.

Though unsuccessful at finding championship points at shows from July 1934 until the Philadelphia show in November, Little Madam won for herself and the breed many fast friends during her show ring appearances.

Perhaps it was due to the fact Welsh Corgis were classified and shown as terriers at the time of Little Madam's first shows that a number of her admirers, who eventually became Pembroke breeders, were terrier people. In Wales, a band of Sealyham Terrier breeders were instrumental in promoting the Pembroke as a show dog. In this country, a group of Cairn Terrier breeders were won over by Pembroke charm. Prefixes associated with the top Cairns of the day, such as Down East, Tapscot and Elphinstone, soon were carried by winning Pembrokes as well.

By the end of the summer of 1935, show entries in the breed were increasing. For the first time in the East, Pembroke exhibitors were able to muster up a three-point major entry, this at the Ox Ridge show in August. The Best of Breed winner, Little Madam, went on to place fourth in the Working Group, the breed having been reassigned to that Group early in the year.

On the weekend following the Ox Ridge event, Rozavel Gwenda, a newcomer owned by Katherine Irvine, won fourth in the Group at the Middletown, New York show. A C.C. winner in England, she followed her first Group placing here with two more, giving her three Group placings in three consecutive weekends.

Gwenda's breeding again demonstrated the high regard breeders held for the combination of Crymmych President and Bowhit Pepper lines. She was sired by Bowhit Pepper and her dam, sired by Crymmych President, was out of a President daughter. When she was imported by Miss Irvine in 1934, Gwenda was in whelp to President. From the resulting litter, Gitana and her brother, Shan Coch, were shown some, but neither equalled their dam in her show ring successes.

Though just a point away from gaining her championship, Gwenda took a leave of absence from the show ring for maternal duties. Sadly for those who knew her and for the breed, itself, Gwenda died shortly after whelping her litter in December 1935.

During 1936, enthusiasm for the breed continued to spread. New dogs were being imported at such a rate that Elizabeth Anderson was prompted to describe in one of her *Gazette* columns the great ship, the Queen Mary, as being the "Mayflower of the Corgi pioneers."

The newly-formed Pembroke Welsh Corgi Club of America's first Specialty was held in conjunction with the prestigious Morris & Essex show in the Spring of 1936. Robin Hood was Winners Dog for five points, and Mrs. Roesler's Defiant Girl of Merriedip went Winners Bitch and Best of Breed.

Another highlight of the year followed the Specialty in June when Mrs. Thelma Gray, owner of the renowned Rozavel Kennels in England and breeder of many American imports, judged an entry of twelve Pembrokes at the Greenwich show. Robin Hood was Best of Breed at that event, another five point win for him, and Defiant Girl was Winners Bitch for three points.

Unfortunately fate was to again take a promising bitch before her true contribution to the breed could be made. Defiant Girl, the daughter of the Cardigan, Ch. My Rockin Mawer, was struck by a truck and died, as did Rozavel Gwenda, a point or two away from being America's second bitch champion.

Waseeka Kennels

Of the kennels that started in the breed during the years 1936 to 1940, two rose rapidly to the foreground, their Corgis sharing prominence in the show ring with those from Merriedip.

The Waseeka Kennels in Ashland, Massachusetts, owned by Miss Elizabeth Loring (later Mrs. Davieson Power) were already known world-

Eng. Am. Ch. Lisaye Rattle (Eng. Ch. Rozavel Red Dragon ex Rozavel Juniper), the first Pembroke Welsh Corgi to win a Working Group in the United States and the winner of two PWCCA Specialty shows.

Robin Hood of Down East, a Bowhit Pivot son, Winners Dog at the first Pembroke Welsh Corgi Club of America Specialty in 1936.

Eng. Am. Ch. Fitzdown Paul of Andely (Eng. Ch. Rozavel Red Dragon ex Pantyblaidd Wonder), whelped 1934.

Eng. Am. Ch. Fire Bird of Cogges of Andely (Eng. Ch. Rozavel Scarlet Emperor ex. Eng. Ch. Tiffany of Cogges), whelped 1937.

A well-known winner with Bests of Breed at three California Specialties, Ch. Am. Byth Anthony Adverse is a direct descendant through his dam, Bundock's All About Eve, CD, of Eng. Am. Ch. Fitzdown Paul of Andely and Eng. Ch. Fire Bird of Cogges of Andely. Jean and Marjorie Walker's Far Away breeding also appears in Tony's pedigree. Owner: Anita Suderman. *Phyl*

wide for the outstanding Newfoundlands bred there when Miss Loring, intrigued by the beguiling Little Madam, decided to add Pembrokes to her kennel.

Immediately after the purchase of a Rozavel Gwenda daughter, Lady Penrhyn, and upon the arrival of Tomboy of Sealy from England, Miss Loring set about producing quality home-bred stock. The Waseeka Pembrokes were to dominate American-bred competition in the breed for some while to come.

The imports judiciously selected by Miss Loring played an important part in maintaining the high quality of the Waseeka Pembrokes. Tomboy, the first of the Waseeka Pembroke imports and a winner of nine Bests of Breed with six Group placings, was the sire of the first Pembroke homebred champion at Waseeka.

The most glamorous of the Waseeka imports was Eng. Am. Ch. Lisaye Rattle, imported in the summer of 1936. Rattle, described as being so close to perfection that she could safely serve as the model for the breed Standard, was undefeated in breed competition in England before coming to the States. Rattle had the honor of being the first Pembroke Welsh Corgi to win a Working Group in this country. She did this at the Brocton show in September of 1936. Rattle collected two more Group wins and a half dozen Group placings in her show career and amassed a total of thirty Best of Breed wins which included top honors at two PWCCA Specialty shows.

Lisaye Rattle was a Red Dragon daughter out of a Crymmych President daughter and should have been useful as a producer. But, as has happened with some of the breed's loveliest bitches, Rattle simply was not a producer.

The hard luck that tested the mettle of other early Pembroke breeders struck again when Rattle, the outstanding winner of her day, met an untimely death when she was suffocated in a kennel fire.

Andelys Kennels

Barbara Lowe Fallass was the force behind the success of the Pembrokes at the Andelys Kennels. Like Waseeka, Andelys rose quickly to the top in Corgi competition during the late thirties. Prior to moving to this country and settling in Cross River, New York, Mrs. Fallass lived in France where the Andelys name, derived from *Les Andelys,* the name of her home in Normandy, was carried by her top-winning Smooth Fox Terriers.

Mrs. Fallass first became acquainted with the Pembroke at the 1929 Crufts show. She subsequently watched the breed's progress with great interest. After determining that the Corgi's popularity was not just a passing fancy following the publicity which the royal family's Corgis had been receiving, Mrs. Fallass purchased Torment of Sealy, an accomplished obedience worker in England.

Torment arrived in the spring of 1937. In the summer of 1938, the Andelys Kennels imported Scarbo of Cogges, a Red Dragon daughter out of Tiffany of Cogges. Scarbo, who lacked but one ticket to make up her English championship, became the first Pembroke champion at the Andelys Kennels.

During the last half of 1938, Mrs. Fallass imported eight Pembroke Corgis. Were that to happen today, cries of "mass breeding" would resound throughout Corgi circles everywhere. Nonetheless, Mrs. Fallass brought to our shores some of the best Pembrokes England had to offer. Included at that time were two notable English champions, Eng. Am. Ch. Fitzdown Paul of Andely and Eng. Am. Ch. Rozavel Traveller's Joy.

The first with a Fitzdown prefix to come to this country, a prefix that is still well to the fore in England today, Fitzdown Paul had started his show career by winning Best of Breed at the 1936 Crufts show. He followed this win by collecting five more Challenge Certificates. After coming to the States, his many wins here included a Working Group fourth at the 1939 Westminster show and Best of Breed at the 1939 PWCCA Specialty show.

Fitzdown Paul, a Red Dragon son, sired a number of winners for the Andelys Kennels, his best known being out of a Dragon granddaughter, Eng. Am. Ch. Fire Bird of Cogges of Andely.

Fresh from a glamorous show career in England where she had the distinction of being the first Pembroke to hold a Junior Warrant from the Kennel Club, Eng. Am. Ch. Rozavel Traveller's Joy joined the growing number of English imports at Andelys late in 1938. This nearly solid flame red daughter of Eng. Ch. Rozavel Scarlet Emperor was Best of Breed at the 1940 Westminster show, completing her American title later that year.

Perhaps the most valuable of the imports at Andelys, in terms of her contribution as a producer, was Eng. Am. Ch. Fire Bird of Cogges. She was another Scarlet Emperor daughter and also a half sister to the earlier import, Ch. Scarbo of Cogges. It is not surprising that Fire Bird proved to be a good producer, as she came from a line noted for its ability to breed on. Eng. Ch. Tiffany of Cogges, dam of both Fire Bird and Scarbo, was from the famous litter that included Australian Ch. Titania of Sealy and Eng. Ch. Teresa of Sealy.

Successful not only as a producer but in the show ring too, Fire Bird completed her English championship in only four months. A highlight of Fire Bird's American show career occurred in 1940 when Derek Rayne placed her Best of Breed over a record entry at the Eastern Dog Club show. The remarkable entry of 44 Pembrokes, making up 49 entries, at that Boston show was a record which was to hold for a number of years to come. The large entry was an obvious tribute to Mr. Rayne as the judge and a good measure of the heights to which interest in the breed had risen.

Pembroke Welsh Corgi registrations at the American Kennel Club indicated, as did show entries, that the breed had become securely established in this country in a phenomenally short period of time. By the end of 1934, the first year the Welsh Corgi was eligible for registration with the American Kennel Club, a total of nine Corgis were registered, and the Welsh Corgi ranked in 76th place among all breeds registered. Within four years, with 135 Pembroke Welsh Corgis registered in 1938, the breed moved up to 45th place.

Except for the brief time when there was a sudden rise in Corgi popularity following the television presentation in 1963 of the Walt Disney film about a Corgi, *Little Dog Lost,* registrations have maintained a ranking for the Pembroke close to that set in 1938. The registration of approximately 2,349 Pembroke Welsh Corgis during 1978, giving the breed a ranking of 48th place, indicates the popularity of the Pembroke has clearly kept pace with the expanding dog scene in America without the breed becoming so popular as to fall victim to commercialism.

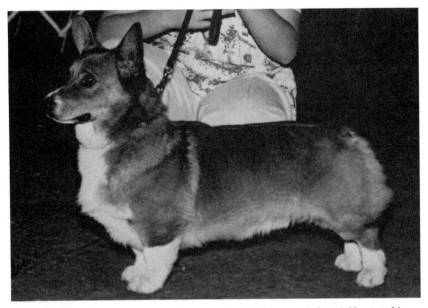

Ch. Menfreya's Classical Jazz, a BIS and Specialty winning son of Ch. Wicklow's Whizzer. Owners: Tina and Rose Dameron. *Petrulis*

Eng. Ch. Teekay's Felcourt Supremacy (Hill Billy of Lees ex Floss), leading stud dog in England 1947-1950.   *Fall*

Eng. Ch. Lees Coronet, winner of nine Challenge Certificates, and said to have had the greatest value of any Supremacy daughter.   *Marjorie Baker*

4

The Post-War Comeback

WHEN THE TRAGEDIES of World War II silenced Corgi activity around the world, many Pembroke kennels were disbanded, some never to resume activity again. Fortunately, the strong foundation of Pembroke bloodlines established prior to the war was carried on by those able to maintain their kennels on a limited scale.

Influential Sires of the Period

Red Dragon breeding survived the difficult times in good strength with two of his most successful sons, Ch. Rozavel Scarlet Emperor and Int. Ch. Rozavel Lucky Strike, proving to be at the head of all prominent bloodlines in America today.

Ch. Rozavel Scarlet Emperor, particularly, suited many of the bitches of his day. Not only was he a Red Dragon son, but also he was out of a Bowhit Pepper daughter, Rozavel Pollyanna, who was heavily bred on Pepper's sire, Caleb.

Whelped in 1935, Scarlet Emperor was just coming into his prime when war broke out. Because of this unfortunate timing, the dog was never used to his fullest potential. Despite his limited use, Scarlet Emperor's impact on the breed through his famous daughters is immeasurable.

As a youngster, Scarlet Emperor sired the winning bitches, Int. Ch. Rozavel Traveller's Joy and Int. Ch. Fire Bird of Cogges, imported by the Andelys Kennels. Three other well-known Emperor daughters remained in England, and it is they who must be given considerable credit for the tremendous quality found in the post-war English bloodlines.

47

Ch. Hollyheath Pilot of Waseeka, the PWCCA Specialty winner in 1951, passed his rich red color on as still seen today in many of his descendants.

Ch. Rozavel Uncle Sam of Waseeka, the first Pembroke Welsh Corgi to win a Best in Show in the United States. This historic milestone occured in 1949. *Brown*

48

Larkwhistle Golden Vanity, following in the wake of her half-sister, Traveller's Joy, was one of the breed's earliest Junior Warrant winners. With one C.C. and a Reserve C.C. to her credit before the war began, Golden Vanity returned to the show ring when championship shows were resumed to gain a second C.C. at the age of ten years but was unlucky never to win the third. All of Miss E. J. Boyt's Larkwhistle dogs descended from Golden Vanity as did the famous post-war dogs, Int. Ch. Formakin Orangeman and Int. Ch. Broom of Ballybentra.

Bronwen of Lees, another of Scarlet Emperor's noted daughters, transmitted the line's ability to breed on to her grandson, Ch. Teekay's Felcourt Supremacy, a particularly valuable post-war sire.

Known as "Old Bob" to his many friends, Ch. Teekay's Felcourt Supremacy was originally registered as Berach Bach. The Kennel Club permitted names to be changed in those days, so when Mr. Gwyn Jones obtained the dog, he became Felcourt Supremacy. With another change of ownership, this time to Anne Biddlecombe, the Teekay was added.

Supremacy was a popular stud for, though a smallish dog himself, he passed on substance and bone to his progeny. These important qualities were lacking in much of the post-war stock. The show ring successes of his offspring earned for Supremacy the Welsh Corgi League's Formakin Stud Dog Cup for four years in succession, 1947 through 1950.

Though Supremacy was primarily noted for his six champion daughters, he figured strongly in many American pedigrees through his grandson, Eng. Ch. Knowland Clipper. Many of our present bloodlines are steeped in Supremacy breeding due to the widely used combination of Knowland Clipper lines and those of the world-famous Int. Ch. Lees Symphony. The Symphony granddams, Eng. Ch. Lees Coronet and Chorus Girl of Cowfold, were both Supremacy daughters.

Scarlet Emperor breeding was consolidated to perfection in Ch. Lees Coronet who was said to be the best of the Supremacy daughters. In turn, Coronet's granddam, Faireyhaze Empress, was the most famous of the Scarlet Emperor daughters.

Miss Anne Biddlecombe, whose Teekay dogs emerged from the war years as a dominant force in the breed, received Faireyhaze Empress from her breeders, the Misses Peat and Harle, when the war broke out. Undoubtedly, Empress would have been another champion added to Scarlet Emperor's record if not for the war. She had proven her quality by winning a strong class at the Kensington championship show while still quite a young puppy. Though Faireyhaze Empress never won a Challenge Certificate, she twice won the Welsh Corgi League's Coronet Brood Bitch Cup, both in 1947 and 1948, and she would have won it in 1946 as well, had the Cup been offered that year. To date, the Coronet Brood Bitch Challenge Cup has not been won three times by the same bitch.

Truly a great brood bitch and the start of the strongest bitch line the breed has ever known, Empress was mated back to her grandsire, Ch. Rozavel Red Dragon, to produce Eng. Ch. Teekay Foxfire, Teekay Vivien, dam of the lovely Ch. Lees Coronet, and the two useful stud dogs, Teekay Marquess and Teekay Pendragon.

Empress was then mated to Ch. Teekay's Felcourt Supremacy for another remarkable litter. This union gave the breed the two notable bitches, Ch. Teekay Diadem and Ch. Teekay Tiara, each the winner of seven Challenge Certificates. Tiara was the first Pembroke Welsh Corgi to win a Non-Sporting Group at an English championship show. She did this at the L.K.A. show in 1947, the show at which she won her first C.C.

Though not possessing the glittering record of her half-sisters, Sally Jane of Dursley, again a Scarlet Emperor daughter, was the dam of an important dog in America, Ch. Hollyheath Pilot of Waseeka. Imported by Mrs. Power in 1951, Pilot had a decided influence on the breed in this country. Several Pilot daughters became the foundation of lines successfully carried on today. Pilot's most celebrated descendant, his grandson Ch. Willets Red Jacket, is honored as the top winning Pembroke Welsh Corgi of all time in the United States.

As Ch. Rozavel Scarlet Emperor was enjoying his retirement years in the company of Mr. and Mrs. Charles Lister-Kaye and their Lisaye Corgis, Int. Ch. Rozavel Lucky Strike was making his presence felt through his glamorous offspring. A number of these subsequently made their way to the United States and Canada.

Post-War Imports

Lucky Strike, one of Ch. Rozavel Red Dragon's last surviving sons, was whelped in 1943 out of Rozavel Land Girl, a Red Dragon granddaughter. Mated to a bitch with the unassuming name, "Snooks," a Red Dragon—Supremacy granddaughter, Lucky Strike sired the noted post-war American champions, Rozavel Lucky Fellow of Merriedip, Rozavel Uncle Sam of Waseeka and Rozavel Miss Bobby Sox, CD.

Of these three renowned litter mates, who with their offspring quite dominated the Pembroke show ring during the late forties and into the 1950s, Uncle Sam was the most successful winner and producer. Uncle Sam covered himself with glory on the 1949 Florida show circuit. By taking top honors at the Tampa Bay Kennel Club show, he became the first Pembroke Welsh Corgi to win a Best in Show in the United States. Following his Florida winning spree, which included three Group firsts in succession, Uncle Sam

Int. Ch. Upperton Corncob of Laggenden (Lisaye Jack's the Boy ex Redwin Candy), whelped in 1946.

Four generations of homebred Macksons Corgis going back to Ch. Rozavel Uncle Sam through Am. Can. Ch. Macksons Coronet (far right). Coronet was BB at the 1957 PWCCA Specialty, with her brother, Am. Can. Ch. Macksons Sceptre, placing BOS.

51

placed second in a strong Working Group at the 1949 Westminster Kennel Club show.

The sire of a number of homebred champions for Waseeka Kennels, Uncle Sam bred on primarily through Ch. Waseeka's Coaltown, the Alexandre Orlowskis' Ch. Esmeralda of Furnace Brook and Ch. Cote de Neige Samson, one of the early Cote de Neige stud dogs. Of today's Pembrokes, only those of Rover Run breeding in this country and of the Macksons line in Canada trace back in any depth to Uncle Sam.

Due to maternal duties upon arrival, Ch. Rozavel Miss Bobby Sox, CD was the last of the famous trio to complete her championship. Miss Bobby Sox was purchased as a foundation bitch by Mrs. Katherine Bartlett (later Mrs. J. Donald Duncan), and she was imported in whelp to Rozavel Thumbs Up.

In her second litter, by Stanley Logan's Int. Ch. Upperton Corncob, a grandson of Int. Ch. Formakin Orangeman and Eng. Ch. Teekay's Felcourt Supremacy, Rozavel Miss Bobby Sox produced the popular winner and showman, Ch. Kaydon's Happy Talk. Happy Talk, whose brilliant career began at 6½ months with a Best of Breed win at the 1950 Westminster Kennel Club show, became the first American-bred Pembroke to win a Best in Show.

Ch. Rozavel Lucky Fellow of Merriedip did not have the same impact on the breed as did Uncle Sam and Miss Bobby Sox. Even so, Lucky Fellow, or "Tubby" as he was known to his friends, won Best of Breed at the 1950 PWCCA Specialty Show under breeder-judge Mrs. William Long, giving the Merriedip Kennels their third such win.

In keeping with family tradition, Rozavel Lucky Fellow sired the striking, deep red, Best in Show winner, Ch. Toelmag's Tommy Lad. Tommy Lad was owned by Dr. Herbert Talmadge.

It is interesting to note that Dr. Talmadge's daughter, Mrs. Thelma von Thaden, still carries on the family interest in Corgis in Mexico where she is now living. Mrs. von Thaden, a well-known judge of Corgis and other working breeds, now owns two Pembrokes of Fox Run breeding. One is an American and Mexican champion and Best in Show winner in Mexico.

The Lucky Strike offspring in America were not alone in capturing Best in Show honors. Ch. Rozavel Rainbow, a lovely Lucky Strike daughter, made breed history in England at the City of Birmingham show in September, 1950 when she became the first Pembroke Welsh Corgi to win Best in Show at an all-breed English championship show.

Purchased for what is said to have been a record four-figure price, Rainbow was subsequently imported by Mrs. Andrew Porter's Tred Avon Kennels in Maryland. Rainbow won Best of Breed at the 1952 PWCCA Specialty held in conjunction with the prestigious Westchester Kennel Club show and went on to win the Working Group at that event. Although Rainbow

Am. Can. Mex. Ch. Toelmag's Tommy Lad, top winning Pembroke of 1954. A BIS winner, Tommy's record includes over 100 BBs and 7 Groups.

Eng. Am. Ch. Rozavel Rainbow, the first Pembroke Welsh Corgi to win Best in Show at an all-breed English Championship show.

Ch. Rozavel Lucky Fellow enjoys a moment of relaxation with owner, Margery Renner.

Shafer

Mr. Edward P. Renner (Merriedip Kennels) with Ch. Rozavel Christmas Gift and Merriedip Rufus Again. The famous Merriedip Old English Sheepdogs, Ch. Ethel Ann and Ch. Downderry Volunteer are portrayed in the painting.

Gladys and John Watson

54

had other Group wins, she was never able to add an American Best in Show win to her laurels. Neither was she a producer, an unfortunate loss for her owners and for the breed.

The imports sired by Int. Ch. Rozavel Lucky Strike marked the end of an era in Pembroke history in America. It was a time when the immortal Ch. Rozavel Red Dragon was well to the fore in the pedigrees of our current winners. Kennels in this country were turning back to England to import offspring of the latest winners, dogs in whose pedigrees Red Dragon was the foundation but also the past.

Post-War Kennels

During the post-war years a number of new kennels began in the breed, many of which continued on to form the backbone of today's fancy. In England the popularity of the Pembroke Welsh Corgi continued to climb with unbelievable momentum, reaching its peak with 8,933 registrations during 1960. New kennels were established at such a rate, it is impossible to single out a few for recognition here.

In America, dogs from Merriedip, Waseeka and Andelys Kennels remained out front in Corgi competition after the war ended.

At the first post-war PWCCA Specialty, held with the Greenwich Kennel Club show in 1946, Thelma Gray was the judge. Mrs. Fallass' Ch. Peppercorn Formakin Fascination of Andely was Best of Breed. This bitch, eight years old at the time, had also been the Winners Bitch at the 1941 PWCCA Specialty before war called a halt to most dog show activities.

Ch. Tormentor of Andelys' Best of Breed win at the 1947 PWCCA Specialty gave Andelys Kennels its fourth PWCCA Specialty Best of Breed win, a record equalled only by Cote de Neige Kennels in later years.

The Pembroke entries at the Westminster Kennel Club shows reflected the strength of the leading kennels of the late 1940s. The Andelys dogs, with Carol Roever (now Mrs. Carol Simonds, owner of the well-known West Coast kennel, Rover Run) in charge as kennel manager, dominated the Pembroke entry at the 1947 Westminster show. Out of a total entry of 18 Pembrokes, 11 were owned by Mrs. Fallass. In addition, two other entries were bred at the Andelys Kennels. The following year, Mrs. Margery Renner judged an entry of 29 Pembrokes at the Garden, 11 of which were owned by Waseeka Kennels and two more entries were Waseeka-bred.

Although Ch. Peppercorn Formakin Fascination was the only entry from the Andelys Kennels in competition at the 1948 Westminster show, five famous Andelys champions were entered for Exhibition Only. What a memorable sight it must have been with Ch. Spring Robin of Andely, Ch. Robin Hood of Andely, Ch. Tormentor of Andeley, Ch. Firelight of Andely and Int. Ch. Fire Bird of Cogges on display for the two days of Westminster.

By 1949, the Andelys Kennels had bowed out of Corgi activities. For reasons of poor health, Mrs. Fallass decided the kennels had to be cut back. Consequently only the Smooth Fox Terriers were retained. Ch. Robin Hood of Andely and Ch. Tormentor of Andely were exported to England where, following quarantine, they joined Rozavel Kennels, making available to England some of the bloodlines lost during the war.

By the mid 1940s, Mrs. Marjorie Butcher's Cote de Neige Pembrokes were beginning to make frequent appearances at the shows. Their wins were just an indication of the strength which was yet to come from Cote de Neige.

Before Mrs. Butcher turned her attention entirely to the Corgis, many of the best known, top-winning Great Pyrenees in this country carried the Cote de Neige prefix. Descriptive of the Great Pyrenees, the name Cote de Neige is translated from the French to mean ''snow drift.''

The first Pembroke to join the Great Pyrenees at Cote de Neige was Far Away Tawny Goch, obtained before the war from Jean and Marjorie Walker's Far Away Kennels. Later, Mrs. Butcher purchased Far Away Goch of Cote de Neige, who became the first champion Pembroke at Cote de Neige, a kennel which was to breed 140 Pembroke champions in the years that followed.

In their early days, Cote de Neige Kennels and Far Away Kennels were located in the Berkshires of Massachusetts. After a move to Connecticut in the late forties, Cote de Neige Kennels permanently relocated to Bedford, New York, in 1953.

Far removed from practically all civilization, Faraway (now one word) Kennels became happily situated on San Juan Island, Washington. Pembrokes bearing the Faraway prefix are still much in evidence on the West Coast.

In 1947, Mrs. Irene Green's Greencorg Kennels, established during the war years, rose to sudden prominence with the arrival of the noted winner from England, Int. Ch. Formakin Orangeman.

Whelped in 1944, Formakin Orangeman was the first Pembroke Welsh Corgi to make up his championship when shows were resumed in England after the war. He gained his title at the first three championship shows held in 1946. Following what was perhaps his greatest win, Best in Show at the Irish Kennel Club championship show in Dublin, ''Paddy'' came to America in search of new victories. Though he won a Best in Show in Sydney, Nova Scotia, a Reserve Best in Show in Halifax and ten Group firsts in the States, he was never quite lucky enough to capture top honors in this country.

It was unfortunate that Orangeman, an exceptionally sound dog of a rich red sable color, did not prove to be a particularly useful stud dog. His only descendant of real note was a grandson, Int. Ch. Upperton Corncob, sire of Ch. Kaydon's Happy Talk.

Mrs. Donald Duncan's Kaydon Kennels, officially established with the importation of Ch. Rozavel Miss Bobby Sox, CD, made a tremendous impact

Corgis awaiting their departure from London's Heathrow airport for kennels in the USA in 1951. Ch. Crawleycrow Coracle of Aimhi (second from the right) mated to Ch. Hollyheath Pilot of Waseeka (far left) produced a number of outstanding bitches, some of whom served as the foundation stock for several successful American kennels.

The 1954 PWCCA Specialty with Ch. Kaydon's Happy Talk (right) BB and Ch. Kaydon Aimhi's Kate BOS. Judge, Derek Rayne. Happy Talk's show record included 91 Group placings, including 22 Group 1s, and five Bests in Show.   *Shafer*

57

Mr. Percy Roberts juding the first PWCCA Sweepstakes in 1953. On the left is Mrs. Marjorie Butcher with Cote de Neige Happy Time, Best in Sweepstakes. At the right is Mrs. J. Donald Duncan with her homebred Kaydon's Anthony. *Shafer*

A BIS winner, Ch. Craythorne's Domino (left) handled by his owner, Mrs. J. Donald Duncan, to BB at the 1953 Morris and Essex show under judge Derek Rayne. Domino, imported from England, went on to win the Working Group at this show. Pictured winning BOS is Mrs. Duncan's Ch. Kaydon's Aimhi Kate, handled by Charles Long. *Shafer*

upon the breed during its brief period of activity. Three Best in Show winners from this kennel, Ch. Kaydon's Happy Talk, Ch. Craythorne's Domino and Eng. Am. Can. Ch. Lees Symphony, stood at the top of Corgi competition up and down the Eastern seaboard until the kennel was closed following Kay Duncan's tragic death during Hurricane Hazel in October 1954.

Through Mrs. Duncan's tireless efforts on behalf of the breed, not only as a breeder and exhibitor but as Secretary of the Pembroke Welsh Corgi Club of America and breed columnist for *Pure-Bred Dogs—American Kennel Gazette* as well, the Pembroke Welsh Corgi made new inroads into the southern and western regions of the country. A number of the Pembroke kennels established in this country during the early 1950s were founded with Kaydon-bred stock. And the phenomenal influence on the breed by the Kaydon import, Ch. Lees Symphony, has yet to be surpassed by any other modern-day Pembroke.

Mrs. Irene Green with Hollyheath Rosebud and Lees Lancelot (right). Lancelot, a son of Eng. Ch. Lees Coronet, sired Ch. Cote de Neige Posy, a favorite house dog at Cote de Neige and a champion before her first birthday.

Eng. Irish Am. Can. Ch. Formakin Orangeman (foreground) with his owner, Mrs. Irene Green, and a kennel mate, Dado of Greencorg.

Eng. Am. Can. Ch. Lees Symphony.

Teekay's Felcourt Autocrat
Lisaye Lees Laurence
Lees Laurel
Lees Laureate
Eng. Ch. Teekay's Felcourt Supremacy
Eng. Ch. Lees Coronet
Teekay Vivien
ENG. AM. CAN. CH. LEES SYMPHONY
Teekay Pendragon
Corker of Cowfold
Larkwhistle Valerie
Cantata of Cowfold
Eng. Ch. Teekay's Felcourt Supremacy
Chorus Girl of Cowfold
Teekay Tansy

5

Breeding On

TODAY'S PROMINENT BLOODLINES stem from three outstanding sources—Int. Ch. Lees Symphony, Eng. Ch. Knowland Clipper and the combination of Stormerbanks Ambrose and Stormerbanks Supersonic breeding.

As would be expected, many of our best dogs represent various combinations of these important lines but, where possible, the top producing dogs and noted winners presented here are grouped together to illustrate the family type and quality that has consistently bred on.

The Symphony Saga

Bred by Miss Pat Curties, Lees Symphony was whelped April 10, 1951. A Junior Warrant winner at eight months of age, Symphony completed his English championship prior to his first birthday.

In 1952, Symphony was imported to the States by Mrs. J. Donald Duncan. Apparently he reacted poorly to the change and was a difficult dog to show here. As Miss Curties was to comment later, Symphony did not look to be the same dog in this country as he did at home for he had become feisty in temperament and hard in eye.

Slower to gain his American title than would be expected of a dog fresh from a fine show career in England, Symphony won his finishing points late in the spring of 1953. Later, a Canadian championship was added as well. Campaigned from 1953 to 1957, Symphony won three Bests in Show and 13 Group firsts out of a total of forty Group placings.

At ten years of age, Symphony was sent back to England to spend his retirement years in the company of his many friends at Lees. Happy to be home, Symphony once again became the gentle, sweet-natured dog he was known to have been as a youngster.

It is as a sire that Symphony will long be remembered and, oddly enough, his greatest impact on the breed came from dogs he sired during the brief time he was at stud in England before leaving for America.

Mated to a Knowland Clipper daughter, Maracas Helarian Gale, Symphony sired the two famous litter mates, Eng. Ch. Maracas Masterpiece and Eng. Ch. Kaytop Maracas Mist.

Eng. Ch. Kaytop Maracas Mist distinguished herself by winning Best Bitch in Show, All Breeds, at Crufts in 1955, and she remains the only Corgi to have such a high placing at that giant of all shows.

The sensational Eng. Ch. Kaytop Marshall, himself the winner of the Gold Trophy for Best in the Working Group at Crufts in 1972, is a direct descendant of Eng. Ch. Kaytop Maracas Mist, the foundation bitch of Mrs. Leila Moore's Kaytop Kennels.

A valuable sire as well as a striking showman, Marshall is found in the pedigrees of countless current winners. His winning progeny in England earned for him the Int. Ch. Lees Symphony Memorial Trophy as runner-up to the Formakin Stud Dog Cup winner in 1970 and 1971. Two of his best known daughters, Eng. Ch. Stormerbanks Mame and Eng. Ch. Stormerbanks Martha have appeared in the Welsh Corgi League's listing of leading brood bitches every year since 1971. In 1975 a Martha son, Eng. Ch. Stormerbanks Vainglory, was England's leading sire and winner of the Formakin Stud Dog Cup. Carrying on the family tradition, Eng. Ch. Lynfarne Pacesetter, a Vainglory son, won the Formakin Cup in 1977.

Eng. Ch. Maracas Masterpiece, one of Symphony's most successful sons, was a legendary sire in his own right. Hesitant in temperament, a condition blamed on illness early in puppyhood, Masterpiece was not everybody's cup of tea. Nonetheless, he sired many outstanding offspring, themselves well off with good temperament. While it is impossible to give credit here to all of the many well-known Masterpiece progeny who have been important to the breed, note must be made of three sons particularly outstanding for their contribution to the breed in America—Eng. Ch. Crowleythorn Snowman, Am. Can. Bda. Ch. Maracas Monarch of Cleden and Am. Ch. Gladiator of Rode, UD, Can. CDX.

The sire of 27 champions, Ch. Maracas Monarch of Cleden ranks third in the PWCCA listing of the all time top ten producing sires in the United States.

Ch. Gladiator of Rode, UD, Can. CDX, is found in the pedigrees of a number of West Coast Pembrokes. Mated to a Symphony daughter, he sired

Eng. Ch. Kaytop Maracas Mist. Reserve Best in Show, Crufts 1955. *Ernest Whiston*

Eng. Ch. Kaytop Marshall, whelped May 8, 1967, breeder-owner: Mrs. L.K. Moore. Marshall is the only Pembroke, either sex, to win a C.C. at Crufts for four years in a row, which he did in 1969 through 1972 when he was retired from the ring.

Sivert Nilsson

Eng. Ch. Lynfarne Pacesetter, whelped July 1, 1973. England's
top Pembroke sire in 1977. *C.M. Cooke & Son*

Eng. Ch. Maracas Masterpiece. Breeder-owner: Mrs. M.T.S.
Thornycroft. Masterpiece was the leading stud dog in England from
1956 through 1960. *Fall*

Eng. Ch. Crowleythorn Snowman, whelped March 4, 1958.
owner-breeders: Mr. and Mrs. Duckworth.

Am. Can. Ch. Gladiator of Rode, Am. UD, Can. CDX, whelped November 23, 1956, breeder: G.L. Mortimer, owner: Douglas Bundock.

Am. Can. Bda. Ch. Maracas Monarch of Cleden whelped August 2, 1956, breeder: Mrs. M.T.S. Thornycroft. Imported and owned by Louise C. Cleland.   *Brown*

Ch. Rover Run Minstrel Man, whelped April 8, 1960, breeder-owner: Carol Simonds. Minstrel Man was a Group and Specialty winning son of Gladiator.   *January*

the stylish tricolor, Ch. Rover Run Minstrel Man. Owned for a time by Derek Rayne before going back to his breeder, Carol Simonds, Minstrel Man won seven Group firsts and the 1961 PWCCA Specialty Show. "Speedie" bred on through his famous son, the captivating Ch. Cote de Neige Derek, a multiple Best in Show and Specialty winner.

Of the three Masterpiece sons, Eng. Ch. Crowleythorn Snowman had the greatest influence on the breed, mainly through his sons, Ch. Halmor Hi-Fi and Eng. Irish and Am. Ch. Crowleythorn Ladomoorlands in this country and in England through his daughter, Evancoyd True Love. True Love is the dam of the celebrated Eng. Ch. Evancoyd Personality Girl, and of England's leading stud dog in 1972 and 1974, Evancoyd Contender. True Love is also the dam of Evancoyd Golden Charm, the leading brood bitch in England in 1972.

America's top winning Welsh Corgi from 1974 through 1976, Am. Can. Ch. Bear Acres Mister Snowshoes, UD, represents a highly successful combination of Hi-Fi and Ladomoorlands breeding. Carried down from his sire, Ch. Bear Acres Two for the Road, the line's ability to breed on successfully through "Mister" has been demonstrated by his two Best in Show winning sons, Ch. Vangard Mr. Ski Bum and Am. Can. Ch. Suzyque's Southern Snowbear. Snowbear broke breed records when he became the youngest American Pembroke champion by finishing his title at the age of six months and 23 days.

Although never receiving the loud acclaim that came to Masterpiece, another Symphony son, South African Ch. Drumbeat of Wyldingtree of Wey, contributed immeasurable quality to the breed. An excellent showman of superb type, Drumbeat was purchased as the foundation dog for the Kenneth Butlers' highly successful Wey Kennels in England. Drumbeat passed on his lovely head quality, refined yet masculine, to his offspring and was in part responsible for the typical "Wey" head which is praised the world over.

Drumbeat's son, Int. Ch. Gayelord of Wey, was a most useful dog in that he did well by bitches of Masterpiece breeding and was also a suitable outcross for bitches of a number of different lines. Likewise, Gayelord's grandson, Pennywise of Wey, has proven himself useful in much the same manner.

In addition to siring the first Pembroke Welsh Corgi to win a Best in Show in the Midwest, Ruth Cooper's Ch. Craythorne's Fleetfoot of Wey, Drumbeat sired a dog who was to head a remarkable line of winners in this country, Ch. Stormerbanks Big Drum, CDX. Big Drum was purchased by the Robert Haights as a family pet. Once he embarked on a show career, Big Drum easily completed his championship, shown by Bill Haight, then a junior handler.

Big Drum combined the foundation breeding of two of England's most

Ch. Cote de Neige Derek with his breeder-owner, Mrs. Marjorie Butcher. Derek was the top-winning Pembroke in the USA in 1964, 1965 and 1966. *Ritter*

Five generations of Derek's descendants owned by Gladys and Doug Bundock. Left to right: a Derek daughter, Ch. Cote de Neige Sugar Treat; Treat's daughter, Ch. Bundocks Mistress Quickly; Quickly's daughter, Ch. Bundocks Apple of the Eye; Apple's daughter, Bundocks Pennies From Heaven, CD, with her daughter, Bundocks Dawn of a New Day.

67

Am. Can. Ch. Bear Acres Mister Snowshoes, UD, whelped March 17, 1972, breeder: Mrs. Stanley Bear, owner: Mrs. Frank Hayward. Fifth Top Working Dog in 1975 and 1976 and Top-winning Pembroke 1974 through 1976. He was Group 1st at Westminster 1976, and the first BIS winning champion UD Pembroke Welsh Corgi. *Callea*

<pre>
                              Eng. Ch. Crowleythorn Snowman
                   Am. Can. Ch. Halmor Hi-Fi
                              Halmor Venus
         Ch. Bear Acres Two for the Road
                              Int. Ch. Crowleythorn Ladomoorlands
                   Ch. Bear Acres One for the Money
                              Ch. Cote de Neige Apron Strings
AM. CAN. CH. BEAR ACRES MISTER SNOWSHOES, UD
                              Ch. Cote de Neige Christmas Candy
                   Ch. Cote de Neige Honey Guide
                              Harham's Golden Honey Pot of Wey & Cote de Neige
         Ch. Cote de Neige Sweet Message
                              Ch. Cote de Neige Newsfront
                   Ch. Cote de Neige Message
                              Ch. Cote de Neige Re-Echo
</pre>

68

famous kennels, Wey and Stormerbanks, through Drumbeat and Eng. Ch. Stormerbanks Dairymaid, one of the breed's finest brood bitches. With excellent quality behind him, it is no wonder we find Big Drum in the pedigrees of a number of our best American-bred Pembrokes.

Big Drum's famous son, Ch. Cote de Neige Sundew was greatly admired by Corgi fanciers everywhere with many believing he more closely represented the Standard for the breed than any Pembroke dog yet to appear in this country. Purchased at the start of his career from Cote de Neige Kennels by Mrs. William B. Long, Sundew piled up an enviable show record which established him as one of the breed's all time top Best in Show winners. His greatest victory, and one which provided a tremendous thrill for the nation's Corgi lovers, was his Best American-Bred in Show win at the 1960 Westminster Kennel Club show.

Sundew's array of top wins might well have been greater still had it not been for the fact he was upstaged by his dashing young son, Ch. Willet's Red Jacket. Red Jacket, or "Barney" as he was known, had not started off as a promising show puppy. He was a gangly, clumsy youngster and had gone off to a pet home. Not only did the fable of the ugly duckling turning into a beautiful swan come true for Barney, but when problems arose in his new home, he was returned to Stephen Shaw, his handler and life-long friend. In Mrs. William Long's ownership, Red Jacket sailed through to his championship and became a leading Working Group and Best in Show contender throughout his entire career. To date, he remains unchallenged as the top Best in Show winning Pembroke Welsh Corgi of all time with 18 such awards to his credit.

In the Midwest a strong line of winning Pembrokes was established by Mrs. Barbara Hedberg at her Cormanby Kennels by linebreeding on both Ch. Drumbeat of Wyldingtree of Wey and Eng. Ch. Stormerbanks Dairymaid, through Cormanby's foundation bitch, Stormerbanks Saucebox. The mating of Ch. Bigdrum's Jewel Tone, a Big Drum daughter, to Ch. Cormanby Commotion, a son of Ch. Craythorne's Fleetfoot of Wey, produced Ch. Cormanby Cavalier, the sire of 13 American and four Canadian champions. A Cavalier son, Ch. Cormanby Cadenza was a noted Midwestern winner whose record included multiple Specialty, Group and Best in Show wins.

Of the American-bred dogs sired by Ch. Lees Symphony, Ch. Kaydon's Anthony and Am. Mex. Ch. Penrick Most Happy Fella stand out as the most noteworthy.

Owned by Mrs. Carol Simonds, Ch. Kaydon's Anthony was campaigned in California during the mid 1950s and many times was the only Corgi entered at the show. Anthony, a Best in Show winner himself, has bred on through his Best in Show winning son, Can. Am. Ch. Macksons Golden

Stormerbanks Big Drum (left) pictured winning BOS under Miss Pat Curties (Lees Kennels, England) with Mrs. McCammon's Ch. Crawleycrow Coracle of Aimhi winning BB at the 1955 PWCCA Specialty show. *Brown*

The illustrious son of Big Drum, Ch. Cote de Neige Sundew, was Best American-Bred in Show at the 1960 Westminster show under George Hartman. Sundew's record included 7 BIS and 54 Group placings of which 23 were Group 1sts. *Shafer*

Sceptre and Sceptre's litter sister, Can. Am. Ch. Macksons Coronet, both owned by Pamela Mack.

Another of Anthony's offspring, Rover Run Romance, became the foundation bitch of the Larklain Kennels. Her breeding has been perpetuated through the Busy B's, Katydid and Larchmont lines, to mention a few.

Mr. and Mrs. J. Liecty had considerable success with closely-bred Symphony stock. Ch. Penrick Princess, a double Symphony granddaughter, mated back to Symphony produced Symphony's second Best in Show winning son, Am. Mex. Ch. Penrick Most Happy Fella, and a Group winning daughter, Am. Mex. Ch. Penrick Belle A' Ringing. Ch. Penrick Flewellyn, CDX, a litter sister of Princess, was mated back to Symphony and gave the Liectys yet another Group winner, Ch. Penrick Sonny.

While the Symphony offspring were making their mark in this country, the pendulum of breed type was in motion, shifting toward a preference for heavier boned, lower-to-ground Pembrokes than had been sought in years past. Masterpiece breeding put with other lines to Eng. Ch. Knowland Clipper provided what the breeders were seeking.

The Knowland Clipper Influence

Mrs. D. E. Foster's homebred, Eng. Ch. Knowland Clipper, was the breed's youngest champion in England. He completed his title at the age of 14½ months in 1950. Clipper was judged Best Puppy at Crufts in 1950, and in March of that year he went Best Dog all-breeds on the first day of the Manchester championship show. By the time he was 18 months old he had amassed a total of 6 C.C.s, 4 Reserve C.C.s and 89 Junior Warrant points. Clipper's total record of 18 C.C.s places him seventh in the listing of Great Britain's top ten Pembroke C.C. winners.

Runner-up for the League's Formakin Stud Dog Cup in 1951, Clipper won the Cup as the leading stud dog in England from 1952 through 1955. His place at the top of the stud dog list was taken over in 1957 by his grandson, Ch. Maracas Masterpiece, a position which Masterpiece was to maintain through 1960.

Although Knowland Clipper appears in the pedigrees of many American-bred Pembrokes, few of his sons and daughters came to this country; of those who did, only a daughter, Ch. Crawleycrow Coracle of Aimhi, has bred on to any significant extent. Coracle, imported and owned by Mary McCammon, was mated to Ch. Hollyheath Pilot to produce a number of outstanding bitches carrying the Aimhi's prefix. Of these Coracle daughters, Ch. Kaydon Aimhi's Kate had the greatest influence as a producer. Bred to Ch. Lees Symphony, Kate produced Ch. Kaydon's Lillabet of Penrick, the Liectys' foundation bitch and Ch. Kaydon's Eversridge Penny, the foundation

Eng. Ch. Knowland Clipper.

Ch. Erhstag's Gage. A BIS winning grandson of Ch. Eversridge
Rum Punch, breeder: Ronald and Jane Shakely, owner: Lawrason
Riggs of J. *Tauskey*

Ch. Benfro Windjammer, by a grandson of Ch. Eversridge Ru...
Punch, Ch. Benfro Lord Gambier, out of Ch. Benfro Robin,
Gambier daughter. His show record includes 95 BBs and tw...
Group 1sts. Breeder-owner: Carolyn C. Bailey. *Kle...*

bitch at Eleanore Evers' Eversridge Kennels. Penny mated to Am. Ch. Stormerbanks Tristram of Cote de Neige produced Ch. Cote de Neige Gold Coin, the dam of an excellent brood bitch at Cote de Neige, Ch. Cote de Neige Penny Wise. From that same Penny-Tris breeding came Ch. Eversridge Rum Punch, a dog who figures strongly in the Ehrstag line bred by Ron and Jane Shakely and in Carolyn Bailey's Benfro line.

Much of the Knowland Clipper breeding in this country was brought in by Eng. Irish Ch. Zephyr of Brome, a Clipper son. Zephyr, bred and owned by Mrs. Rose Johnson, was a Junior Warrant winner at eight months and a champion at twelve months, thus taking over his sire's position as the breed's youngest champion in England. Zephyr's total wins included 27 C.C.s and a Best in Show at an all-breed Championship show.

In a very short period of time Philip and Louise Cleland established a successful and readily identifiable line of Cleden Corgis by using a carefully selected nucleus of imported linebred Masterpiece-Zephyr-Clipper stock. Their two foundation stud dogs, Am. Can. Bda. Ch. Maracas Monarch of Cleden (a Masterpiece son out of a Zephyr daughter) and Am. Bda. Ch. Maracas Gale Force of Cleden (a Zephyr son out of a Clipper daughter) proved tremendously useful as sires in this country.

Although Gale Force with 14 champions to his credit had to relinquish his placing on the ten top producing sires listing to current sires, two of his offspring out of Ch. Cote de Neige Garland, namely Ch. Cote de Neige Christmas Candy and Ch. Cote de Neige Christmas Rush, are all time top ten producers.

A Christmas Candy grandson, the famous Ch. Cote de Neige Pennysaver, and a Pennysaver son, Ch. Cote de Neige Instant Replay, appear on the current top ten sires listing, each with 18 champion offspring. Out of a Christmas Rush daughter, Instant Replay is from a repeat of the breeding that produced the Best in Show winner, Ch. Cote de Neige Chance of Fox Run. Following the death of Marjorie Butcher "Savers" and "Play" went to the Goldwick Kennels in the co-ownership of Mrs. F. A. Howard and Marjorie's son, Christopher Butcher. Savers remained a favorite house dog at the Howards' Meadowville Farm until his death in June 1978.

Elaine Swinney Erganbright, the breeder of well over a hundred Pembroke champions bearing the Larklain prefix, made what appears to be the most concentrated use of Zephyr lines of any breeder in this country. Her imported stud dogs included Ch. Viceroy of Brome, a Zephyr son; Ch. Red Envoy of Brome CD, sired by Red Major of Brome—a Zephyr brother, and out of a Zephyr daughter; and Ch. Enterprise of Brome, again sired by Red Major and out of a Viceroy daughter.

As the sire of 51 champions, Red Envoy remains at the head of the all time top sires listing, comfortably ahead of all others. Not only has Red

Envoy sired the most champions of any Pembroke in this country, but his record of siring three Best in Show winners has not, to date, been equalled. Of his three Best in Show sons, Ch. Larklain's Firebright, Ch. Larklain's Red Desaster and Ch. Larklain's Emblem, Firebright was the best known winner with a total of 2 Bests in Show, 30 Working Groups, 70 Group placements and 175 Bests of Breed.

A number of today's active breeders owned as their first Corgi, a Larklain-bred dog or bitch. As a result, lines to Zephyr and Clipper became widely dispersed around the country as the foundation stock for many of the new kennels formed during the late 1950s and early 1960s.

The Ambrose—Supersonic Combination

Quite apart from the Clipper-Masterpiece-Zephyr breeding which was being carried out the world over was the emergence of a powerful line in England. Miss Patsy Hewan's Stormerbanks line first made its presence felt late in the 1930s. Stormerbanks dogs have continued right to the present to rank among the top winners and producers of the day. The success of the line is evidenced by the annual listings of England's top producing sires and dams in which at least one dog or bitch carrying the Stormerbanks prefix can be found every year for the past twenty-five years.

The ability to breed on was undoubtedly transmitted to the Stormerbanks Pembrokes in part by the noted post-war winner and sire, Eng. Irish Ch. Broom of Ballybentra through his son, Churchleigh Ballybentra Cowboy. Broom appears in many pedigrees through his well-known sons, Ch. Lisaye Disturbance and Ch. Crawleycrow's Bannow Master Broom, and through his famous grandson, Ch. Zephyr of Brome. Many of the Wey and Hildenmanor dogs trace back to Master Broom which explains the compatibility often found between these lines and those of Stormerbanks breeding.

Churchleigh Ballybentra Cowboy sired Eng. Ch. Stormerbanks Cowbelle, the first of a long line of champions at Stormerbanks, and Eng. Ch. Stormerbanks Dairymaid. Dairymaid mated to Stormerbanks Parmel Audacity, a dog Miss Hewan brought in after Cowboy's untimely death, produced Stormerbanks Ambrose and Stormerbanks Amanda. Bred to Eng. Ch. Sonec of Rode, one of England's leading stud dogs throughout the 1950s, Amanda produced Stormerbanks Supersonic. In the Dairymaid son, Ambrose, and grandson, Supersonic, Miss Hewan had a nucleus from which careful line breeding would produce generations of famous Stormerbanks winners.

In a personal letter, Miss Hewan modestly writes of the Ambrose-Supersonic combination:

> I think it was just one of those lucky bits of line breeding that seemed to work out exceptionally well, and the influence has carried on over the years. I suppose you could say that the combination produced what people call the

74

Int. Ch. Broom of Ballybentra, great grandsire of Eng. Irish Ch. Zephyr of Brome and grandsire of the first champion at Stormerbanks, Eng. Ch. Stormerbanks Cowbelle, and of Eng. Ch. Stormerbanks Dairymaid. Broom was worked regularly as a cattle dog while in his native Ireland. He was the first Irish bred dog to become an English champion and was runner-up for the Formakin Stud Dog Cup in 1948 and 1949. *Fall*

Stormerbanks Ambrose.

Fall

Am. Can. Ch. Stormerbanks Tristram of Cote de Neige was the
leading sire in 1960, 1961, 1962, 1964 and 1965 (tied with Envoy
in 1962 and 1964). He sired Ch. Country Miss of Hillview, the
second Pembroke bitch to go Best in Show in the United
States.   *Tauskey*

Can. Am. Bda. Ch. Welcanis Adulation, breeder-owners: Dr. and
Mrs. G. Wilkins (Ch. Stormerbanks Tristram of Cote de Neige ex
Ch. Corgana Fascination). She was the top-winning Corgi in
Canada in 1964, 1965 an 1967 and BB at the Golden Gate PWCF
Specialty show 1963.   *January*

Lees Jackpot.   *C.M. Cooke*

Stormerbanks Supersonic.   *F.W. Simms*

Eng. Ch. Stormerbanks Sabreflash, a Supersonic grandson out of an Ambrose daughter, and a winner of 18 C.C.s.   *F.W. Simms*

Eng. Ch. Stormerbanks Invader, leading stud dog in 1961 and 1962. His last champion son, Eng. Ch. Stormerbanks Vainglory, appears on the list of England's leading stud dogs, 1977.

C.M. Cooke

Stormerbanks type, and I think each of the dogs had an equal influence on the offspring. One of the main good things from the breeding of these two was that they never produced (and would actually correct) all the serious faults like fluffies, bluies, mismarks, sharks etc. I don't think either of them ever sired one, which didn't make such an impression on me at the time.

Of the Ambrose-Supersonic breeding imported into the United States, Ch. Stormerbanks Tristram of Cote de Neige stands out as the most important producer. Whelped in June, 1956, Tris was sired by Stormerbanks Supersabre, a Supersonic son. His dam, Tresarden Trinket, was an Ambrose daughter who already had proven herself to be a producer as the dam of one of the breed's prettiest bitches, Eng. Ch. Stormerbanks Superfine. Superfine, sired by Supersonic, bred on through her son, Eng. Ch. Stormerbanks Indigo, the sire of Eng. Ch. Stormerbanks Invader.

Stormerbanks Tristram was imported in January 1957 by Marjorie Butcher. With a Group first and frequent Group placings enroute, "Tris" completed his championship undefeated in the classes at 11 months of age. With a total of forty champion offspring to his credit, Tris ranks as the second top producing sire of all time in the United States.

Of the many Tris offspring who have bred on well for their owners, Am. Can. Ch. Welcanis Adulation heads the list. She is well-known not only for her record as a producer but for her successes in the show ring as well. An Adulation daughter, Am. Can. Ch. Welcanis Duplication has been an important producer at the Leetwood Kennels owned by Mr. and Mrs. Elwin Leet. Another Duplication daughter, Am. Can. Ch. Welcanis Constellation Faraway, is prominent in many pedigrees through Faraway and Schaferhaus breeding.

Perhaps one of the best known dogs to represent Ambrose-Supersonic breeding outside of the Stormerbanks Kennels is Lees Jackpot, owned by Miss Pat Curties. Whelped in September, 1956, Jackpot was sired by Ambrose and was out of a Supersonic daughter, Stormerbanks Supersweet. Unlucky to never make up his championship, Jackpot proved himself a consistent producer instead. His name appears on the listings of England's leading stud dogs every year from 1959 through 1965.

Jackpot breeding is found more frequently in American pedigrees through his son, Eng. Ch. Lees Sunsalve, than directly by himself. Sunsalve, a grandson of Int. Ch. Gayelord of Wey, brings the familiar breeding of Ch. Drumbeat of Wyldingtree of Wey into the pedigrees of a number of our winning dogs.

A top winner bred and owned by Mr. and Mrs. Dennis Van Velzer, Ch. Wicklow's Whizzer, is a line bred Sunsalve grandson. His granddam, Lees Lizette, has more recently produced a line of champion offspring for the Royal Mark Kennels, owned by Mr. and Mrs. Neil McLain.

78

Lees Jackpot, Lees Firefly and their daughter, Eng. Ch. Lees Firefairy. Firefly was the winner of the League's Coronet Brood Bitch Cup in 1959. *C.M. Cooke*

Eng. Ch. Lees Sunsalve (Lees Jackpot ex Lees Firefly), whelped August 24, 1960. *Sally Anne Thompson*

Am. Can. Ch. Lees Briardale Midnight (Eng. Ch. Lees Sunsalve ex Lees Tessa), whelped May 13, 1967. Breeder: Miss B. Woods. *Booth*

**Ch. Wicklow's Whizzer, (Am. Can. Ch. Lees Briardale Midnight ex Ch. Fox Run's All Bets Down),
whelped August 13, 1971. A Specialty and BIS winner, Whizzer was the top Pembroke Welsh Corgi for
1974. Breeder-Owners: Mr. and Mrs. Dennis Van Velzer.**

Lees Jackpot

Eng. Ch. Lees Sunsalve

Lees Firefly

Am. Can. Ch. Lees Briardale Midnight

Eng.Ch. Lees Wennam Eagle

Lees Tessa

Lees Sonatina

CH. WICKLOW'S WHIZZER

Ch. Cote de Neige Pennysaver

Ch. Cote de Neige Chance of Fox Run

Ch. Cote de Neige News Item

Ch. Fox Run's All Bets Down

Eng. Ch. Lees Sunsalve

Lees Lizette

Lees Eugenie of Bulcorig

80

Am. Can. Ch. Llanfair Night Owl holds the breed record with Bests of Breed at one Canadian and six American Specialty shows. He has also won BOS at one American and one Canadian Specialty. He has been owner-handled to all of his wins.

<pre>
                                    Eng. Ch. Winrod Peregrine
                        Eng. Ch. Lees Wennam Eagle
                                    Wennam Snowbunting
            Am. Can. Ch. Lees Mynah, CD, TD
                                    Lees Jackpot
                        Lees Brunette
                                    Lees Sonatina
AM. CAN. CH. LLANFAIR NIGHT OWL
                                    Eng. Ch. Winrod Rob Roy
                        Ch. Halmor's Winrod Spencer
                                    Winrod Belinda
            Llanfair Bee Balm, CD, TD
                                    Ch. Cyclone of Cowfold
                        Cappykorns Carousel, CDX
                                    Lees Gaiety Girl
</pre>

Ch. Larchmont's Golden Triumph, CD, (Ch. Halmor's Winrod Spencer ex Ch. Kem's Candy), whelped December 6, 1965. breeders: Bob and Esther Britain, owner: Mrs. Pat Jensen. He sired 15 champions including the 1970-71 top-winning Corgi in the U.S., Ch. Nebriowa's Miss Bobbisox.

```
                                    Eng. Ch. Kentwood Cogges Woodpecker
                       Eng. Ch. Winrod Rob Roy
                       Winrod Vanessa
          Ch. Halmor's Winrod Spencer
                            Eng. Ch. Maracas Masterpiece
                       Winrod Belinda
                            Stormerbanks Emma of Corig
CH. LARCHMONT'S GOLDEN TRIUMPH, CD
                            Ch. Cleden's Portrait of Force
                       Ch. Larklain Toddy
                            Larklains Token
          Ch. Kem's Candy
                            Ch. Enterprise of Brome
                       Larklain Coquette
                            Ch. Larklain's Cinderella
```

Am. Can. Ch. Llanfair Night Owl is one of this country's most successful Specialty show winners and popular stud dogs. Night Owl, or "Hooter" as he is affectionately known, was bred by Henrik and Irene Sorley, and is co-owned by Irene Sorley, Fred Omer and Don Christie. Ambrose-Supersonic breeding is found mainly through Jackpot in Night Owl's pedigree, as the Winrod breeding also goes back to Jackpot.

Another popular English stud whose name appears frequently in American pedigrees is Eng. Ch. Lees Wennam Eagle. Wennam Eagle was brought into Miss Curties' Lees Kennels to serve as an outcross for Jackpot and Sunsalve daughters. Through Eng. Ch. Kentwood Cogges Woodpecker on both sides of his pedigree, Wennam Eagle combines heavy Masterpiece breeding with Supersonic breeding. Additional Ambrose-Supersonic breeding is found behind Wennam Eagle's granddam, Eng. Ch. Winrod Rhapsody, a Jackpot granddaughter.

Not only did Wennam Eagle prove to be a successful outcross for bitches of Jackpot and Sunsalve breeding, but his son, Ch. Lees Craythorne's Golden Plover has been a useful sire, for different outcross lines in this country.

A combination, similar to what is behind Wennam Eagle, of Winrod breeding with Masterpiece lines has been perpetuated by the Pimlotts' Ch. Halmor's Winrod Spencer, grandsire of Ch. Llanfair Night Owl.

In turn, a Spencer son and a well-known West Coast stud dog, Ch. Larchmont's Golden Triumph, CD, combines the Masterpiece-Supersonic lines of the Winrod stock with his dam's Masterpiece-Clipper breeding and a line to Ch. Stormerbanks Tristram of Cote de Neige, the sire of Larklain Token. "Britt's" pedigree, probably as well as any, represents a complete integration of Symphony, Clipper and Ambrose-Supersonic lines.

Today's Trends

In contrast to the depth of quality seen in English Pembrokes, a number of our American Pembrokes from the mid-1950s through the 1960s were sadly lacking in over-all quality. Coarse, heavy-headed dogs with overly long muzzles, small eyes and hard expressions were seen with alarming frequency. Unfortunately, newcomers to the breed during that time, be they future breeders or judges, had no way of knowing the Corgis they were seeing did not represent the ideal in Pembroke type.

Perhaps due to wider exposure to different dogs from a variety of geographical areas made possible by the increasing number of annual Specialty shows, most of today's breeders have a better understanding of what constitutes desired Pembroke type and quality.

Breeders across the country have made good use of English imports to

Ch. Bekonpenn Count Doronicum, CD, whelped October 12, 1971. Breeder: Mr. L.F. Needham, owner: Mrs. Elaine Swinney Erganbright. A Crown Prince-Duskie Knight grandson, Count Doronicum is also a successful sire.

Hildenmanor Bonilad
Eng. Ch. Hildenmanor Crown Prince
Hildenmanor Gold Crown
Carabana Foxash Milord
Eng. Ch. Caswell Duskie Knight
Foxash Bright Star
Foxash Winrod Juliet
CH. BEKONPENN COUNT DORONICUM, C.D.
Caswell Marcus
Eng. Ch. Caswell Duskie Knight
Mynthurst Duskie Princess
Anemone of Bekonpenn
Eng. Ch. Stormerbanks Invader
Candytuft of Bekonpenn
Stormerbanks Fuchsia of Bekonpenn

Eng. Ch. Kathla's Dusky Sparkler of Blands, whelped November 4, 1971, breeders: Mr. and Mrs. E. Lacey, owner: Mrs. Peggy Gamble. One of England's leading stud dogs since 1974, Sparkler won the League's Formakin Stud Dog Cup in 1976. *Diane Pearce*

<pre>
                          Int. Ch. Corgwyn Shillelah
               Eng. Ch. Jomaro Midnight Special
                          Jomaro Winrod Juno
       Eng. Ch. Jomaro Midnight Sun
                          Eng. Ch. Blands Ambassador
               Jomaro Blands Candida
                          Blands Caroline
ENG. CH. KATHLA'S DUSKY SPARKLER OF BLANDS
                          Pennywise of Wey
               Blands Telstar
                          Corgwyn Lucky Lady of Blands
       Dusky Rosaday of Kathla
                          Blands Duskie Knight
               Kathla's Roxi of Edlands
                          Kathla's Super Star
</pre>

upgrade the level of quality within their own lines. While many of the names beginning to appear in pedigrees of American-bred Corgis would seem to represent new bloodlines, they all trace back in some degree to one or more of the early greats, Symphony, Masterpiece and Clipper.

Eng. Ch. Hildenmanor Crown Prince is found in the pedigrees of some of our best known dogs—Ch. Velour of Rowell, Ch. Bekonpenn Count Doronicum, CD and Ch. Cappykorns Bach, to name a few. Crown Prince, bred-owned by Mrs. Dickie Albin, was one of England's leading stud dogs during the late 1960s and into the 1970s. He carries Ambrose-Supersonic breeding through his grandsire, Eng. Ch. Lees Sunsalve and also has a line back to Masterpiece. The attractive head quality for which the Hildenmanor dogs are known can be traced back to Laddie of Veryan, the dog from whom all the Hildenmanor Pembrokes descend.

Both Ch. Bekonpenn Count Doronicum, CD and Ch. Cappykorns Bach combine Crown Prince breeding with that of the famous and extremely useful English stud dog, Ch. Caswell Duskie Knight. Duskie Knight lines, in turn, bring in the additional lovely type and head quality for which his grandsire, Pennywise of Wey is noted.

Another new name which is appearing with considerable frequency today is Blands, Mrs. Peggy Gamble's kennel prefix. The Blands line has been astutely built on a foundation of Zephyr lines heavily crossed with Masterpiece breeding. The foundation bitch at Blands Kennels, Dawn of Brome, was a Zephyr daughter and out of a Clipper daughter. Dawn bred to Eng. Ch. Sonec of Rode, a dog found in the foundation breeding at Stormerbanks as well, produced Blands Satinette. Line breeding Dawn and Satinette together with a popular stud dog in the north of England, Thornbelle Cointreau of Trewake, has given Mrs. Gamble the well-known English sires, Blands Telstar, Eng. Ch. Blands Ambassador and Ch. Kathla's Dusky Sparkler of Blands. As so many breeders have done, and are still doing, Mrs. Gamble turned to Pennywise of Wey breeding to successfully strengthen head quality and expression in her Blands line.

The top winning Corgi in England for 1976, Ch. Blands Solomon of Bardrigg, represents concentrated line breeding on Pennywise of Wey through his two sons, Blands Telstar and Eng. New Zealand Ch. Corgwyn Shillelah.

Pennywise breeding has been further intensified in American bloodlines through Ch. Leonine Leprechaun, a son of Int. Ch. Corgwyn Shillelah, and the foundation stud dog at Schaferhaus Kennels. The pedigrees of Ch. Faraway The Magic Kan-D-Kid, CD and Am. Can. Ch. Schaferhaus Yul B of Quanda nicely illustrate the successful combination of Leprechaun breeding with the lines which come down from the early Ambrose-Supersonic breeding. The depth of quality within these lines is attested to by the fact that Kan-D-Kid has four champion sisters. Yul has, to date, at least seven

Ch. Cappykorns Bach, whelped October 8, 1973, breeder: Dorothy Lacy, owners: Ken and Patricia Pettipiece. Bach was BB at the 1977 Golden Gate Specialty under Margaret Cole. One of the outstanding sires of the late 1970s, he is pictured as WD at the 1975 Cascade Specialty under Mrs. Dickie Albin. *Smith*

Eng. Ch. Lees Sunsalve

Eng. Ch. Lees Orpheus

Eng. Ch. Lees Opalsong of Treland

Carabana Foxash Offenbach

Eng. Ch. Caswell Duskie Knight

Foxash Bright Star

Foxash Winrod Juliet

CH. CAPPYKORNS BACH

Corgay Badger

How's That of Ormareon

Hildenmanor Glamour Girl of Atlast

Ch. Ormareon Grace and Favour

Carabana Foxash Milord

Raymardene Marchioness of Ormareon

Camelot Black Princess

Ch. Faraway The Magic Kan-D-Kid, CD, whelped October 19, 1970, breeder: Jean Walker. co-owners: Judy Zimmerman and Robert Simpson. In the one year Stoney was shown as a Special, he won two BIS five Group 1sts, 12 Group placings and 20 BBs. *Robert*

Pennywise of Wey
Int. Ch. Corgwyn Shillelah
Corgwyn Lucky Lady of Blands
Am. Can. Ch. Leonine Leprechaun
Leonine Christopher
Leonine Golden Maid
Leonine Gay Witch
CH. FARAWAY THE MAGIC KAN-D-KID, CD
Eng. Ch. Stormerbanks Indigo
Can. Ch. Royalbrae Nocturn
Royalbrae Infatuation
Am. Can. Ch. Welcanis Constellation Faraway
Ch. Stormerbanks Tristram of Cote de Neige
Am. Can. Bda. Ch. Welcanis Adulation
Can. Ch. Corgana Fascination

Am. Can. Ch. Schaferhaus Yul B of Quanda. Whelped December 10, 1975, breeders: G.A. and M. Clarke and Schaferhaus Kennels, owners: Schaferhaus Kennels and G.A. Clarke. At three years of age, Yul has five BIS and ten Group 1sts. He was BB at the PWCCA and Cascade Specialties and was BOS at two other Specialties.

Eng. Ch. Lees Orpheus

Carabana Foxash Offenbach

Foxash Bright Star

Ch. Cappykorns Bach

How's That of Ormareon

Ch. Ormareon Grace and Favour

Raymardene Marchioness of Ormareon

AM. CAN. CH. SCHAFERHAUS YUL B OF QUANDA

Int. Ch. Corgwyn Shillelah

Am. Can. Ch. Leonine Leprechaun

Leonine Golden Maid

Ch. Schaferhaus Aeroglend Tupence

Leonine Call Boy

Schaferhaus Honey n' Cream

Ch. Faraway The Magic Flame

Ch. Midon's Billie The Kid, (Cl
Halmor's Winrod Spencer ex Cl
Cappykorn's Sonnet), whelpe
April 27, 1965, breeder: D. Pric
owners: M.D. and L.E. Thaxter. H
was owner-handled to BB at th
1967 Golden Gate Specialty und
Miss Patsy Hewan (Stormerbanks
He repeated this win in 196
under Arthur Bridge (Daleviz
Schle

Ch. Halmor's Winrod Spencer, whelped August 30, 1963, breeder: Mrs.
E.J. Busby, co-owners: Nell Merrick and Eileen Pimlott. Spencer is the
sire of 10 champions and his descendants include the Westminster
Group winner, Ch. Nebriowa Miss Bobbisox, and the multiple Specialty
winner, Ch. Llanfair Night Owl. He is pictured at the 1965 Golden Gate
Specialty where he was WD under Mrs. Dickie Albin (Hildenmanor),
handler: Roy Pimlott. *King*

champion brothers and sisters. Both Kan-D-Kid and Yul have proven themselves to be quality sires, each with a number of champion offspring to their credit.

Today's breeders are much more aware of, and concerned with, sound movement in the Pembroke Welsh Corgi than at any other point in the history of the breed. Not realizing that it was not only desirable but also entirely possible for the Corgi to have the free, seemingly effortless movement associated with larger breeds, many breeders overlooked the stilted, mincing, or shuffling movement which was all too common in the breed. Now, with the quality of stock at hand, coupled with generally increased understanding of correct movement as it relates to proper body structure, breeders today are in a position to establish lines from which true Corgi type, character and soundness will breed on for generations to come.

Eng. Ch. Gilburn Supermac (right) and his son Eng. Ch. Fitzdown Cygnus of Rowell, both owned by Miss Paddy Date. Supermac, Pembroke Welsh Corgi of the Year in 1975, is by Eng. Aust. Ch. Kydor Cossack ex Gilburn Fantasy. Breeder: Mrs. A. Gibson. Supermac won the Working Group and Reserve Best in Show at Birmingham National and was 13th top-winning dog, all breeds, in 1975 in England. Fitzdown Cygnus of Rowell, ex Fitzdown Cygnet, is a breed Championship show winner with seven C.C.s to his credit. Breeders: T. and A. Gibson.   *Diane Pearce*

C H. STORMERBANKS
DAIRYMAID

FISHER & POTTER LTD.
LEICESTER.

Eng. Ch. Stormerbanks Dairymaid
Whelped April 21, 1948
Breeder: Mr. H. Whitworth
Owner: Miss P. Hewan

A granddaughter of both Int. Ch. Broom of Ballybentra and Eng. Ch. Teekay's Felcourt Supremacy. Dam of Ch. Stormerbanks Big Drum, CDX, Stormerbanks Ambrose and Stormerbanks Amanda (Stormerbanks Supersonic's dam). The son-grandson combination of Dairymaid has been successful for Miss Hewan.

Crawleycrow Banjo
Int. Ch. Broom of Ballybentra
Teekay Bramble
Churchleigh Ballybentra Cowboy
Eng. Ch. Bowhit Prince
Teekay Mistress Quickly
Teekay Quicksllver
ENG. CH. STORMERBANKS DAIRYMAID
Hill Billy of Lees
Eng. Ch. Teekay's Felcourt Supremacy
Floss
Sandra of the Butts
Int. Ch. Rozavel Lucky Strike
Foxy of Helpric
Red Vixen

6

Outstanding Pembroke Bitches

As WITH MOST BREEDS, male Pembroke Welsh Corgis have reaped the lion's share of show ring glory. The bitches pay the penalty for changing coats between seasons and for taking time off for maternity duties. They do not have the size or the heavy, glamorous coats of many of the breed's flashy males that make for top wins. Thus the bitches may appear less impressive to some eyes. Yet, the outstanding bitches in the breed, rather than most of the top winning males, are the ones who have gained the universal approval of Pembroke connoisseurs. Bitches such as Rockrose, Personality Girl, Fergwyn Frith and Red Rose come as close to being "everybody's cup of tea" as any animal ever could.

Space does not permit coverage for every bitch that has made an important contribution to the breed. Some of the breed's well-known bitches that have obtained impressive show records and/or have proven to be important producers have been selected for presentation here.

Ch. Crawleycrow Coracle of Aimhi (Eng. Ch. Knowland Clipper ex Crawley-crow Cloverhoney), whelped August 27, 1950. This noted import finished with Group placements after three litters all by Ch. Hollyheath Pilot of Waseeka. She was the dam of Ch. Kaydon Aimhi's Kate and was BB at the 1955 PWCCA Specialty under Miss Curties. Breeder: Mrs. Christopher Firbank. Owner: Mrs. M. D. McCammon. *Shafer*

A group of Mrs. Eleanore Evers' Corgis (from left) Ch. Eversridge Sherry Flip, her dam Ch. Kaydon's Eversridge Penny and Penny's dam Ch. Kaydon Aimhi's Kate. Kate, bred by Mrs. McCammon, was whelped April 3, 1952, and was by Ch. Hollyheath Pilot of Waseeka ex Ch. Crawleycrow Coracle of Aimhi. Mrs. Evers considers these bitches the source of the quality at her Eversridge Kennels still seen eight generations later.

Ch. Cote de Neige Penny Wise
Whelped September 10, 1958
Breeder-Owner: Mrs. Marjorie Butcher

A granddaughter of Ch. Kaydon's Eversridge Penny. Dam of Best in Show winners Ch. Cote de Neige Derek and Ch. Cote de Neige Pennysaver. Through Penny Wise and her sons descended numerous Cote de Neige champions.

Eng. Irish Ch. Zephyr of Brome
Am. Bda. Ch. Maracas Gale Force of Cleden
Maracas Helarian Gale
Ch. Cote de Neige Christmas Candy
Ch. Cote de Neige Shadow
Ch. Cote de Neige Garland
Ch. Cote de Neige Posy
CH. COTE DE NEIGE PENNY WISE
Stormerbanks Supersabre
Ch. Stormerbanks Tristram of Cote de Neige
Tresarden Trinket
Cote de Neige Gold Coin
Eng. Am. Can. Ch. Lees Symphony
Ch. Kaydon's Eversridge Penny
Ch. Kaydon Aimhi's Kate

Ch. Nebriowa Amber Mist

Whelped January 13, 1967
Breeders: Thomas Mathiesen and Mrs. Eileen Pimlott
Owner: Thomas Mathiesen

Tied for Seventh Top Producing Dam in the United States (1935–1977) for her seven champions from six litters by four different studs. Dam of Best in Show and Specialty winner Ch. Nebriowa Miss Bobbisox and several other champions particularly successful in the show ring such as Ch. Nebriowa Duskie Lad and Ch. Nebriowa Jonathan. One of her daughters, California's Golden Poppy, is a dam of three champions.

Eng. Ch. Crowleythorn Snowman
Am. Can. Ch. Halmor Hi-Fi
Halmor Venus
Am. Can. Ch. Dogdene Cochise of Halmor
Sportsman of Wey
Can. Ch. Falaise Kittiwake
Falaise View Hullo of Almadee

CH. NEBRIOWA AMBER MIST

Eng. Ch. Crowleythorn Snowman
Am. Can. Ch. Halmor Hi-Fi
Halmor Venus

Halmor Bonny Bess

Ch. Gerona's Sundowner
Ch. Gerona's Sundancer
Tia Maria of Gerona

Ch. Nebriowa Miss Bobbisox (Ch. Larchmont's Golden Triumph, CD ex Ch. Nebriowa Amber Mist), whelped September 25, 1968, breeder: Thomas Mathresen, owners: Mr. and Mrs. Derek Rayne. Bobbisox won a BIS, BB at the PWCC of Southern California Specialty in 1972 and 15 Working Groups. Three times BB followed by Group placings at Westminster, she is shown winning the Group at Westminster in 1972 under Hayworth F. Hoch, handler Frank Sabella. *Shafer*

Eng. Am. Ch. Rockrose of Wey (Red Rock of Wey ex Michele of Wey), whelped November 20, 1962, breeder: E. Evans. owners: Mr. and Mrs. Derek Rayne. Her outstanding show record includes five all-breed BIS, five Specialty BBs, two Specialty BOS wins, and 27 Working Groups. She was the top-winning bitch in England in 1964 and won the same honor in America in 1965. She is shown winning the 1967 PWCC of Southern California Specialty under judge Jack Liecty, handled by Derek Rayne. *Henry C. Schley*

Ch. Brideholme Jordonian Sunlight (Playboy of Brideholme ex Jordonian Miranda), whelped July 3, 1956, granddaughter of both Eng. Irish Ch. Zephyr of Brome and his sire Eng. Ch. Knowland Clipper. Breeder: Mr. A. Jordan, imported and owned by Mrs. F.A. Howard. A dam of seven champions, she is tied for seventh place on the top producing dams list.

Ch. Cote de Neige Posy (Lees Lancelot ex Brendon Myrtle of Cote de Neige), whelped October 8, 1950, was heavily line-bred on Eng. Ch. Teekay's Felcourt Supremacy. Breeder-owner: Marjorie Butcher. She was the grand-dam of Ch. Cote de Neige Sundew and many other Cote de Neige champions most notably through her daughters Petal and Garland. Posy will be remembered by those who knew her as the "official greeter" at Cote de Neige Kennels.   *Shafer*

Ch. Busy B's Cherry Bark Key
Whelped January 25, 1967
Breeder-Owner: Lynn Brooks

All Time Top Producing Dam with 17 champion offspring to her credit. Out of five litters she whelped between the ages of two and seven, there were thirty living puppies. Five puppies from one litter alone finished their titles. Several additional offspring are pointed; and others have earned advanced obedience titles. Her record will be difficult to surpass.

Eng. Ch. Maracas Masterpiece
Ch. Coster of Cowfold
Cherryripe of Cowfold
Ch. Larklain's Prince Charming
Ch. Red Envoy of Brome, CD
Ch. Larklain's Cinderella
Ch. Larklain Babeta
CH. BUSY B'S CHERRY BARK KEY
Ch. Hi Ho Ranger, CD
Corwyne Arwr of Bi Lu
Ch. Larklain's Illusion
Busy B's Really Moxie, CD
Cormanby Cabin Boy
Gold Star's Blondie
Vagabond's Gold Star

Larklains Token (Ch. Stormerbanks Tristram of Cote de Neige ex Ch. Cote de Neige Sweet As Honey), whelped October 15, 1957, breeder: Marjorie Butcher. For her owner Mrs. Elaine Swinney Erganbright, she produced nine champions, placing her in a tie for second top producing dam in the United States in 1935-1977. She is the dam of BIS winner Ch. Larklain's Firebright.

Ch. Larklain Babeta (Ch. Cleden's Portrait of Force ex Larklain Red Flirt), pictured at 11½ years of age, whelped December 31, 1959, breeder: Mrs. Elaine Swinney Erganbright, owner: Mrs. Molly Langerak Schwarz. Bred four times to Ch. Red Envoy of Brome, CD, she produced nine champions including Ch. Larklain's Cinderella, granddam of Ch. Busy B's Cherry Bark Key and tied for second top producing dam.

Eng. Ch. Evancoyd Personality Girl
Whelped February 18, 1967
Breeder-Owner: Mrs. Beryl J. Thompson

Winner of the greatest number of Challenge Certificates in the history of the breed. By the time she was retired in 1974, Personality Girl had won forty C.C.'s. She was Pembroke Welsh Corgi of the Year in 1968, 1969 and 1973. Her son, Am. Ch. Evancoyd Something Special, sired Eng. Ch. Evancoyd Audacious, Pembroke Welsh Corgi of the Year in 1972.

                                 Pennywise of Wey
                    Caswell Marcus
                                   Eng. Ch. Caswell My Fair Lady
          Eng. Ch. Caswell Duskie Knight
                                 Mynthurst Artful Dodger
                    Mynthurst Duskie Princess
                                 Eng. Ch. Mynthurst Carousel of Cellerhof
ENG. CH. EVANCOYD PERSONALITY GIRL
                                 Eng. Ch. Maracas Masterpiece
                    Eng. Ch. Crowleythorn Snowman
                                 Crowleythorn Snowdrift
          Evancoyd True Love
                                 Evancoyd Brokencote Benedictine
                    Eng. Ch. Evancoyd Cover Girl
                               Evancoyd Romance

Am. Can. Ch. Glynea Red Rose
Whelped June 16, 1969
Breeder: D. Charles Lewis
Owner: Janet Robinson

The lovely "Rosie" has had notable success at Specialties. Her PWCCA Specialty wins include BOB in 1972 and 1974 plus BOS in 1975 and 1977 (from the Veterans Bitch class). BOS at Lakeshore in 1977 and Potomac in 1978. Consistent winner of the Brood Bitch class with her three champion offspring by her beloved kennel mate Ch. Velour of Rowell. Her record in all-breed competition certainly would have been far greater had she been an outgoing show girl.

<pre>
                          Eng. Ch. Stormerbanks Indigo
            Eng. Ch. Stormerbanks Invader
                          Stormerbanks Flashback
      Imperial of Pendcrest
                          Pennywise of Wey
            Isolda of Pendcrest
                          Stormerbanks Ice Magic of Pendcrest
CH. GLYNEA RED ROSE
                          Stormerbanks Boniface
            Hildenmanor Bonilad
                          Hildenmanor Mermaid
      Belroyd Skylark
                          Corporal of Cowfold
            Belroyd Orange Blossom
                          Belroyd Kittiwake
</pre>

Ch. Ormareon Grace and Favour

Whelped May 17, 1972
Breeder: Mrs. M. J. Carlyle
Owner: Dorothy Lacy

Imported in whelp to Carabana Foxash Offenbach, her first litter included two well-known champions, Ch. Cappykorns Ravel and Ch. Cappykorns Bach, who has proven himself useful as a stud. "Kirsty" was Winners Bitch and Best of Breed at the two California Specialties in 1974. In 1975 she was BOS to her son Cappykorns Bartok at the Southern California PWCC Specialty and BOS to her son Bach at the Golden Gate Specialty in 1977.

Pennywise of Wey
Corgay Badger
Banhaw Balm
How's That of Ormareon
Eng. Ch. Hildenmanor Crown Prince
Hildenmanor Glamour Girl of Atlast
Chloe of Atlast
CH. ORMAREON GRACE AND FAVOUR
Eng. Ch. Hildenmanor Crown Prince
Carabana Foxash Milord
Foxash Brightstar
Raymardene Marchioness of Ormareon
Eng. Ch. Lees Sunsalve
Camelot Black Princess
Belroyd Redwing

Ch. Schaferhaus Danielle
Whelped October 10, 1971
Breeders: C. C. Kruger and Louise Vantrease
Owner: Margaret C. Shepard

With seven all-breed Bests in Show, she has gone to the top more than any other Pembroke Welsh Corgi bitch of all time. A two-time Specialty winner. BOB and Group Two at the 1977 Westminster Kennel Club Show. Dam of two champions from her first litter. She lives with her handler and former co-owner, Robert Simpson.

Pennywise of Wey
Int. Ch. Corgwyn Shillelah
Corgwyn Lucky Lady of Blands
Am. Can. Ch. Leonine Leprechaun
Leonine Christopher
Leonine Golden Maid
Leonine Gay Witch

CH. SCHAFERHAUS DANIELLE

Aust. Ch. Elmoran of Elsdyle
Lodestar of Elsdyle
Double Star of Elsdyle
Am. Can. Aust. Ch. Rryde Symphony
Cogges Peregrine
Rryde Lyrebird
Rryde Warbler

Eng. Ch. Wey Blackmint (Wey Magic ex Caramel of Wey), whelped September 6, 1975 breeder-owner: Mrs. K. Butler. Mint has in a short time amassed 22 C.C.s, a BOS to BIS at an all-breed Championship show, several Working Groups and Reserve Working Groups. The Pembroke Welsh Corgi of the Year for 1977 and Top Working Dog in England in 1977, ranking seventh in all breeds that year, she took time out for a litter after winning BB at Crufts in 1978. *Sally Anne Thompson*

A young bitch with a great future, Ch. Pegasus Lori of Pennington started by winning two Specialty Sweepstakes in 1977 and finished in 1978 with three 5-point majors from Lakeshore PWCC, Potomac PWCC and Golden Gate PWC Fanciers. She was BB at the 1978 Lakeshore Specialty. Whelped October 19, 1976, she is by Can. Am. Ch. Revelmere Cordoba ex Pegasus Lady Heather. Breeders: Mr. and Mrs. D.R. Timmins, owners: John and Sue Vahaly. *Earl Graham*

A trio of Lees Corgi champions: (from left) Can. Ch. Lees Moonlight of Brow (at seven months), Eng. Ch. Lees Joker and Eng. Ch. Lees Coronet.

Can. Am. Ch. Daleviz Red Ink, the first Canadian-owned Corgi to win a Best in Show in North America.

7

The Pembroke Welsh Corgi in Other Countries

ONCE PEMBROKE CORGIS began to be seen away from their Welsh farmlands, they soon attracted the attention of dog-minded folk from many parts of the globe. The little Welshmen traveled to new owners, breeders and exhibitors throughout the world, and thus became the foundation stock for major centers of Corgidom in Canada, Australia, New Zealand, South Africa and continental Europe.

No one volume could attempt to include the many details of individual dogs, contributing bloodlines and development of type necessary for a thorough, world-wide study of the Pembroke Welsh Corgi. Only the most outstanding dogs and their influence on the breed in each country can be given recognition in this chapter.

Canada

It is not surprising that Miss Thelma Evans (later Mrs. Gray) of Rozavel Kennels was involved in exporting the first Pembroke Corgis to both Canada and Australia in the 1930s. Her ad in the League Handbook in 1957 states, *Exports a Specialty*. Rozavel Foxyface and Rozavel Pimpernel were imported by Mr. Ralph H.M. Gardener to Sundance, Alberta, in February 1932, and were mated to produce the first Canadian litter. Two more Rozavel dogs joined Mr. Gardener's Tamarac Kennel. In 1937, 14 additional Corgis with the Tamarac prefix were imported. From this nucleus in 1935 Mr. Gardener bred the first Canadian Pembroke champion, Ch. Tamarac Red Duke (Rozavel Red Admiral ex Rozavel Foxyface). Mr. Gardener was such an avid exhibitor that he traveled in a truck on a single lane gravel road through the Rockies with five Corgis and seven children to attend a show in British Columbia.

Another early breeder, Mr. Charles Batten, also of Alberta, started his Alsagar Kennel with stock brought from Mr. Gardener, as did Mrs. Dorothy Barrie (now Morlang) of North Vancouver, B.C., to found her Rador strain. One of the outstanding dogs of the 1940s was Ch. Rador's Golden Harvester, who quickly gained his championship. At the age of 8½ he went to Mrs. Barbara Fallass' Andely Kennels in New York, where he completed his American title and was used extensively at stud.

In 1947 Sheilah Parry (now Mrs. Sheilah Roberts) founded her Bhilwara Kennels, again with stock out of Rozavel bitches. Mrs. Roberts imported Ch. Lees Moonlight of Brow (Lees Cracker ex Erica's Bertha) in 1949. This dog had a grand show career topped by the first Best in Show in Western Canada at the Pacific Exhibition Show in 1952 under Derek Rayne. A CD in obedience also became part of his title.

In Eastern Canada the Upperton Kennels of Reginald Foster and Cam Baxter were founded in 1946. Can. Am. Ch. Upperton Corncob was well-known and sired Am. Ch. Kaydon's Happy Talk for Mrs. Duncan in New York.

Another prominent exhibitor in Ontario in the 1940s was Cmdr. Peter Hopkinson of the Uxmore prefix. His import Can. Am. Ch. Daleviz Red Ink was the first Corgi bitch in North America to win a Best in Show. This was at Coburg, Ontario in 1951. The win also made her the first Canadian owned Corgi of either sex to win that award. (The first Best in Show-winning Corgi in Canada was Int. Ch. Formakin Orangeman, owned by Mrs. H.L. Green, an American.) Cmdr. Hopkinson's Can. Am. Ch. Desmor Happy Landing was the first Corgi on this side of the Atlantic to leave a champion son in England, Ch. Miles of Glyntirion, and Can. Am. Ch. Lucky Anne of Cadno, owned by Hopkinson, was the first to win a Working Group in Canada. She captured the Brood Bitch class three times at PWCCA Specialties.

In the mid 1950s Mrs. Pamela B. Mack of Quebec began showing Corgis under her Macksons prefix. Many of her dogs had splendid show careers not only in Canada but also in the United States. Of particular note are Can. Am. Ch. Macksons Golden Sceptre, Can. Am. Ch. Macksons Coronet and Can. Am. Ch. Macksons The Young Pretender. The latter did a great deal of stud work in both countries, won the PWCCA Specialty in 1968, was top-winning Corgi in Canada in 1968 and 1969 as well as top Working dog in 1967 and 1968.

Can. Am. Ch. Tiverton Talk of Th'Town (Can. Am. Ch. Cleden's Gale Storm ex Can. Ch. Colwyn's Copper Coin).   *DNH*

Can. Am. Bda. Ch. Macksons The Young Pretender, owned and bred by Mrs. Pamela Mack, shown with handler Peter Green after winning the 1968 PWCCA Specialty under Mrs. Eileen Pimlott. He sired 19 champions in Canada and the USA.
Gilbert

Can. Am. Bda. Ch. Convista Sunsabre of Lees with Miss Helen Timmins.   *H.R. Cauldwell*

Several other Canadian Corgis of recent years are noteworthy. Can. Am Bda. Ch. Welcanis Adulation, bred and owned by Dr. and Mrs. George Wilkins, was the top winning Corgi in 1964, 1965 and 1967. This outstanding bitch had a number of Specialty wins as well as eight Bests in Show, including one in Bermuda.

Can. Am. Ch. Tiverton Talk of Th'Town, owned by John and Rod Heartz, has a record number of 14 Bests in Show, 44 Group firsts and 128 Bests of Breed in two countries. She was Top Corgi in 1971 and 1973, and winner of the 1973 Purina Invitational Show of Shows for the title of Canada's Best Show Dog of the Year - 1973.

Can. Am. Bda. Ch. Convista Sunsabre of Lees, owned by Mr. and Mrs. D. R. Timmins, gained three titles in ten months, was the top winning Corgi in 1974, and has multiple Best in Show wins as well as a Specialty win. Sunsabre has proven to be a successful sire of champions.

Other winners of Specialties or top winning Corgis both in Canada and the United States include Can. Am. Ch. Schaferhaus Aeroglend Tupence (Clarke and Kruger), Can. Am. Ch. Revelmere Cordoba (Timmins), Can. Am. Ch. Tehidybarton Tigbourne Snowshoes (Huggins), Can. Am. Ch. Bhilwara Golden Charmer (Roberts), Ch. Ruardeans Loa of Willoan (Kennedy), Ch. Crosslands Ceilidh (Eadie) and Ch. Mackson's The Instigator (Mack).

Australia

Although not Rozavel dogs nor even the first Corgis to arrive, the foundation of the breed in Australia was sent to Mrs. V. Nish and her son Ian of Victoria in 1934 via Mrs. Gray. Mrs. Nish adopted the kennel prefix Benfro and began the breed there with Titania of Sealy, who became an Australian champion. She was imported in whelp to Eng. Ch. Rozavel Red Dragon. Titania was one of the three famous "of Sealy" litter sisters sired by Ch. Trier of Sealy out of Tea Rose of Sealy. Ch. Tiffany and Ch. Teresa did much in England, while Titania virtually founded the breed in Australia. Subsequently, Mrs. Nish imported Ch. Jubilee Girl also in whelp to Red Dragon.

The first Corgis to come to New South Wales, Aust. Ch. Rozavel Ranger and Ch. Rozavel Pipkin, were originally imported by Mrs. Nish. Benfro Anwyl can be traced back to Pipkin and was mated to Benfro Bronelydan to produce the very promising early sire Benfro Gelert. Two well-known breeders who bought puppies from Mrs. Nish in the early days were Mrs. C. Smith, originally of Werribee, and Mrs. A. E. Bridgford of Taumac fame.

One of the first dogs bred in New South Wales was Mrs. J. M.

Can. Am. Ch. Revelmere Cordoba breeders: Mrs. D. Mason and Mrs. V. Deer. He was BB at the 1976 Cascade PWCC Specialty and sired Ch. Pegasus Lori of Pennington, the 1978 Lakeshore PWCC Specialty winner. *Robert*

Can. Am. Ch. Willoan's Cecelia of Ruardean, owners: Jayne and Jim Chalmers. She is shown going BB over 99 Corgis under judge Mrs. Seaver Smith at the Berks County KC. *Gilbert*

Campbell's Ch. Picton Bronelydan, sired by Benfro Gelert. Picton Bronely-dan went to the Taumac Kennels in Victoria where he sired Ch. Boyanda Golden Blossom, Ch. Benfro Sal, and the sensational bitch Ch. Rrac Seren, a challenge winner at three successive New South Wales Corgi Club shows and the Sydney Royal.

During the war English importations ceased and the breed became somewhat static. Ch. Bowhit Purser was the first to arrive once the flow resumed. Mrs. Darlington of the Radnor Kennel soon brought out Ch. Scarlett Pimpernel and Ch. Red Pavon of Elsdyle, both sired by Eng. Ch. Red Pennon of Elsdyle. Mated to a third import, the influential stud Rozavel Prime Minister, Red Pavon produced Ch. Radnor David, who did much for the breed in the late 1950s. The Bridgford's Rrac Kennels added Ch. Lees Jasper of Wyldingtree.

A great winner and four states champion, Mrs. Stevens' Ch. Scotby Sergeant Major, was a great-grandson of Red Dragon and was used at stud in Victoria, New South Wales and Queensland. His sire was Ch. Copshaw Torquil, also influential throughout Australia. From New Zealand came the first tricolor, Ch. West Country Flight. Ch. Tyn Coed Cherie became the first Corgi winner of Best Exhibit, All Breeds, at the Melbourne Royal show.

In the late 1950s Mrs. Beryl Cornwell of Aurglyn Kennels was influential to the breed in the Sydney area. Her import, Brockencote Best Man, an Eng. Ch. Maracas Masterpiece son, was a top sire and the foundation of a good line when combined with bitches descending from Knowland Clipper. Ch. Aurglyn Clipper, sired by Knowland Clipper, also figured into this line.

Perhaps the most famous Aurglyn bitch from an outstanding litter sired by Maracas Masterpiece was Ch. Aurglyn Damask Rose, owned by Mrs. Gordon McKay of Carbeth Kennels. "Teena" won 54 Challenge Certificates including four at Royal shows, and was the dam of several champions who continued to breed on particularly in combination with Mrs. McKay's Ch. Wiseguy of Wey. A Damask Rose granddaughter by Wiseguy, Ch. Carbeth Misty Morn Rose, in 1963 was the only Corgi to have won Best Puppy at the Sydney Royal.

A most successful Pembroke was Aust. Ch. Chetwyn Merthytidvill. His sparkling show record was climaxed by a Best Exhibit in Show at the 1961 Sydney Royal Easter show under judge Percy Roberts from the United States. As a product of such greats as Ch. Lymepark Orange Fire of Gedney, Ch. Lymepark Rideacre Rose, Ch. Scarlett Pimpernel, Ch. Red Pavon of Elsdyle, and Ch. Radnor David, Merthytidvill was proof that quality begets quality. Superb conditioning and handling also contributed to his stardom.

During the 1960s several imports added new strength to the growing Corgi population in Australia. Ch. Cogges Perriwig, by Stormerbanks Indigo out of a Masterpiece bitch, was used a great deal. Ch. Stormerbanks Viking

Can. Am. Bda. Ch. Cote de Neige Commentator II, breeder: Mrs. Marjorie Butcher, owner: Mrs. Pamela Mack. He finished his championship with Group placings and went on to be Canada's top-winning Corgi for 1975 and ninth top Working dog.

Can. Ch. Crosslands Ceilidh, Canada's top-winning Corgi in 1976, with over 120 BBs and 40 Group placings.

Aust. Ch. Rrac Seren, breeder: C. Carr, owner: Miss B. Wilhelm.

Aust. Ch. Aurglyn Damask Rose.

Aust. Ch. Wiseguy of Wey.
Glenn A. Keep

and Carolette of Wey were imported by Charles Corlis and produced Ch. Mbula Intruder and Ch. Mbula Vagabond, two prominent studs. Ch. Stormerbanks Bonaparte followed.

Into South Australia, Ivor Snaith imported Ch. Lees Kettledrum (Eng. Ch. Lees Sunsalve ex Lees Glamour), whose line is still dominant in winning stock in New South Wales. David Tidswell brought out Cwellyn Garter King, son of Am. Ch. Stormerbanks Winrod Fergus. In 1969 Ch. Crowleythorn Maccason, by Eng. Ch. Falaise Maccaboy, came to Mrs. Barbara Ludowici (Fergwyn) and produced 17 champions among them a Pembroke of the Year. Mrs. Vicki Scott (Scottholme) acquired Ch. Lees Picador, who, put to Cwellyn Garter King bitches and Stormerbanks Bonaparte stock, sired excellent quality including 15 champions. Picador won the challenge at two Royal Shows and is the grandsire of Ch. Tamerai Royal Bronze.

Important bitch imports from the late 1960s to the early 1970s were Mrs. McKay's Eng. Aust. Ch. Donna Rosa of Rowell of Wey and Mrs. Ruth Hutchin's Ch. Wyeford May Princess, Brood Bitch of the Year in 1972. A third, in whelp to Eng. Ch. Kaytop Marshall, brought by Mrs. Vi Palmer-Cummings and later sold to Mrs. Ludowici, was Braxentra Quite Contrary of Camcounty. "Mary" made her mark as a brood bitch when mated to Ch. Crowleythorn Maccason, as together they produced three Best in Show-winning sisters, Ch. Fergwyn Frith, Ch. Fergwyn Serena and Ch. Fergwyn Fairy Fable. Frith has won 82 C.C.s, 11 Bests in Show and 18 Runner Up Bests in Show. Her dam also was granddam of Ch. Bowmore Mark Time, Best in Show at the 1976 Melbourne Royal. Mrs. Carleigh Jobson of Bowmore Kennels has worked with Braxentra stock, including Ch. Braxentra Time Tag, to achieve a strain known for its soundness.

Another interesting import is Eng. Aust. Ch. Wyeford Black Tweed, the first champion dog out of England. He has sired ten champions in several Australian states and New Zealand, where a son was named Pembroke of the Year in 1976.

A new star in New South Wales is Ch. Tamerai Royal Bronze, three times Pembroke of the Year, and in 1977 Working Dog of the Year. His record includes 14 Bests in Show, 11 Runner Up to Best in Show, Runner Up Champion of Champions, and 65 Challenge Certificates. He is a grandson of Ch. Lees Picador and Cwellyn Garter King with Ch. Lees Kettledrum in the background.

Imported into Victoria in 1973 by Mrs. D. Lawes and Mrs. J. Exell, Eng. Aust. Ch. Kydor Cossack, "Duskie" continued his thriving show career begun in England with Australian Bests in Show and Group wins under specialist judges. His progeny include at least 18 champions in England, Australia and New Zealand with more on the way to their titles. He is known to pass on his lovely head.

Aust. Ch. Lees Kettledrum. *Evening Standard*

Braxentra Quite Contrary of Camcounty (Eng. Ch. Hildenmanor Crown Prince ex Peggoty of Camcounty).

Eng. Aust. Ch. Donna Rosa of Rowell of Wey, an Eng. Ch. Caswell Duskie Knight daughter. Breeder: Miss P.A. Date.

C.M. Cooke & Son

Aust. Ch. Crowleythorn Maccason.

Aust. Ch. Fergwyn Frith (Aust. Ch. Crowleythorn Maccason ex Braxentra Quite Contrary of Camcounty).

Eng. Aust. Ch. Wyeford Black Tweed (Eng. Ch. Brocade of Rowell ex Wyeford October Flame). Breeders: Mr. and Mrs. Joe Ford, owners: Mr. and Mrs. Max Schmarr.   *Kelly*

Mrs. Ludowici has written to suggest that three or four English sires have dominated the breeding in Australia. Stormerbanks Boniface and Invader, Pennywise of Wey and Lees Sunsalve appear in the pedigrees of all the prominent imports. For example, two English bitches by Eng. Ch. Hildenmanor Crown Prince, Ch. Wyeford May Princess and Braxentra Quite Contrary of Camcounty, were Brood Bitch of the Year; and Crown Prince combines both the Boniface and Sunsalve lines.

New Zealand

In New Zealand imports also played the major role in the development of the breed. Ringbourne Owain, bred by Miss B. A. Talmondt, was the first to arrive on the South Island in 1939. Not much is known about pre-war New Zealand Corgis, but in the early 1950s the flow from England brought several prominent studs. Mrs. E. M. Adamson imported a tricolor son of Int. Ch. Formakin Orangeman, Ch. Scarab from Shiel, who in turn sired several New Zealand champions for her West Country Kennels. A West Country dog was sent to Australia and completed his title there; and many Australian dogs were added to the New Zealand population. For example, Aust. Ch. Stormerbanks Bonaparte, an English import, was brought to New Zealand from Australia by Mrs. S. C. Skurr of the Oakbridge prefix.

By the mid 1950s Mr. and Mrs. M. S. Russell began receiving dogs from the Rozavel Kennel to add to their earlier imports. New Zealand Ch. Rozavel Kind Regards and Ch. Rozavel Rebel Maid were winners and producers at the time.

Ch. Snowman of Wey came to Miss E.L.J. Davis' Kings Ride Kennel in the late 1950s. He was followed by other notables including the outstanding Ch. Costons Consequence of Wey, winner of two Bests in Show plus four Runners Up, and a top dam. New Zealand Ch. Corgwyn Shillelah, also brought out by Miss Davis, was New Zealand's top stud dog in 1967 and 1968.

The Tintagel kennels of breeders Mr. and Mrs. Stewart Lusk were well-known in the 1960s, putting to use such imports as N.Z. Ch. Crusader of Cowfold. Ch. Tintagel Mister Tody won three Bests in Show, ten Runners Up, and was Corgi of the Year in 1963, 1964 and 1965. Mated to imported Ch. Dronlow's Sarah Thompson, he sired Aust. New Zealand Ch. Tintagel Salvation Yeo, winner of at least 12 Bests in Show and Corgi of the Year in 1969. Sarah Thompson also was the dam of Ch. Tintagel Cutty Sark.

Messrs. B.M. Giles and L. Ellis of Leea-Von fame have been active and brought out from England Int. Ch. Sealord of Wey, featured in many pedigrees. And Mr. and Mrs. Bruce Hyde of Stormwey Kennels are the proud owners of Ch. Crocket of Wey, a top winner and influential stud in the 1970s.

Eng. Aust. Ch. Kydor Cossack, sire of Eng. Ch. Gilburn Supermac, Pembroke Welsh Corgi of the Year in England, 1975. *Neilson*

Aust. Ch. Tamerai Royal Bronze (Aust. Ch. Scottholme Merrimarti ex Tamerai Temptation), owner: Mrs. C. Laing.

119

South African Ch. Hillhead Lucky Strike of Waycliff, owner: Mrs. C.M. Beeby.

South African Ch. Oldlands Ponsonby of Hillhead, owner: Mrs. C. Gordon-Creed.

South African Ch. Kimfield Tumbles, owner: Shirley Bloomfield.

It would appear that most of the aforementioned Corgis have been English imports or first or second generation descendants from imported stock. However, the listing has been pieced together without a genuine, first-hand knowledge of the Pembroke Welsh Corgi in far away New Zealand.

South Africa

Taking a large leap, we find South Africa is the next center of Corgi activity. Many fine English dogs have been exported to this country and have formed the basis of its winning stock today. Once again, the name Rozavel crops up in the earlier imports, notably Rozavel Supersinger and Rozavel Yours Sincerely of Southwell.

Mrs. Gray was not the only one to send dogs to Africa. South African Ch. Morzine Mosaic of Wey, by Eng. Ch. Knowland Clipper, was dominant in the 1950s. Such famous English prefixes as Wennam, Wey, Lees, Stormerbanks and Falaise can be found in the names of South African champions.

Int. Ch. Daleviz Copperfield of Ballyvoreen, at first in Kenya, was bought by Mr. and Mrs. C.G.A. Bowring, who have established a strong line of Hillhead Corgis. Some of these dogs are behind the South African winners from the American breeder, Mrs. Gordon-Creed's Oldlands Kennels. Other active kennels are Norsongula operated by Mrs. S. Palmer, Roodedraai of Mrs. Y du Preez, and Stuartfield of Mr. K. W. King.

Holland

By the time Corgis from England became established on the shores of nearby Holland, many breeders other than the pioneer Mrs. Gray were exporting quality animals, as it was after the war. The two Pembrokes at the Delft Championship Show in 1950 were Radnor Robin Goodfellow, a son of Eng. Ch. Red Pennon of Elsdyle, and Larkwhistle Mirella, daughter of Eng. Ch. Teekay's Felcourt Supremacy. Both finished their Dutch titles. The first litter in Holland was out of Daleviz Kay imported in whelp to Eng. Ch. Woodvale Woodpigeon. The first litter bred on Dutch soil was sired by Mrs. J. M. van Ommen Kloeke's Ch. Radnor Robin Goodfellow and whelped on the last day of 1951.

Four years later Felcourt Choirboy, the son of Eng. Ch. Knowland Clipper out of a Rozavel Lucky Strike daughter, topped an entry of 21 Pembrokes in Rotterdam. Later, as a champion, he contributed to the progress of the breed. Dutch Ch. Cadnoaidd Cadno was a Choirboy son.

Another dog used extensively at stud was Ch. Shucks of Bablake, an Eng. Ch. Zephyr of Brome son. He went on to sire Int. Ch. Flame's Gwendolyn van 'T Hooyvelt.

Int. Nordic Ch. Crawleycrow Prank.

Int. Nordic Ch. Ryttarens Narcissos.
Lasse Rudberg

English dogs continued to be prominent in Holland. Mrs. C. M. de Weerd-Schippers' Int. Ch. Lees Berry has done well. A top winner in recent years, Dutch and Int. Ch. Beau of Humdinger, owned and bred by Merv. A. v-d. Burg-Buitendarp, is a combination of Helarian and Wey bloodlines.

Sweden

An early Swedish Corgi in the 1930s was Bucklers Megan, sired by Crymmch President, and mated to imported Rozavel Tuck and for a later litter to Wolfox Walker. In 1945 an Eng. Ch. Teekay's Felcourt Supremacy son, Teekay Mannikin, was imported. He never gained his title but sired three Swedish champions to Megan daughters. Nonetheless, Corgis were rare until 1953-54, when 12 arrived from leading English kennels.

The first really top sire was Int. Nordic Ch. Crawleycrow Prank (Int. Ch. Crawleycrow Bannow Master Broom ex Crawleycrow Perky) owned by Per Erik Wallin. Prank lived to the age of 17 and did much to benefit the breed. He sired the first Corgi to win a Best in Show at an all-breed event, not an International show, Int. Nordic Ch. Benedicts Belinda.

The top winning Pembroke of all time in Sweden is Int. Nordic Ch. Ryttarens Narcissos (Butterybar of Braxentra ex Ch. Gerona's Killarney Rose) again owned by Per Erik Wallin. He was the Corgi Club's Corgi of the Year in 1972, 1973, 1974 and 1976, and sire of the top Corgi, Swed. Finn. Norw. Ch. Red Sheila, in 1977. Narcissos was the first Corgi to win Best in Show at an International show, which he did twice, once in Sweden and then in Finland. He has won the Corgi Club show twice as well.

An outstanding bitch and top producing dam, Int. Nordic Ch. Moonrocks Binette, is a direct descendant of Bucklers Megan. Binette's sire, Ch. Rittarens Iller, was sired by Eng. Ch. Zephyr of Brome, and her bloodlines in combination with Narcissos have come up with constant winners.

Two recent imports from England have already made a positive contribution to the breed. Ch. Fanara Foil (Evancoyd Contender ex Eng. Ch. Falaise Teazel) was top Corgi in 1975. Wennam Audacity (Eng. Ch. Evancoyd Audacious ex Wennam Firethorn) also has been useful. In fact, it is reported by Mrs. Terry Dillenbeck that most of the current winners are either imports or second generation at least on one side.

Norway

Corgis were slower to penetrate Norway to the west, not arriving until about 1950 from England for Mrs. E. Galtung. She and Mrs. Anspach were the only breeders until 1967. This year marked the arrival of Mr. Knut S. Wilberg's Norw. Swed. Ch. Yorken Gallant Knight (Blands Duskie Knight ex Yorken Ramona of Kathla). His impressive wins include the Norwegian

Kennel Klub's highest award for the top winning dog of any breed at the Kennel Klub's Championship shows in 1968. At a time when there were only seven championship shows a year, he earned three Bests in Show and five Group firsts. As a sire he produced 12 champions and many other C.C. winners.

The first Corgi in Norway to become an International Champion is Int. Nordic Ch. Siggen's Dusky Queen (Wennam Sea King ex Norw. Swed. Ch. Yorken Dusky Mandy of Kathla), owned by Mrs. L. Wilberg. As a top dam, six of her ten puppies became champions. Her most famous daughter is Mr. L. H. Wilberg's Int. Nordic Ch. Siggen's Treasure, top winning Corgi in 1974 and 1975. Treasure, herself, was the dam of two winners of Corgi of the Year in 1976 and in 1977, sired by different studs.

Other Countries

Other countries have had Corgis of which to be proud, as the breed has found its way into Belguim, Italy, Switzerland, Finland, and Germany among others. Corgis also reside in Rhodesia, India, Kenya and East Africa. South America and Mexico claim Corgi greats as well.

For the most part, the Pembroke Welsh Corgi has become established in the various countries with stock imported from England. Mexico is a notable exception, for its Corgi population, while admittedly small, consists mainly of dogs coming from the United States. American Pembrokes owned and exhibited by Dr. Herbert Talmadge became the first Mexican champions of the breed, when Dr. Talmadge took his Ch. Toelmag's Tommy Lad and Toelmag Telmie on a Mexican show circuit in 1958.

Int. Nordic Ch. Moonrock's Binette.

Norw. Swed. Ch. Yorken Gallant Knight.   *Brenna*

Int. Nordic Ch. Siggen's Dusky Queen.

Ch. Shonleh Song and Dance Man moves in on a straggler.

Callea

8

The Pembroke Welsh Corgi—A Working Dog

THE CORGI'S REPUTATION as a working dog was established clearly from the start. The Welsh farmer found he had a superb cattle dog, ratter, guardian and clever companion all in one. The Corgi's characteristic intelligence, determination and agility served him well as he performed a variety of tasks around the homestead.

The Corgi as a Farm Dog

It is to the Corgi's ability as a herder that we look first. Many are the amazing tales of this little dog's effectiveness with cattle. Many are the skeptics won over to hearty respect for his abilities.

Most Pembroke Welsh Corgis seem to be born with a special sense about working with other animals. Miss Eve Forsyth-Forrest, in her charming book, *Welsh Corgis* (Edited by S. M. Lampson, A. S. Barnes and Company, New York), says:

> Corgis who like working with cattle and ponies have a great gift of getting the confidence of other animals. They are quick to realize where one wants or does not want the herd or an individual beast, and their way of collection or removal is by the nose-and-heel method. When herding they single out the leader and appear to have a little conversation on the desirability of

Ch. Shonleh Song and Dance Man working Black Angus heifers and Angus/Whiteface crosses at a seminar for all herding breeds. This was Dandy's first exposure to cattle. *Callea*

Ch. Shonleh Song and Dance Man in his show ring attire. Whelped April 24, 1974, breeder: Sharon Curry, owner: Kathy Miramontes.
Callea

128

obeying instructions. Usually the horse or cow puts its head down and follows, and any insurrections in the rank and file calls forth more persuasive conversation, a great deal of threats and an occasional nip at the heels.

Under more demanding circumstances it is the Corgi's low, agile build, ever alert mind and indefatigible spirit which are called to the fore. According to John Holmes, famous in the field of working breeds, in his article, "All in the Day's Work," *1955 Welsh Corgi League Handbook,* the Corgi's small size is an advantage in several ways:

> First of all, by keeping up close to the heels the cattle kick over him, and so long as he keeps his head down, he does not seem to have to duck at all.

Too, the Corgi's lowness puts him in the correct position to grab the tender part of the heels rather than the more dangerous hind tendon higher up the leg. And finally:

> Their small size also makes them more difficult to see, which means that the cattle have something, they know not quite what, which they can only hear and feel tearing around their heels, here, there and everywhere. As a result they have much more respect for the Corgi than for the enemy they can see.

Exaggerated lowness and heaviness can be a disadvantage, though, as all-important agility is lost, and the stamina to last the full day in the field is diminished. Holmes says, ". . . The real working type Corgi had speed quite out of proportion to his size and build."

Above all, Mr. Holmes stresses an agile mind is essential, for ". . . if the cattle dog does not keep his wits about him every minute and every second, he is liable to collect a hoof in the ribs or on the side of the head." Yet a good working dog must know how to sneak in a moment of relaxation and rest.

He goes on to the state, "Combined with agility of mind must be levelheadedness, otherwise the dog is sure to get over-excited and land in trouble."

With mind and body in order, the Corgi adds an extra portion of courage and determination. Once again we quote Mr. Holmes with his description of a Corgi escorting a drove of wily, somewhat frightened steers or heifers down a country road to market:

> For that sort of work one needs a dog with what is known as "plenty of force" to keep the cattle moving. . . . There is nothing "wide run" or "stylish" in the Corgi's work. He stays right in amongst their heels, and in deep

Ch. Peterkin of Pen-y-Bont goes about his chores on the Pen-y-Bont ranch. *Phyl*

Sinbad of Wey, TD Ex, UD, CD Ex, with his owner Kenneth Butler after a successful day in the field.

Eng. Ch. Rozavel Golden Corn.

mud such as forcing through gateways, he sometimes - seems to be lost altogether. Another point is that he does not stick to one beast and let all the others scatter. He tears round from heel to heel, biting and barking, never relaxing for a second, thereby preventing the cattle from collecting their wits until they are where they are wanted—through the gate, past the traffic or whatever it happens to be. Of course, if one turns its head and charges, he does not "heel" that, he "moves" it.

Here in the United States today the Corgi is not likely to be called upon to offer his skills as a drover. There are, nonetheless, a number of farmers or ranchers who still work their dogs actively with cattle. Miss Virginia Farr and Miss Vivien Jeffery of the V2 Ranch in Templeton, California, turned to raising purebred Hereford cattle after a career as flyers in World War II's "Bombers to England delivery program." They acquired two Corgi puppies as working dogs in 1959. Many of their prize-winning dogs shown under their Pen-y-Bont prefix add their special version of help around the ranch.

Mrs. Lynn Brooks and her husband raise Black Angus beef cattle on their Busy B's Ranch in Wisconsin. Three to six Corgis at a time are used as a team to work the cattle, which as a breed are known to be highly excitable animals. She describes their style of working in the March 1974 *Pembroke Welsh Corgi Newsletter:*

> If we want a particular animal or animals put somewhere, the dogs when sent will usually rush the cow or cows to get them moving. Then they circle at a run and with what seems like wild, uncontrolled foolishness drive the cow where it's supposed to go. Often one or the other of the dogs will lead the cattle, cavorting and teasing, which entices the lead cow to chase it. Often cows with calves or the bulls will get in a fence corner or against a building and turn to face the dogs, lower its head and refuse to move. This is about the only time the Corgis do bite and then they will occasionally draw blood.
>
> As for ducking flat, I have yet to see one do it. Animals do not kick that high and they are fairly accurate in hitting what they kick at. I'm sure a dog that practiced this method would be in a constant state of injury. Our dogs depend on their quickness and agility to keep out of flying hooves' way. They dash and dart around, always on the move and *always* barking. They are absolutely fearless, taking on the biggest bull, if asked.

Mrs. Brooks reports a few drawbacks she has experienced with her dogs, however. Heavy coats lovely in the show ring become a hazard in the mud. Not all dogs are endowed with an equal herding instinct, a trait which usually can be determined by three months of age, and join the others only to heckle. And a few get carried away with their zeal, going so far as to take delight in stuffing too many cows in one barn.

131

Corgis do not limit their herding activities to large hoofed creatures. Although reportedly less reliable with skittish sheep, several Corgis in various parts of the world have coped admirably. Mrs. Brooks bought her first Corgi from a breeder who used them to herd pigs—not cattle. This skill is not uncommon; as John Holmes wrote, ". . . they are said to be the only dogs for which a pig has any respect at all." Often a young Corgi will turn his attention first to herding poultry of various sorts. Ducks, geese, turkeys and chickens all have been sorted out and moved here and there in perfect safety. Sometimes a dog will be a boon in fetching eggs as well.

The versatile Corgi has other useful tricks in his bag. Right from the start he has earned praise as an indomitable ratter. The Welsh farmers could count upon him to control the vermin with a short pounce, lethal nip and rapid shake. Some barns today are equally blessed; and even a suburban back yard offers opportunity to a proficient moler. Farm stock and well-bred show dogs alike have shared this occupation with great success. Back in the 1950s Miss E. Boyt's prize-winning Larkwhistle Golden Vanity and her dam proved themselves handy one afternoon by dispatching 56 rats flushed out by the threshing.

Even more impressive is the feat described in a letter from Mrs. Thelma Gray appearing in the April 1952 *Pure-Bred Dogs—American Kennel Gazette*. It tells of Eng. Ch. Rozavel Golden Corn:

> It will amuse you to know that since we started to farm, Golden Corn has become a super farm dog. She fetches all the cows daily as if she had done it all her life, and is so crazy to do so we can't keep her in; she scales a five and six foot wall to get out when she knows milking time is near. When we were threshing out a few ricks of corn, she killed over 200 rats and mice, and was so worn out at the end of the day that she quite literally couldn't stand, but by 8 A.M. next morning was chewing at her kennel door to get out and be on the job again. Nothing remarkable in this, of course, excepting that for a bitch that has lived in a kennel and show life until eight years of age, to take to farming in such a big way, is a tribute to the inborn abilities of the breed and a sock in the jaw for the people who say that show dogs have no brains. She is still one of the leading Chs. with her eight Challenge Certificates.

The Corgi as a Guard Dog

Another plus for a Corgi earning his keep is as a guardian of the home. Provided with a rural life, he uses his extremely keen sense of hearing and his vigilance to protect not only his owner but also the livestock on the farm. He repels thieves and prowlers of both the two and four-legged kind. Even in an urban environment a low growl or the tone of his bark clearly indicates something is amiss. Foolhardy is the maurader who does not heed this warning. A letter from Mrs. Branson of Ravenna, Ohio, published in the January 1954 *Gazette,* reports the effectiveness of Dugoed Queen:

> It was about an hour after the family had retired, when Queen awakened them with her restless short, sharp barking—she would not be hushed. A series of burglaries had nervous citizens bolting and barring their doors securely at night. With this in mind, my brother-in-law decided to investigate. Queen became extremely agitated as he came down, ran to the door scratching furiously; convinced that something was seriously amiss, he first called the police and then flicked the switch to the yard lights, opened the door, and away went Queen.
>
> Within a moment or so, he heard loud angry shouts, deep furious growls of anger from Queen. Stepping outside, the sight that greeted him was almost unbelievable. One prowler, so frightened by the little Corgi, had run blind, and unthinking into a tree, and was lying unconscious beneath it, the second was firmly held by the pants leg—an infuriated Queen determined never to let go.
>
> The police arrived, and the prowlers were taken off to jail. Now the citizens of this small Wisconsin town sleep at peace these nights always with a thought of the brave little Corgi that had accomplished so much.

In line with his role as a guardian, the watchful Corgi sits beneath the baby carriage, minds the toddlers, turns tears to smiles, and even separates sibling squabbles. It is no chore, of course, to tidy up the spills and rejects from the children's plates.

The list of small services, taught or self-assumed, which Corgis all over the world perform is lengthy. Whether or not these efforts can be classified as work is questionable, for Corgis obviously derive much pleasure in their execution. Bringing in the paper, fetching the slippers, even supplying "the boss" with filched tomatoes from the neighbor's yard—there is room for endless and amusing variation from the Corgi's fertile mind.

The Corgi as a Gun Dog

As a jack-of-all-trades many a Corgi steps over into the realm of the Sporting breeds. Major Branson, in the 1959 *Gazette* column recommends:

> For the sportsman who is looking for a dog that is useful, as well as ornamental, the very talented Corgis is a happy solution. He is a natural hunter of game and birds found throughout the United States. His keen ear, remarkable sense of smell, interest in the game and strong aptitude for obedience all combine to make the Pembroke an outstanding partridge and pheasant hunter. These characteristics have made Ch. Tobbe Petworth one of the outstanding pheasant hunting dogs in recent years. His ability to trail, locate and recover is unexcelled in the field.

Schulhaus Billy The Kid, CDX, TD, SchH II, owned and trained by Margery Malseed, retrieving a 1½ pound dumbell over the 40 inch jump.

Putting the Corgi (Billy) before the cart.

Billy performs a protection exercise in the Shutzhund training routine. He has a good bite!

Others have found the Corgi to be a suitable hunting companion. Mr. Kenneth Butler's Sinbad of Wey was well-known in hunting circles. Brigadier Brown's Falaise Fanfare, as described in Miss Forsyth-Forrest's book [ibid] was trained and at nine months of age took in his first day of hunting, soon found the fallen birds without direction, had a gentle mouth, retrieved equally well from the water, and gained the respect of other hunters in spite of his unorthodox appearance for a gun dog.

Corgis with very little training will work in the thickest cover and retrieve with speed. The short, thick coat is a boon in this regard.

The Corgi and Schutzhund Work

In 1975 a new element was added to the Corgi's list of achievements. In April of that year Schulhaus Billy The Kid, CDX, TD., SchH II, became the first Corgi in the world to earn a degree in the sport of Schutzhund training. Billy went on two years later to gain his Schutzhund II degree. He is owned and trained by Margery Malseed of Olympia, Washington, under the direction of the Puget Sound Schutzhund Association.

Schutzhund training basically is threefold, specifically tracking, obedience and protection. The rules are stringent. The obedience section features such tests as retrieving over a 40″ jump, heeling through a milling group of people, and steadiness under gunfire. As there are no exceptions made for short-leggedness, Billy had to forfeit 20 points because he had to omit the 64″ scaling wall and he touches the 40″ hurdle, which he bounces over from a dead stop. The rest of his work had to be exemplary for him to pass.

It was in the protection section that Billy accomplished something new for the breed. In spite of his size and the skepticism of several Schutzhund fans used to working with more conventional guard dogs, Billy learned exercises involving locating and guarding a suspect, attack on command and defense of his handler who is under attack. The illustrations of Billy at work leave no doubt that a Corgi can be formidable. It certainly is one more example of the old adage, ''A Corgi is a big dog in a small package.''

Something Really Unique

Perhaps the most unusual work a Corgi has been asked to do so far draws upon a dog's incredibly acute sense of smell. Research scientists from the Sloan-Kettering Institute for Cancer Research in New York have been conducting experiments with dogs trained to differentiate the scents of closely related people, even genetically identical twins. The object is to determine if dogs can be used to distinguish tissue types by scent. It is hoped this would help in understanding the body's immunity system, which acts upon germs, renegade cells and tissue transplants. Ultimately, it may be possible for dogs to seek out compatible tissue or organ donors.

Miss Molly Bruce's Pembroke, Heretoday Chorus Girl, CD, TD, is involved in the Sloan-Kettering research. "Corey" was selected because of her obedience and tracking prowess. She is being trained to recognize tissue types of mice. Miss Bruce writes:

> Dr. Peter Andrews comes to Baltimore to do the experiments with us in an environment the dogs are used to. The dogs are able to discriminate between mice that are only one gene apart. Up until now we have used the bedding from the mouse cages, saturating the gauze with the odor just by stirring pieces of gauze around in two different cages, A and B. We lay down two or three pieces of gauze with nothing on them, then, among them place a piece from A and a piece from B. The dog is pre-scented with the odor we desire and is told to find it. The handler does not know the correct one (except in the training period where one could get the praise in). Sometimes we do a blind test which even Dr. Andrews does not know the answer to until he calls Sloan-Kettering late at night. I find this all very exciting.

It is indeed thrilling to think that Corgis may contribute to this important work.

Heretoday Chorus Girl, CD, TD, owned and trained by Miss Molly Bruce, takes the scent from a piece of gauze in a Sloan-Kettering research experiment. *Bales*

9

The Pembroke Welsh Corgi—A Companion

THE STANDARD for the breed describes a Corgi as "Outlook bold, but kindly. Expression intelligent and interested. Never shy nor vicious." This nutshell version of Corgi personality cries out for elaboration when the dog's whole entity is being considered—not just his conformation.

To begin with, the Corgi is an energetic dog, full of life, quick in movement and mind—a lover of activity. Yet, while a Corgi is always ready for the task at hand or a rollicking game with a friend, human or otherwise, he does not indulge in tiresome perpetual motion. Rather he is happy to enjoy as well quiet moments of companionship.

The Corgi's quick intelligence expresses itself in many ways. Just to look at a Corgi's face is to sense his bright mind. Curiosity, a component of intelligence, coupled with persistence, will lead a Corgi to explore and discover new meanings and solutions. An object when first confronted will be evaluated with an inquisitive nose, tactile whiskers and searching paw. Of course, there are variations in the minds of individuals and in their reactions to something new. One clever bitch coming upon a temporary barrier to protect wet paint pushed by it quite obviously thinking, "Humph! What is this for?" Others in the family inspected the barrier but sensibly realized it was to serve some purpose and pressed no further.

Am. Can. Aust. Ch. Rryde Symphony. The foundation bitch at Schaferhaus Kennels, Bambi is the dam of an Australian BIS winner, Aust. Ch. Lanney Barngremlin, and of the top American BIS bitch of all time, Ch. Schaferhaus Danielle.

A Willets puppy shows inquisitiveness begins at an early age.

A Corgi's curiosity is never-ending.

Whether they are house dogs or kennel dogs, Corgis love a routine. A friend's story about her first Corgi, Casey, not only illustrates what creatures of habit we and our Corgis can be, but it also demonstrates how unbelievably observant the Corgi is. It was this friend's custom to watch one particular soap opera on television everyday and then call another friend to discuss the events of the day's program. Casey, upon hearing the start of the commercial at the end of the program and before his owner had moved from her chair, would dash to the phone and bark in anticipation of the inevitable phone call he knew would be made to the friend.

Corgis eavesdrop on phone conversations as well. The dogs here are up and stirring the instant they hear the "Well, I have to" without even waiting for the "go now" which means the end of a long call and signifies a possible trip outside for them.

The typical Corgi takes a particular pride in knowing, practically before you do, exactly what your next move will be. Small actions you may not even be aware of tip the dog off as to your plans. For instance, there is the Corgi who would run to the front door and bark because he knew his mistress was going out and chances were good he would get to go with her. It took the dog's owner a long time to figure out how the Corgi knew when she was ready to leave, but she finally discovered that the dog was responding to the click of her lipstick case as it was being closed. And sure enough, the last thing she always did before going out was to put on her makeup.

Dinner time here is a time of high voltage excitement, as the Corgis can barely stand to wait for the food to be served once it has been prepared. One would hardly think that in the fervor of the moment a dog would ever notice whether he was given his food from the left or right hand. Corgis are aware of every little detail, though, and one dog here will balk at eating from a dish put down with the left hand. He knows his daughter eats at his left side, therefore it is her dinner, not his. Pick the same dish up and put it down with the right hand, and the dog will dive in without a moment's hesitation.

Miss Caldwell writes in the *1955 Welsh Corgi League Handbook* of another observant Corgi:

> A well-loved bitch of an earlier generation used to enjoy showing off to visitors. She would strum on the piano keys, delighted with the inevitable applause rolling her eyes round and laughing with her audience. She was a great *poseuse,* and everybody spoilt her. This dog was the only one I have known who could really see a picture or photograph. She showed special interest in pictures of dogs, and was indifferent to those of people or scenery. She was tested many times. We tried out our other Corgis, but it never worked; they only sniffed politely at what was to them merely a piece of paper."

The ability to learn easily is another Corgi trait. However, there is a difference between learning and training. John Holmes of Formakin fame comments:

First a grin . . .   . . . and then a little foot work.

Am. Can. Ch. Lees Mynah, CD, TD. Owners: H. and I. Sorley.

140

So far as the Corgi is concerned, I cannot put it very high on the list of those easy to train. Of the breeds capable of being trained to do almost anything and do it well I put it right up near the top. My experience has been that it is easily trained dogs who are often stupid dogs who do what they are told because they are too dim to think of anything else.

The Corgi is far from stupid. Although it is biddable, a working dog must be self reliant and able to think for himself in an emergency.

Corgis can let self reliance play into the tendency to be independent. They are not above being too busy to heed a command—at least not the first command. Although vagrancy is not usually a problem, some easily become engrossed in their own pursuits just a bit beyond the perimeter which is allowed. The best control is to guard against relegating a Corgi to a boring existence which drives him to find activity elsewhere.

Speaking of boredom, when training a Corgi it is important to maintain a brisk, variable schedule of exercises. Endless drill quickly bores and brings out a strong streak of stubbornness. Along with an independence of spirit goes an independence of mind. That equates with stubbornness when handled inadroitly.

Most Corgis have a great sense of humor. Many games are devised for self-amusement when things get a bit dull. And when frolicsome ways elicit a laugh, the trick is repeated. Anyone who has lived with a Corgi can tell of many individual versions of mirth—eyes laughing, paws waving, rolling and woofing, dashing and darting. Playfulness prevails. Two Corgis carry out boisterous games of tag, ambush, tug and tussle. Fun loving and fun giving, that is a Corgi! Humor stems from a bright mind.

Swimming is popular, too. It begins with sloshing and pawing in the water dish and leads to summer dips in any available puddle or stream. For the lucky Corgi it is great sport to circle around the head of one's owner who has been herded purposely into the lake, or to attempt to pursue the water skiers.

This sense of fun can spill over into teasing and heckling. According to Mrs. Lynn Brooks, one of the reasons her dogs are good herders is that they tease the cattle and thereby move them. One scamp overdid, though, and decided ". . . to keep the feeder calves away from the feeder. She'll guard it for hours if she's not reprimanded. She does this with the horses and their water tank, also."

All this cleverness can have its disadvantages, and a Corgi's energy, like any energy can become disruptive if it is misdirected. Mrs. Beryl Morgan writes of Corgi naughtiness in her article "Corgi Traits" in the *1946 Welsh Corgi League Handbook*:

> Some Corgis develop an annoying habit of nipping ankles and I understand this is the working instinct coming out. Not being a cow myself I fail to appreciate it and think it a habit to be checked at once. I find some of them

also get the trick of "minding" things. This is excellent if kept within bounds. Once when I had given a seven-months puppy a dose of medicine, I carelessly left the bottle in the kennel. In the morning I found him sitting in the corner growling quietly and couldn't understand what the trouble was about. He was "minding" his medicine, and as soon as I picked up the bottle, which he allowed me to do without demur, he came out of his kennel and seemed glad to be relieved of his self-appointed task.

I don't think any dog without plenty of intelligence and reasoning power would respond to obedience training in the way the Corgi does, and in my opinion six weeks is not too young to begin teaching a puppy manners. Corgis are definitely not one of the breeds that can bring themselves up. To get the best out of them they must have a master. Once they understand they cannot do exactly what they like, they take pleasure in obliging, even sometimes forestalling their owners' demands, and quite often even a look is enough. But if not checked as youngsters they are likely to turn into bossy little dogs that will rule a whole household with a rod of iron.

Mrs. Morgan continues:

This hard streak in them is what appeals to me personally. I could never like an animal without the brain to discriminate between the things he may and may not do, and I so admire that look in his eye when sometimes he just wonders if you still remember you said "he must NEVER . . ." whatever it is, and then the sedate way he semi-apologizes.

Some people call the breed noisy, but I have never found them so. Good house dogs, yes, but when properly disciplined they never indulge in that aimless yapping which is so infuriating.

Miss Patsy Hewan, of Stormerbanks fame, supports Mrs. Morgan's assessment of Corgi temperament when she writes in the *1949 Welsh Corgi League Handbook* the following:

Although a Corgi is a sensitive dog, and can be ruined with ill-treatment, he is also extremely intelligent and determined, and will do his best to get the better of you, so you must be firm, and sometimes even strict with him if you are to get good results from your labours. Always make him realize that you are the master, and he will respect you ever afterwards.

An adaptable dog, the Corgi will accept kennel life with all the eagerness and energy typical of the breed. If bored, he will find his amusement fence running, hurling insults at a kennel mate in another run, or in the creative pastimes of making a mud hole of his water bucket (and a mud ball of himself) or playing barber. A barber in the kennel busies himself by neatly chewing off the lovely show coats of his kennel mates.

Unless he has plenty of freedom outside the kennel to develop both mentally and emotionally, the kennelled Corgi remains just a dog. Whereas there seems to be no limit to the depth of the personality and character of a Corgi lucky enough to have at least one human companion to live with and look after. The much-loved Corgi becomes almost human, but without the human foibles that make the friendship somewhat less than perfect.

Beach bums.

"I got it!"

Eng. Ch. Rozavel Red Dragon, a leading show dog of his day, demonstrates the Corgi's natural aptitude for obedience work.

Am. Ch. Rozavel Rufus of Merriedip, a Red Dragon son, was the first Corgi to earn a CD both in England and in the United States.

Ch. Sierra Bruin, CD, owned and trained by Derek Rayne.

10

The Pembroke Welsh Corgi

in Obedience

CORGIS AIM TO PLEASE and like to be doing something. With active, intelligent minds they quickly learn and eagerly approach a job which brings them praise. They work cheerfully at the designated task relishing success as much as their owners do. Their trainability has attracted obedience fans to the breed, and some splendid performers have emerged.

The Right Approach

Whether being trained for a specific job or for the formal exercises required in obedience trial competition, a Corgi should be handled with clear, consistent commands, gentle firmness and lavish praise. The heavy corrections often used on some larger working breeds or inattentive individuals definitely will have a negative effect upon a Corgi. They are anxious to comply but resent bullying and become balky or apprehensive. It is much better to encourage with pats and words, making only well-timed, light corrections with the lead or with a stern-sounding voice when necessary.

Corgis also thrive on variety. They rapidly become bored when subjected to ho-hum routine or repetitive drilling on one exercise. Training sessions should be brief, interesting and fun for the dog. The result will be a happy worker.

Just because a Corgi is busy on the obedience routines should not relegate him to his work-a-day attire. At any obedience trial a Corgi in the limelight should be well-groomed for his own sake and that of the breed.

Milo and Margaret Pearsall, noted obedience authorities, with their Corgi Wakefield Margo's Happy Talk.

Ch. Furnace Brook Eniwetok, CDX. A son of Ch. Rozavel Uncle Sam of Waseeka, Tony is found in the pedigree of many of today's Macksons Corgis.

Ch. Capt. Jinks Wiggs, UDT, an early West Coast obedience worker, owned and trained by Miss Margaret Downing. *Lineer*

146

Many excellent books have been written on training dogs in obedience. Most libraries will have a good selection which give detailed advice. We recommend *The Pearsall Guide to Successful Dog Training* by Margaret E. Pearsall (Howell Book House, New York). Mrs. Pearsall and her husband Milo have been prominent obedience trainers, handlers and teachers for many years, and they have shared their lives with Pembroke Welsh Corgis.

Early Obedience Corgis

Back in the early days of competition it was easy enough for the Corgi to step over from farm work to the more rarified obedience exercises. However, Corgis were given no special treatment just because they were small. They were required to retrieve two-pound wooden dumbells and scale four-foot jumps in competition with German Shepherd Dogs and Great Danes. Later concessions in the rules were made both in the United States and England to shift the emphasis in trials to the quality of training in a small dog rather than almost impossible physical capabilities. Jumps and dumbells now are tailored to size.

The first Corgi shown in English obedience tests was Chalcot Bruin, owned by Mr. W. R. Lee. In spite of the odds against a dog of his stature, Bruin managed to win a Certificate of Merit.

An excellent description of early obedience Corgis on this side of the Atlantic is given by Mrs. Thelma Gray in the 1952 *Welsh Corgi League Handbook*.

The first Corgi to demonstrate obedience in the U.S.A. was Am. Ch. Rozavel Rufus CDX. Owned by Mrs. Gray and trained and handled by Mrs. Montgomery, he made history by being the first Corgi to win an obedience class in England, and had qualified as a CDX at the Associated Sheep, Police and Army Dog Society (ASPADS) working trials. Bought by Mrs. E. P. Renner, as Am. Ch. Rozavel Rufus of Merriedip he made his title in the beauty ring, and then won his American CD degree, becoming the first international CD Corgi and, his owner believes, the first Corgi to win an obedience class in the U.S.A. All his performances were characterized by very high scores. He drew an enormous number of people to the breed when he took part in a multi-breed demonstration at the Westminster show in New York, where he was handled by the late Miss Esther Bird, and his performance almost "brought the roof down." Rufus was followed to the U.S.A. by Torment of Sealy, also trained and handled in England by Mrs. Montgomery and bred by Mrs. Victor Higgon. Torment did a lot of winning at trials and in obedience classes, and distinguished himself on arrival in the U.S.A. by winning the first obedience class in which he competed. These two Corgis were the breed's pioneers of obedience work in the U.S.A.

Cymmwyn II, UDT, owned and trained by Mrs. Phyl Young, with a classmate. *Phyl*

148

Another noted English obedience Corgi was "James," the Kenneth Butlers' Sinbad of Wey, TDX, UD, CDX, by Ch. Rozavel Scarlet Emperor out of Jill of Pem. Born May 12, 1946, he was an "only child" and soon developed a personality which merited him the ranking position of house dog with bed privileges. His obedience career was impressive, and he went on to sire several top obedience workers as well. He qualified for his UD in 1949, was the first Corgi to do tracking, and made TDX in 1950, often in competition with the top working police dogs. James served double duty, for as a gun dog he put to practical use his ability to retrieve, track and jump.

The first Corgi bitch to gain a TD in Britain (1951) was Mr. and Mrs. Harrison's Bunty of Buzzard, CDX, UD Bunty, when bred to Sinbad of Wey, produced the Harrison's Chorister of Fentimen, TD, UD, CD. Obviously brains as well as beauty can breed on.

To become an obedience champion in England a dog has to win three Challenge Certificates for Highest Scoring Dog in Trial. The first Pembroke Corgi to gain this most distinguished honor was Obed. Ch. Ambrose of Kingstead, whelped March 13, 1954, sired by Stormerbanks Ploughboy out of Charmaine of Wey, owned and trained by F. Strutt.

"Johnny Boy" began in competition by winning the Novice class at the Welsh Corgi League's championship show in 1955. He had over 40 tickets (prizes) between that first show and his first C.C. The third and final C.C. was earned at the Southern Alsatian show in June 1959.

The first Corgi obedience champion bitch was Obed. Ch. Dawnway Busy Bee, owned by Mr. A. E. Hutchinson. A granddaughter of Sinbad, she was out of Tansy of Fentimen, linebred to Bunty of Buzzard, TDX, UD, CDX.

To return to early obedience Corgis in the United States, it is interesting to note that Derek Rayne entered his Ch. Sierra Bruin, CD, in Open A at the North Westchester Kennel Club show in Katonah, New York in 1939.

Mrs. William B. Long, whose dogs carry the well-known Willets prefix, owned and trained one of the outstanding obedience Corgis in the East, Waseeka's Megan. In 1940 Megan earned the breed's first UDT and was also the first small dog to win this combined degree. It was not until about 1947 that tracking became a separate event from the Utility routine, and the UD degree was established. Megan and three other dogs competed as the New England Dog Training Club's team against six other clubs for large cash prizes at the 1940 Westminster show.

Obedience Corgis scored high marks in other parts of the country. In the Southwest, Mr. and Mrs. Jack Liecty's first Corgi, Sierra Penryn, entered three Arizona obedience trials in March 1948. She won Novice B in each of the three shows, received High Score of all entries in two and tied for High Score in the third.

In the late 1940s a Canadian dog amassed a string of titles longer than

Am. Can. Ch. Bundocks Mellow de Rover Run, Am. Can. UD, owned by Douglas Bundock, was nine times Highest Scoring Dog in Trial.

Am. Can. Ch. Bundocks Rover Run Concerto, Am. Can. UD (left) and Bundocks Sonata de Rover Run, Am. Can. UD.

Ch. Merwyn's Proud Patrick, UDT, owned and trained by Irene Enger.

his name. Int. Ch. Windrush Redwing, Int. CD, CDX and UD plus UDT in the United States. He was the first dog of any breed to win all the obedience trial degrees in two countries. With his American championship he became the first international bench champion and obedience trial degrees winner combined. He was never defeated for Best of Breed in Canada. This remarkable dog was bred by Dr. A.R.B. Richmond of Toronto and owned by Mrs. M. H. Page of York Mills, Ontario.

On the West Coast Miss Margaret Downing had excellent success with her "Cappy," or more formally, Ch. Capt. Jinks Wiggs, UDT. This famous fellow, born in 1944 from a family of obedience Corgis, began his Novice work in 1948 and had finished all four degrees two years later. Miss Downing writes in the January, 1959, *Gazette* column of Cappy's championship in 1956:

> . . . The greatest joy, however, was Captain Jinks Wiggs' championship, which he received at 12 years of age! For years I have shown him where there was only himself or two Corgis at most. Until two years ago a major for Corgis was a rarity and although he had many points he had no majors. It wasn't until 1954 at the age of ten that he made his first major and then in July his second. I had made up my mind not to show him any more if he didn't make it in July because of his age. At the July show he never looked more handsome nor moved better.
>
> Captain Jinks Wiggs (Cappy) has been a real Western pioneer. His temperament, appearance and performance have done much to increase interest and ownership of Pembrokes around the San Francisco Bay area. I have had him since he was five weeks old and he has been a healthy, happy and wonderful companion all of these years and I look forward to many more with him.

Cappy was the first Pembroke Welsh Corgi champion to earn a UDT once tracking had been separated from Utility. Cappy lived to be 14½.

Other early UDTs were Tamarac Cadno (1941), Charles of Wrexham (1959), Ch. Dusky Wrexham (1959) and Willow Farm Grass Hopper (1960).

Mrs. Phyllis Young's bitch, Cymmwyn II, finished her UD with a third leg score of 199 out of a possible 200 points. "Kim" earned her Utility degree one year and ten months after entering her first obedience trial despite time out to raise a litter. She was originally enrolled in an obedience training class to learn basic manners, but did so well she completed her CD before the 12-week-class was over. For her Novice work she was given the *Dog World Award of Canine Distinction* for gaining scores of 195, 196½ and 197½ in three straight shows. She was 11 months old at the time.

Mrs. Young writes:

> We then formed a tracking class ourselves, and she got her degree at the very first local tracking test, just before her fourth birthday. The amazing part

about passing it was that about a quarter of the trail through, she sat down and sneezed and sneezed and sneezed. Practically sneezing her head off. Then while still sneezing, she continued to work the remainder of the track and passed with flying colors! The test was held in a very dry field . . . and she had picked up a foxtail in her nose! It had to be surgically removed the next morning! We truly marveled at this fantastic girl, continuing to "do her thing" with a painful, hazardous foxtail up her nose.

More Recent Standouts

Several other California dogs have proven to be outstanding workers and have brought fame to themselves, their trainers and the breed. High on the list are three bitches owned and trained by Douglas and Gladys Bundock, Amer. Can. Ch. Bundocks Mellow de Rover Run, Amer. Can. UD, and her two daughters, Amer. Can. Ch. Bundocks·Rover Run Concerto, Amer. Can. UD, and Bundocks Sonata de Rover Run, Amer. Can. UD. Between them these three girls racked up a total of 35 Highest Scoring Dog in Trial awards in the United States and Canada. Mellow and Sonata each had a 200 score; and Concerto earned no less than an incredible six perfect scores! At one show under judge Margaret Downing there was a run-off for first place in Open B between Sonata and Mellow with Doug Bundock handling them both as a brace. The tied score was 199½. Sonata won.

Sonata and Concerto were trained further by Mr. Bundock to do the Walt Disney film, *Little Dog Lost*. Mrs. Bundock writes, "Sonata did the bulk of the work in the picture, but the official star was Concerto . . . because Concerto was the extrovert and better able to take the adulation of her 'fans'."

Ch. Merwyn's Proud Patrick, UDT, a tri owned and trained by Mrs. Irene Enger, also had a notable career in California. "Riki" was whelped in January 1968 and had completed his UD by August 1970. The bench championship and T were added by September 1972. He won 14 Highest Scoring Corgi in Trial honors, was several times Highest Scoring Champion of Record, and passed three tracking tests.

A well-known tri father and daughter combination belonging to Miss Olive Gardiner of Los Angeles is Ch. Gardiner Jones, UDT and Gardiner Djinn, UDT. "Djinn" earned three obedience titles in the period of 7½ months at an early age. Her father, "Jones," finished his championship in 1972 and four weeks later completed his UD. After seven months of training he passed his tracking test. Jones has always been a high scoring obedience dog and a happy, speedy worker. Miss Gardiner says:

> Crowds always collect to see the "funny, little black dog" in the ring. I don't think I've ever left a trial without being asked: "Where can I get a dog

Ch. Devonshire's Royal Flush, UDT, Can. UD, Bda. CD, the sire of two UDT offspring, owned and trained by Mrs. Oliver J. Hart, Jr.

Ffafryn Cyntaf O Brenhinol, UDT, Can. Bda. UD, Mrs. Hart's son of Royal Flush.

153

Ch. Gardiner Jones, UDT, and his daughter Gardiner Djinn, UDT, owned and trained by Miss Olive Gardiner.

Ch. Larklain Katy-Did, UDT, the first champion UDT bitch in the United States. Owned and trained by Mrs. Carole-Joy Evert.

154

A daughter of Royal Flush, Thurlow's Little Lizajane, UDT, a spectacular worker with several 200 scores on her record. She is owned by J. and V. Thurlow.

Am. Can. Ch. Katydid's Top Von Bart Starr, CDX (left) and his dam Ch. Larklain Red Venus Amour, UDT, a Katy-Did daughter, both owned by Mrs. Evert.

155

exactly like yours?" He is really a ham, and he passed this on to his daughter. Recently, Djinn got a standing ovation, but her score was 58!

Another family of obedience whizzes descends from the late Mrs. Roz Hart's Ch. Devonshire's Royal Flush, UDT, Can. UD, Bda. CD. "Royal" gained his Canadian UD in his first three straight trials in Utility. His son, also trained by Mrs. Hart, is a triple UD winner and carries the title of Ffafryn Cyntaf O Brenhinol, UDT, Can. Bda. UD. His Bermudian title was won in three straight shows.

To be a consistent scorer of 197 or better is rare, and Royal's daughter, Thurlow's Little Lizajane, UDT, deserves accolades. This bright little lady, owned and trained by Joan and Virgil Thurlow, has set a fantastic record of several 200 scores, many 199 and 199½ scores, and a number of Highest Scoring Dog in the Regular Classes (as the HIT award is now known) awards—six in 1976 alone. She is still being shown in competition at the time this is written.

In Colorado a family of top performing Corgis has been trained by Mrs. Carole-Joy Evert. The first champion UDT bitch in the country, Ch. Larklain Katy-Did, UDT, shone in the breed ring as well as in obedience. Her daughter, Ch. Larklain Red Venus Amour, UDT, is the only second generation champion UDT bitch to date. "Venus," herself, has produced champions and obedience titleholders and has a Stock Dog I Certificate of Working Ability. Venus' son, Am. Can. Ch. Katydid's Top Von Bart Starr, CDX, is well on his way to becoming a third generation champion UDT. Other Katydids are starting their obedience training to carry on the tradition.

Two final records must be mentioned. Am. Can. Ch. Calusa's Brandy Alexander, CDX, TD, owned by Mrs. Jacobsen in Florida, passed his Tracking test at the tender age of seven months. And at the age of 12½ years Munna of Greenshome was trained by her owners Donald and Eva Green to complete her CD degree with such high scores that she was awarded the *Dog World Award of Canine Distinction.*

There have been many very successful obedience Corgis across the country. As of mid 1978, the UD degree has been earned by a total of 87 Pembrokes, many of which are champions and include the multiple Best in Show winner, Amer. Can. Ch. Bear Acres Mister Snowshoes, UD. There are 53 TDs. Of these, 24 have won both titles to become UDTs. The number of champion UDTs is nine. The records leave no doubt the Pembroke Welsh Corgi has proven, indeed, its ability to star in the demanding field of obedience trials.

156

11

The Pembroke in the Spotlight

To THOSE OF US who love the breed it is not at all surprising that people of fame share our admiration, for a Pembroke Welsh Corgi is certainly special. Quite a few Corgis have shared the spotlight with their illustrious owners.

Queen Elizabeth's Corgis

By far the most well-known Corgi owner in the world is Her Majesty, Queen Elizabeth II, of England. The royal family long has been interested in purebred dogs of several breeds and always has had groups of dogs around.

It was in 1933 that the Duke of York, later King George VI, purchased a Corgi puppy from Mrs. Thelma Gray to be a playmate for his daughters Elizabeth and Margaret. The puppy was royally bred himself, as he was a son of Ch. Crymmch President out of Ch. Rozavel Golden Girl. His call name "Dookie" evolved during the month he was being housebroken by Mrs. Gray prior to his move to the royal household. It is a derivation of "The Duke," which he was dubbed to match his "snooty" airs supposedly assumed over his good fortune. Dookie, or more regally Rozavel Golden Eagle, soon joined the little princesses in all their play as well as during more ceremonious occasions.

It is said the King, too, was captivated by the Corgi's great personality. Dookie was such a success that Rozavel Lady Jane joined the royal dogs as his prospective bride. These two Corgis became dearly loved companions, but, alas, no litter resulted. Eventually in 1938 Jane was bred to Mrs. Gray's Tafferteffy. The puppies arrived on Christmas Eve, and "Crackers" and "Carol" were added to the family.

Another early favorite was "Sue," who replaced Jane, tragically struck down by a car in 1944. Sue, or as an adult, Susan, had the honor indeed of joining the future Queen Elizabeth and Prince Philip on their honeymoon. Susan was mated to the renowned Int. Ch. Rozavel Lucky Strike, and two puppies were retained. Descendants of these Corgis and others surround the royal family today.

Although the Queen always has insisted on well-bred dogs of good quality, the royal Corgis usually are not shown. An exception is Windsor Loyal Subject, a Ch. Kaytop Marshall son bred by the Queen and owned by Mrs. Gray, who won a Challenge Certificate in 1973.

Queen Elizabeth has continued her interest in the breed. In 1978 one of her bitches produced a nice litter bred to Miss Pat Curties' Aust. Ch. Scottholme Red Ember. No doubt Her Majesty's enthusiasm for Corgis will last a lifetime. After all, how many of us can say we have been "in the breed" since 1933?

Corgis also have graced the homes of other heads of state. In 1954 Mrs. Helen Sheldon sent a puppy by Critic of Cowfold out of Craythorne's Good Tender to General de Gaulle in Paris.

Larry Sullivan's Corgis

Francis L. Sullivan, better known as Larry, gained fame on the stage and screen. Some of his most memorable roles were in *Witness for the Prosecution, Great Expectations* and *Oliver Twist*. Although London born, Mr. Sullivan moved to New York and ultimately became an American citizen.

According to Mr. Sullivan's close friend David Wainwright, in the 1930s Larry became a Corgi owner quite reluctantly. Upon returning to his dressing room on one special occasion, he found "a small reddish object with large paws, larger ears, and a still larger bow around his neck, with a yet even larger sign attached, 'I am Quoodle, please be good to me!' " In spite of a fearful fuss, this gift from his wife soon was ensconced in Larry's lap and in his heart. Quoodle lived in London and traveled with Larry all over Britain. He soon was joined by "Mrs. Quinn" and "Quirrip," the Sullivans' country Corgis.

In the late 1940s Mrs. Van Beynum, of the Willow Farm prefix, offered the Sullivans Willow Farm Quest, who immediately set off with them for Bermuda. Quest traveled back and forth between New York and California on the train with the famous actor, sharing the fanciest accommodations. He

H.M. Queen Elizabeth II holds Buzz, the great grandson of Susan.
Studio Lisa Ltd.

Sherry and H.R.H. the Prince Andrew having a tete a tete. Sherry and Whiskey were the two nursery Corgis in 1962.
Studio Lisa Ltd.

Actor Larry Sullivan with Willow Farm Quest aboard ship en route to Europe.

Tasha Tudor and a *Corgiville Fair* Corgi.

Actress Shelagh Fraser relaxes with Mynthurst Shemoy Albertine.   *Westminster Press*

160

crossed the Atlantic on the Mauretania to tour Europe, where ". . . he had *his* dinner served to him in something like eight of the twelve 3-Star Michelin Restaurants in the whole of France."

In Paris Mr. Wainwright, while walking Quest on the Champs Elysees, noticed several people in front of Cunard's window, and discovered there was a photograph of Larry and Quest on the Mauretania.

> . . . Quest with his dazzling "smile" had managed to upstage a famous actor, who certainly knew how to upstage any human soul. . . . The same picture stopped crowds in London, New York, and wherever Cunard had an office. The head of the NYC office of Cunard told us that if we ever took him on a Cunard ship again his passage was free.

Mr. Wainwright relates another story:

> At the Meurice . . . we got on [the elevator], Larry, Quest and I, and there was a small, rather pudgy woman already in the car, who exclaimed, "Oh my a Corgi!", and promptly got down on her knees and had an animated conversation with Quest. As we got to the street, I asked Larry if he had realized who she was, and he said that he had not. "Dorothy Parker," I said. Larry remarked, "You mean that woman who is so brittle and tough in her writings?" "The same." "Good God."

There is also the story of Richard Burton reciting long Welsh poems in the native tongue to Quest; and of Jerry Lewis—". . . *he too* got down on his knees and had a long chat with Quest." Larry Sullivan died in 1956, but Quest lived on with David Wainwright to the age of 17 as a true "Bon Vivant . . . yet ever the gentleman."

Shelagh Fraser's Corgis

A famous lady of the English stage, screen, TV and radio is Shelagh Fraser, with a long list of theatrical credits to her name. Ms. Fraser started out with Corgis under the encouraging eye of fellow actor Leslie Perrins, who steered her to Mrs. Maureen Roberts and the Mynthurst stud dogs. In spite of busy rehersal schedules, on location filming, and a London flat, Ms. Fraser in cooperation with Mrs. Roberts raised several litters from her Shemoy bitches.

A pinnacle of success was reached in 1975 with the championship of Mynthurst Peach Blush (Ch. Lees Chico ex Mynthurst Shemoy Albertine), four generations down from Ms. Fraser's original Corgi. "Albertine" is the actress' constant companion. Ms. Fraser writes:

> She appeared with me in certain episodes of "Family at War" (Shown in America) and, characteristically, is just (as) at home in a theatric dressing room

Bundocks Sonata de Rover Run as Candy pauses in the daily route in search of food to make sure the coast is clear.

Bundocks Rover Run Concerto, Candy of *Little Dog Lost,* stares adoringly at the old man who befriended "him."

162

as she is in film or TV Studios. As the TV series was a great success in Scandanavia, Albertine's photograph has been blazoned, in full colour, across many Scandinavian magazines (with her owner).

A brother, "Tom," belonged to the distinguished theater star Beatrix Lehman and once accompanied his owner onto the stage while she did scenes from Shakespeare for a university lecture.

Other Famous Owners

Other cinema celebrities to have owned Corgis are Gary Cooper with a Cote de Neige dog; Kay English, a featured MGM actress, whose Corgi was named "Rosebud;" and Ava Gardner, who owned several Corgis while living in Hollywood and purchased the tricolor, Nona of Wey, from the Butlers in 1968.

Tasha Tudor

In America the person with whom most associate the charming little red and white Corgi dog is artist-author Tasha Tudor. Her enchanting illustrations appear in many joyful books including the tiny, leather bound *The Twenty-Third Psalm*. Prince Philip purchased a copy while visiting America, and the Queen ordered more through a British bookseller. The Corgi model for each of the illustrations is Mrs. Tudor's Megan.

Christmas and other holidays are featured in Tasha Tudor's work. At least 65 different designs showing Corgis have been circulated on colorful Christmas cards. She has prepared several books treasured by people the world over at Yuletide, particularly her version of *The Night Before Christmas* (Rand McNally & Co.). Completely unique and fanciful is *Corgiville Fair* (Thomas Y. Crowell Company, New York), wherein all the characters are animals, and every detail is worth studying. Tasha Tudor fans can find a whole room devoted to her work at The Dutch Inn Gift Shop in Mill Hall, Pennsylvania. Mrs. Tudor lives in Vermont in a setting as quaint as the scenes she so artfully depicts.

Little Dog Lost

Undoubtedly the greatest publicity ever given the Pembroke Welsh Corgi surrounded the Walt Disney, full-lenth color film, *Little Dog Lost*. First shown on television on January 13, 1963, the story concerns a Corgi puppy separated from his family and his adventures as he tries to cope on his own. The movie is an adaptation of Meindert de Jong's book *Hurry Home Candy*. Most of the scenes were shot in Northern California by Perkins Films, Inc.

163

Mellow de in *Little Dog Lost*.

Fferm Corgwyn Lucky Lady Bug played Candy in the cattle sequences.

164

Little Dog Lost was an instant success, and the breed went straight to the heart of a vast viewing audience across the nation.

The star of the show, glamorous Amer. Can. Ch. Bundocks Rover Run Concerto, Amer. Can. UD, was owned, trained and handled by Douglas Bundock. Concerto was ably assisted by her litter mate Bundocks Sonata de Rover Run, Amer. Can. UD, who did many of the scenes demanding split-second timing between the "actress" and her handler. The girls' mother, Amer. Can. Ch. Bundocks Mellow de Rover Run, Amer. Can. UD, got into the act and even peeked through the camera used for the aerial shots.

Two other of Mellow's puppies contributed to the movie. Bundocks Cathl, CD, was called upon to howl on command, and Bundocks Colwyn supplied a tail-wagging scene with a somewhat longish appendage.

The beginning of the story called for pictures of the Corgi, "Candy," as a puppy. Mrs. Marjorie Butcher sent out two Cote de Neige youngsters with similar markings named, appropriately, "Candy Bar" and "Candy Tuft."

The major herding sequences were acted by yet another Corgi, Fferm Corgwyn Lucky Lady Bug, Am. Can. CD, belonging to Mrs. Jean Robocker of Kalispell, Montana. Lady Bug had been practicing by herding chickens and other animals on her farm and living up to the Corgi's reputation as a good ratter.

It is interesting to note that while the script called for a male "Candy," almost all the Corgis participating were bitches. It is doubtful the public noticed the discrepancy as it became caught up in the drama of an endearing little dog.

Ch. Cottleston Card of Fox Covert. A homebred BIS winning son of Ch. Llanfair Night Owl. Breeders: Michael Sauve and Ruth Cooper.
Booth

A Study in General Appearance. Note the lovely over-all balance, good bone and substance yet with nice refinement throughout, and head and expression which illustrate perfectly the dictates of the breed Standard.

12

An In-Depth Look at the Pembroke Welsh Corgi Standard

THE PRESENT Pembroke Welsh Corgi Standard, revised to provide a more comprehensive and realistic description of the desired breed characteristics, was approved by the Directors of the American Kennel Club on June 13, 1972. The changes from the previous Standard make the Standard currently in use in the United States differ slightly from the Standard which is used in other countries, such as England, Canada, Australia and New Zealand. The official English Standard is presented at the end of this chapter.

The drawings accompanying the breed Standard are reprinted from the booklet, *An Illustrated Study of the Pembroke Welsh Corgi Standard,* prepared and published by the Pembroke Welsh Corgi Club of America.

Official AKC Standard for the Pembroke Welsh Corgi

General Appearance—Low-set, strong, sturdily built and active, giving an impression of substance and stamina in a small space. Should not be so low and heavy-boned as to appear coarse or overdone, nor so light-boned as to appear racy. Outlook bold, but kindly. Expression intelligent and interested. Never shy nor vicious.

167

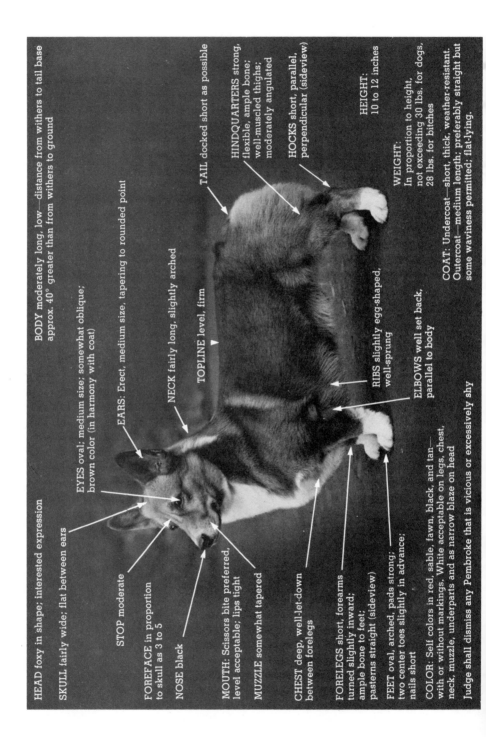

HEAD foxy in shape; interested expression

SKULL fairly wide; flat between ears

BODY moderately long, low—distance from withers to tail base
approx. 40° greater than from withers to ground

EYES oval; medium size; somewhat oblique;
brown color (in harmony with coat)

EARS: Erect, medium size, tapering to rounded point

STOP moderate

NECK fairly long, slightly arched

FOREFACE in proportion
to skull as 3 to 5

TOPLINE level, firm

NOSE black

TAIL docked short as possible

MOUTH: Scissors bite preferred,
level acceptable; lips tight

HINDQUARTERS strong,
flexible, ample bone;
well-muscled thighs;
moderately angulated

MUZZLE somewhat tapered

HOCKS short, parallel,
perpendicular (sideview)

CHEST deep, well-let-down
between forelegs

RIBS slightly egg-shaped,
well-sprung

FORELEGS short, forearms
turned slightly inward;
ample bone to feet;
pasterns straight (sideview)

ELBOWS well set back,
parallel to body

HEIGHT:
10 to 12 inches

FEET oval, arched, pads strong;
two center toes slightly in advance;
nails short

WEIGHT:
In proportion to height,
not exceeding 30 lbs. for dogs,
28 lbs. for bitches

COLOR: Self colors in red, sable, fawn, black, and tan—
with or without markings. White acceptable on legs, chest,
neck, muzzle, underparts and as narrow blaze on head

COAT: Undercoat—short, thick, weather-resistant.
Outercoat—medium length; preferably straight but
some waviness permitted; flat-lying.

Judge shall dismiss any Pembroke that is vicious or excessively shy

Size and Proportions—Moderately long and low. The distance from the withers to base of tail should be approximately 40 percent greater than the distance from the withers to the ground. *Height* (from ground to highest point on withers) should be 10 to 12 inches. *Weight* is in proportion to size, not exceeding 30 pounds for dogs and 28 pounds for bitches. In show condition, the preferred medium-size dog of correct bone and substance will weigh approximately 27 pounds, with bitches approximately 25 pounds. Obvious oversized specimens and diminutive toylike individuals must be very seriously penalized.

Head and Skull—Head to be foxy in shape and appearance, but not sly in expression. Skull to be fairly wide and flat between the ears. Moderate amount of stop. Very slight rounding of cheek, and not filled in below the eyes, as foreface should be nicely chiseled to give a somewhat tapered muzzle. Distance from the occiput to center of stop to be greater than the distance from stop to nose tip. The proportion being five parts of total distance for the skull and three parts for the foreface. Muzzle should be neither dish-faced nor Roman-nosed. *Nose*—Black and fully pigmented.

Eyes—Oval, medium in size, not round nor protruding, nor deep-set and piglike. Set somewhat obliquely. Variations of brown in harmony with coat color. Eye rims dark, preferably black. While dark eyes enhance the expression, true black eyes are most undesirable, as are yellow or bluish eyes.

Ears—Erect, firm, and of medium size, tapering slightly to a rounded point. Ears are mobile, and react sensitively to sounds. A line drawn from the nose tip through the eyes to the ear tips and across should form an approximate equilateral triangle. Bat ears, small cat-like ears, overly large weak ears, hooded ears, ears carried too high or too low are undesirable. Button, rose or drop ears are very serious faults.

Mouth—Scissors bite, the inner side of the upper incisors touching the outer side of the lower incisors. Level bite is acceptable. Lips should be tight, with little or no fullness, and black. Overshot or undershot bite is a very serious fault.

Neck—Fairly long, of sufficient length to provide over-all balance of the dog. Slightly arched, clean and blending well into the shoulders. A very short neck giving a stuffy appearance, and a long, thin or ewe neck, are faulty.

Body—Rib cage should be well sprung, slightly egg-shaped, and moderately long. Deep chest, well let down between forelegs. Exaggerated lowness interferes with the desired freedom of movement and should be penalized. Viewed from above, the body should taper slightly to end of the loin. Loin short. Firm level topline, neither riding up to nor falling away at the croup. A slight depression behind the shoulders caused by heavier neck coat meeting

169

the shorter body coat is permissible. Round or flat rib cage, lack of brisket, extreme length or cobbiness are undesirable.

It is impossible to have either a correct front or the desired front action with an incorrectly shaped rib cage. The desired egg-shaped rib cage will permit freedom of front action while providing ample heart and lung space.

Forequarters—Legs short; forearms turned slightly inward, with the distance between the wrists less than between the shoulder joints, so that the front does not appear absolutely straight. Ample bone carried right down into the feet. Pasterns firm and nearly straight when viewed from the side. Weak pasterns and knuckling over are serious faults. Shoulder blades long and well laid back along the rib cage. Upper arms nearly equal in length to shoulder blades. Elbows parallel to the body, not prominent, and well set back to allow a line perpendicular to the ground to be drawn from the tip of the shoulder blade through to elbow.

Hindquarters—Ample bone, strong and flexible, moderately angulated at stifle and hock. Exaggerated angulation is as faulty as too little. Thighs should be well muscled. Hocks short, parallel, and when viewed from the side are perpendicular to the ground. Barrel hocks or cowhocks are most objectionable. Slipped or double-jointed hocks are very faulty.

Tail—Docked as short as possible without being indented. Occasionally a puppy is born with a natural dock, which if sufficiently short is acceptable. A tail up to two inches in length is allowed, but if carried high tends to spoil the contour of the topline.

Feet—Oval, with the two center toes slightly in advance of the two outer ones. Turning neither in nor out. Pads strong and feet arched. Nails short. Dewclaws on both forelegs and hind legs usually removed. Too round, long and narrow, or splayed feet are faulty.

Movement—Free and smooth. Forelegs should reach well forward, without too much lift, in unison with the driving action of hind legs. The correct shoulder assembly and well-fitted elbows allow the long, free stride in front. Viewed from the front, legs do not move in exact parallel planes, but incline slightly inward to compensate for shortness of leg and width of chest. Hind legs should drive well under the body and move on a line with the forelegs, with hocks turning neither in nor out. Feet must travel parallel to the line of motion with no tendency to swing out, cross over, or interfere with each other. Short, choppy movement, rolling or high-stepping gait, close or overly wide coming or going are incorrect. This is a herding dog which must have the agility, freedom of movement, and endurance to do the work for which he was developed.

Color—The outer coat is to be of self colors in red, sable, fawn, black and tan, with or without white markings. White is acceptable on legs, chest, neck (either in part or as a collar), muzzle, underparts, and as a narrow blaze on head.

Very Serious Faults—

Whitelies—Body color white with red or dark markings.

Mismarks—Self colors with any area of white on back between withers and tail, on sides between elbows and back of hindquarters, or on ears. Black with white markings and no tan present.

Bluies—Colored portions of the coat have a distinct bluish or smokey cast. This coloring is associated with extremely light or blue eyes and liver or gray eye rims, nose and lip pigment.

Coat—Medium length; short, thick, weather-resistant undercoat with a coarser, longer outer coat. Over-all length varies, with slightly thicker and longer ruff around neck, chest and on the shoulders. The body coat lies flat. Hair is slightly longer on back of forelegs and underparts, and somewhat fuller and longer on rear of hindquarters. The coat is preferably straight, but some waviness is permitted. This breed has a shedding coat, and seasonal lack of undercoat should not be too severely penalized, providing the hair is glossy, healthy, and well groomed. A wiry, tightly marcelled coat is very faulty, as is an overly short, smooth and thin coat.

Very Serious Fault—

Fluffies—A coat of extreme length with exaggerated feathering on ears, chest, legs and feet, underparts and hindquarters. Trimming such a coat does not make it any more acceptable.

The Corgi should be shown in its natural condition with no trimming permitted except to tidy the feet and, if desired, remove the whiskers.

OVER-ALL PICTURE

Correct type, including general balance and outline, attractiveness of head-piece, intelligent outlook and correct temperament, is of primary importance. Movement is especially important, particularly as viewed from the side. A dog with smooth and free gait has to be reasonably sound and must be highly regarded. A minor fault must never take precedence over the above desired qualities.

A dog must be very seriously penalized for the following faults, regardless of whatever desirable qualities the dog may present:

Whitelies, Mismarks or Bluies; Fluffies; Button, Rose or Drop Ears; Overshot or Undershot Bite; Oversize or Undersize.

The judge shall dismiss from the ring any Pembroke Welsh Corgi that is vicious or excessively shy.

Approved June 13, 1972

171

Common Faults in General Outline

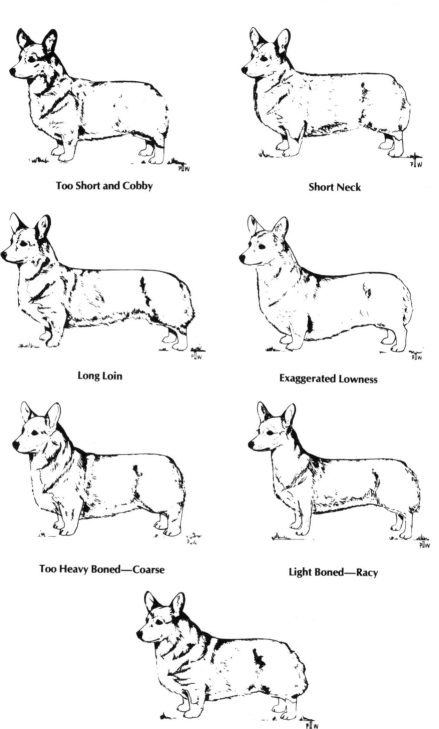

Too Short and Cobby

Short Neck

Long Loin

Exaggerated Lowness

Too Heavy Boned—Coarse

Light Boned—Racy

Stuffy

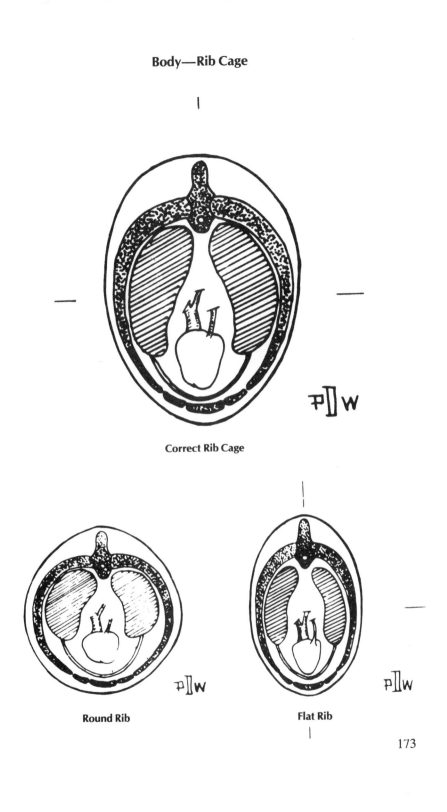

Correct Rib Cage

Round Rib

Flat Rib

Correct Head Proportions

The true foxy head, the intelligent and interested expression, and the kindly outlook are essential characteristics of the Pembroke Welsh Corgi. The four head studies presented here nicely illustrate the desired head quality. Note the moderately wide spread of ears, the refinement under the eyes and the correct head and ear proportions which give the imaginary wide triangle.

Very Serious Ear Faults

Button Ear

Drop Ear

Rose Ear

176

Bites

Correct Scissors

Acceptable Level Bite

Overshot Bite

Undershot Bite

177

Fronts

Correct front. Note how the forearm turns in slightly to compensate for and fit around the deep brisket.

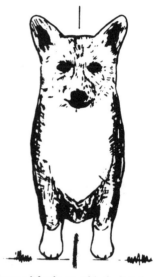

Terrier-straight front. This fault is becoming increasingly prevalent both here in the States and in England with some judges mistakenly selecting it out as a virtue.

Crooked Front.

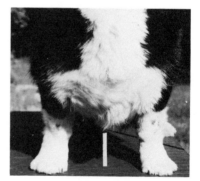

Wide Front.

178

Angulation

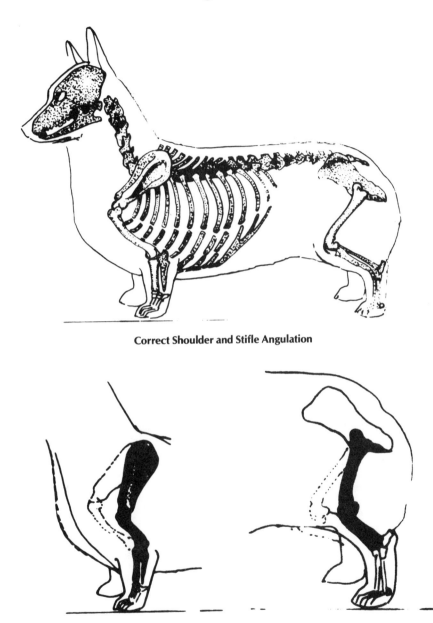

Correct Shoulder and Stifle Angulation

Straight Shoulder and Short Upper Arm

Insufficient Angulation—Straight Stifle

(A) Desired line drawn perpendicular to the ground from the tip of the shoulder blade through to the elbow. (B) Well developed forechest; brisket well let down between forelegs   *Tauskey*

Elbows well forward of the desired line (A) drawn from tip of shoulder blade perpendicular to the ground. (B) denotes lack of forechest.

(A) Strong, level topline, Correct proportion of length to height.
Tauskey

(A) Correct turn of stifle. (B) Hocks short.   *Tauskey*

(A) Lacking the desired turn of stifle. (B) Overly-long in hock by present day standards. The straight stifle and long hocks account for the "high in the rear" topline.

Two famous dogs in the history of the Pembroke Welsh Corgi have been selected to illustrate the Standard's specifications for forequarter and hindquarter angulation and correct topline. Ch. Rozavel Red Dragon, considered by many to have been the progenitor of the breed, represents the foundation from which our present-day Pembrokes stem. A modern-day Pembroke, Ch. Willet's Red Jacket, the top Best in Show winning Pembroke of all time, demonstrates the sound construction breeders are continually striving to obtain.

181

Hindquarters

Nice view of a champion Pembroke from behind, showing good hindquarters, short hocks, good bone, good tail set and finish, nice length of neck, good ear set and lovely coat. *Phyl*

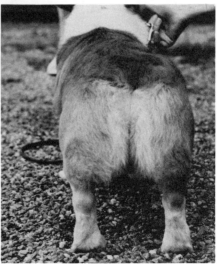

Over-wide behind

Faulty Hindquarters

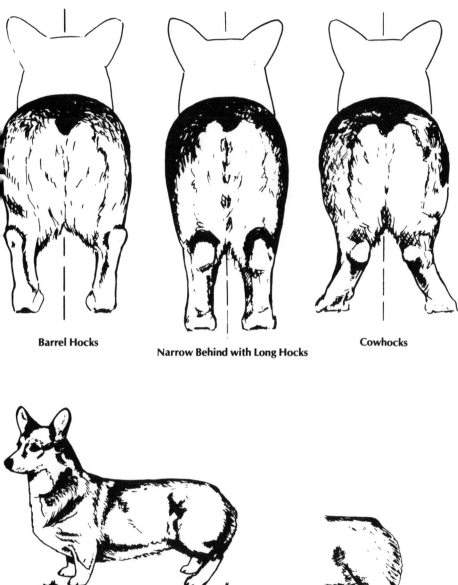

Barrel Hocks

Narrow Behind with Long Hocks

Cowhocks

Over-angulated Hindquarters—Sickle Hocks

Double-jointed Hock

183

Correct side movement. Note low, sweeping forward reach in front, the driving thrust behind, and the strong, level topline. *Phyl*

Another example of free, smooth, purposeful movement. *Phyl*

184

Side Movement

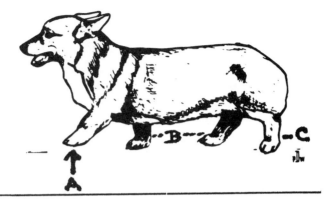

Short Stride. Note (A) lack of forward reach, (B) short distance covered in a single stride and (C) lack of thrust behind.

Poor side movement. A poor topline and body sway appear with faulty, inefficient movement.   *Phyl*

Another example of undesirable side movement. Note the high, flipping action of the far front foot and the high stepping action of the near hind leg.   *Phyl*

Front Movement

Correct front movement

Wide front movement

Paddling

Plaiting

Rear Movement

Correct Rear Movement

Hocks Turning Out—Toeing in Movement

Close Hind Movement

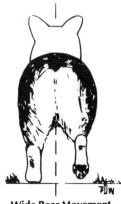

Wide Rear Movement

Weaving Rear Movement

Feet

Correct Foot

Round Foot

Long, Narrow Foot with Weak Pastern

Splayed Foot with Long Nails

A Very Serious Coat Fault

A typical Fluffy.

Fluffy head study. Long wisps of hair on the inside of the ears became apparent at five weeks of age. *Phyl*

White markings on the body should not extend above the dotted line. *Harper*

Mismark—The side marking extends well up above the level of the elbow, and the stifle trim continues in a marking up to the base of the tail. This dog also appears to be short coated as well as mismarked.

190

Color and Markings

This tricolor illustrates the maximum acceptable extent of white markings. *Phyl*

Whitely—The white body color with red or dark markings. (Note the lovely eye and expression of this striking fellow.) *Phyl*

Applying the Standard

The photographs of four dogs are presented here, each with a brief critique to illustrate how a judge might evaluate these dogs were they to appear as entries in the show ring.

A bitch of nice over-all balance and quality. Good head and expression. Level topline here and satisfactory length of body. The bitch is standing wide in front and behind. She would have to be examined for a wide front (A) and the topline would have to be rechecked when she was standing properly behind. She is perhaps a shade long in hock (B) which could be due to the angle at which the photograph was taken.

Another sweet type, this one a puppy. The head can be faulted slightly for the filled in cheek area under the eye (A). Ears are just a shade rounder at the tips than would be desired for perfection. What may be close to perfection someday are the forequarters. Note correct slant of forearm (B) and parallel pasterns. The chest will let down between the forearms with maturity. This puppy possesses lovely bone and looks to be coming into a nice coat of correct texture.

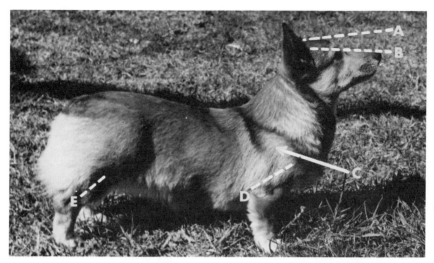

This two-year-old bitch demonstrates several quite common faults seen in the ring today. An otherwise nicely proportioned head—though possibly a shade masculine—is marred by the lack of parallel planes between the skull (A) and muzzle (B). The topline is obviously faulty, riding up badly behind. Shadings indicate a possible short shoulder blade (C) but the bitch would have to be examined to be sure of this. She also appears to be unbalanced in angulation, having more front angulation (D) than rear (E). Movement would undoubtedly give away a lot here. Over-all, not wholly unattractive but a hard bitch to win with because her faults are so obvious.

This poor fellow should remain out of the ribbons regardless of what his competition may be. Coarse all over and extremely overdone in head, the dog is much too low in front for the rest of him. The front appears crooked and the hindquarters with the overly long hocks are probably cowhocked. This dog is completely lacking quality and correct type.

193

Current Official English Standard
for the Pembroke Welsh Corgi

General Appearance

Low set, strong, sturdily built, alert and active, giving an impression of substance and stamina in a small space, outlook bold, expression intelligent and workmanlike. The movement should be free and active, elbows fitting closely to the sides, neither loose nor tied. Forelegs should move well forward, without too much lift, in unison with thrusting action of hind legs.

Head and Skull

Head to be foxy in shape and appearance, with alert and intelligent expression, skull to be fairly wide and flat between the ears; moderate amount of stop. Length of foreface to be in proportion to the skull as three is to five. Muzzle slightly tapering. Nose black.

Eyes

Well set, round, medium size, hazel in colour and blending with colour of coat.

Ears

Pricked, medium-sized, slightly pointed. A line drawn from the tip of the nose through the eye should, if extended, pass through or close to the tip of the ear.

Mouth

Teeth level, or with the inner side of the upper front teeth resting closely on the front of the under ones.

Neck

Fairly long.

Forequarters

Legs short and as straight as possible. Ample bone carried right down to the feet. Elbows should fit closely to the sides, neither loose nor tied.

Body

Of medium length, with well-sprung ribs; not short-coupled or terrier-like. Level top line. Chest broad and deep, well let down between the forelegs.

194

Hindquarters

Strong and flexible, slightly tapering. Legs short. Ample bone carried down to the feet. Hocks straight when viewed from behind.

Feet

Oval, the two centre toes slightly in advance of two outer ones, pads strong and well arched. Nails short.

Tail

Short, preferably natural.

Coat

Of medium length and dense; not wiry.

Colour

Self colours in Red, Sable, Fawn, Black and Tan, or with white markings on legs, chest and neck. Some white on head and foreface is permissible.

Weight and Size

Dogs 20 to 24 lb.; Bitches 18 to 22 lb. Height from 10 to 12 inches at the shoulder.

Faults

The following are serious faults: white on the body giving a piebald or skewbald effect, or hound-like markings. Long fluffy coat, accompanied with feathering on ears and feet. Overshot or undershot mouth.

Male animals should have two apparently normal testicles fully descended into the scrotum. Non entirety should be regarded as a fault in the same way as the absence of any other external part of a dog.

The Beauty Treatment

13

Showing Your Corgi

A HEALTHY, properly conditioned and trained Corgi is an easy dog to prepare for the show ring and a joy to show. Even though the Corgi does not require the endless hours of brushing or trimming that many long-coated breeds must have before a show, the night before the show is not the time to wake up to the realization your Corgi is not looking his best. True, vibrant show condition is a product of months of good diet, ample exercise and conscientious health care. All the chalk powders, coat conditioners and coat dressings in the world, by themselves, will not give your dog true bloom. A lovely coat and sparkling good health come from within, not from a spray can or bottle.

Grooming

If your Corgi has been kept in good condition right along, his nails have been trimmed routinely, and his teeth have been kept free of tartar, there is really very little you must do the night before. In fact, if the breed judging is not scheduled for the crack of dawn, our Corgis are permitted their usual run in the woods and even a session of frogging down at the pond if it is the appropriate time of year. It is not until they come back to the house and see the towels and soap out that they realize they are about to have a day's outing at a show.

What we do to ready our Corgis for a show is quite simple. First wash the white parts on the feet, chest and collar with a mild soap. The soap is *thoroughly* rinsed out and the wet areas are vigorously dried with a towel. The

197

Rough, ungroomed coat. *Spengler*

Improperly combed with a wide-toothed comb. *Spengler*

Ready for the show ring. *Spengler*

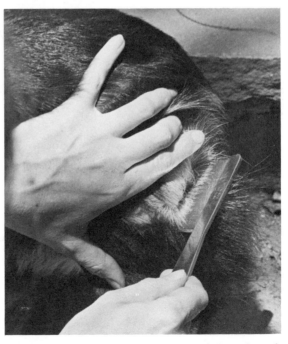

For a thorough grooming, lift the top hair and comb through the undercoat. *Spengler*

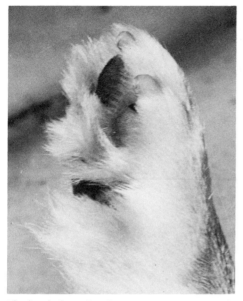

The foot before trimming. *Spengler*

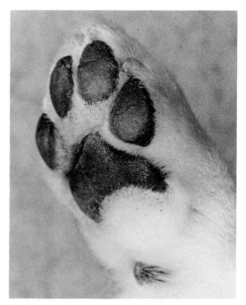

The foot after trimming. *Spengler*

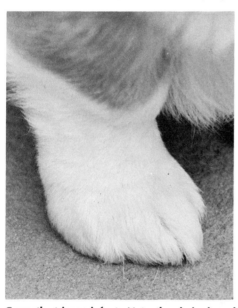

Correctly trimmed foot. Note the desired oval shape and the short toenails. *Spengler*

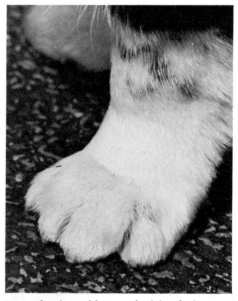

An overly-trimmed foot emphasizing the incorrect round shape. *Spengler*

dampened towel is used to give the dog a thorough body rub. This will remove the surface grime and also fluff the coat out just a bit, adding to the overall impression of a luxuriant depth of coat. To bathe the entire dog the night before the show usually is a frightful mistake, as when the coat dries it will be unmanageably fluffy, curly and go every which way. If for some reason a dog has to be given a complete bath before a show, it should be done at least two or three days ahead.

When the dog's white marked areas are nearly dry, white chalk powder can be brushed into the coat and left until just before show time. Some Corgis have crystal white markings. Others have markings that are a duller white. Yellowish white markings will be whitened somewhat with the use of chalk. When it is brushed out before the dog is taken into the ring, the chalk will carry with it the dirt and soot picked up on the way to the show. A slight chalk residue will remain after the brushing and will help give the white parts of the coat a fuller look, as the remaining chalk separates the individual hairs from one another.

Even though all Corgis here have their nails trimmed at least once a week, there always seems to be a little bit a nail that can be sanded off before the dog is ready to go to the show. The excess hair on the foot is trimmed off at the same time.

Many exhibitors remove the whiskers on their Corgis before a show. British breeders abhor this practice, as it does somehow alter the over-all impression of the head and expression. It is not done with our dogs because we dislike the prickly face washes while the stubble is growing in, and whiskers are an impossible nuisance to keep short. Plus we learned eventually that few judges ever noticed whether a dog's whiskers were trimmed and the presence of whiskers certainly made no difference in the eventual placing of the dog.

The last and most time consuming part of grooming the dog for the show ring consists of an absolutely meticulous combing. We start at the back end of the dog at the very bottom of his pants and work up over his back and sides to the front and end with combing the chest coat. An English fine comb is used, and the coat is combed from the skin out in the direction the hair grows. Be careful to not scratch the skin as you work. With a dense undercoat, only a very small section can be combed at a time. Combing the coat in this manner will get the undercoat and guard hairs all going in the same direction and will give a smooth, even, rich appearance to the coat. If the coat is full of static electricity, making it difficult to comb because of the fly-away hairs, dampen the coat slightly with a fine spray of water as you work. After all your efforts are done, the dog will give himself a good shake, letting you know he prefers to go dressed his own way, and you are ready to set off for the ring.

Ch. Stokeplain Fair Chance of Cote de Neige with his owner-handler, Marjorie Butcher, and breeder-judge Stanley Logan as Chance wins Best in Sweepstakes at the 1963 PWCCA Specialty. Chance sired the well-known winner Ch. Cote de Neige Pennysaver. His Stokeplain breeding traces back to Masterpiece-Clipper lines.   *Shafer*

A poor pose. The dog is too close to the handler which forces her to hold her head back to see her handler's face. Compare the resulting poor topline with the one in the next photo of the same dog.   *Phyl*

Properly posed the overall picture is greatly improved.   *Bennett Associates*

Handling

Even though the Corgi is a relatively easy dog to prepare for exhibition, he is not necessarily an easy dog to handle in the ring. The Corgi is a natural working breed and should be shown on an absolutely loose lead to give the dog a chance to show off his free, easy movement. And the Corgi should pose himself just as naturally. He should never be shown artificially posed or strung up by the neck on a taut lead.

It takes a little doing to train a Corgi to stand patiently in front of you all the while looking alert and full of energy. A Corgi will quickly learn to bait if you make a practice of giving him food treats only when he is standing squarely. The competition for the treats from other dogs will keep a youngster really on his toes. The baiting game will become great fun for the dog, and he soon will enjoy practicing his catching skills in the ring. Experiment with different foods to see which one is most certain to keep your dog's attention in the presence of many distractions. Dogs here do best with beef liver that has been thoroughly cooked - usually boiled and then dried slightly in a low oven. Other dogs are known to prefer pieces of hot dogs, potato chips or a variety of tidbits.

Table training should begin during the puppy's early grooming sessions. Without making a big production of it, train the puppy to stand calmly on a table while you examine him from head to tail. Take your time in training a puppy to allow his mouth to be examined. At first do little more than lift the sides of his lips and tell him what a good boy he is to have such pretty teeth. Gradually work him up to the point where you can have other people approach him while he is standing on the table and examine in his mouth in the way a judge will do at a show.

Lead training a youngster for the show ring need consist of little more than teaching him to take you for a walk. This does not mean he should be allowed to pull you all over kingdom come, but rather he should proudly step out ahead of you, though still to your left side, as you walk along.

The fun of actually going someplace rather than walking around in a circle, as in a show ring, in your back yard will make a vast difference to how your dog reacts to show training. Once he is confident on the lead, he can be taught in a few brief sessions the patterns of gaiting used in the show ring, such as the straight out to the end of the ring with a U-turn and back, the L-shaped and the triangle patterns. More potentially good show dogs are ruined by over-practice at home than by lack of training.

A Corgi is easily bored and what is worse, a Corgi will take special delight in letting the whole ringside know just how bored he is. The more you try to pep up a Corgi who refuses to show, the worse he will get. With luck he will come to life if you studiously ignore him and make him work to get your

Ch. Vangard Mister Ski Bum with his breeder-handler, Robert Simpson, whelped October 15, 1975, owner: Margaret Shepard. He was a winner of three Group 1sts and a BIS at 17 months.   *Robert*

Eng. Ch. Lees Joker (left), handled by his breeder-owner, Miss Pat Curties, and Eng. Ch. Lisaye Mariella, handled by her owner, Charles Lister-Kaye, winning the C.C.s at Brighton, 1952. In England Corgis are usually handled by their owners and are more casually presented than in the American show ring.   *Klein*

attention. If you find you have one of those few Corgis who simply cannot be tricked into being a "showing fool," then it is best to put him aside and go with a dog who thoroughly enjoys the whole dog show scene.

If you decide to have a professional handler to show your dog, write or phone the Professional Handlers Association for recommendations. When this book went to press, the President of the PHA was Ted Young, Jr., Rocky Hill, CT 06067, phone 203-529-8641. If no longer President, Mr. Young will refer you to the current PHA Officer to contact.

This winning team of BIS winner Am. Can. Bda. Ch. Velour of Rowell and owner-handler Mrs. Janet Robinson has achieved great success. Spock is always shown in impeccable condition which has contributed to his remarkable record of over 200 Bests of Breed. He is shown winning the Working Group at the Central New York KC under Dr. Richard F. Greathouse.   *Klein*

Ch. Cote de Neige Posy and Cote de Neige Early Glow, handled by owner Marjorie Butcher, winning Best Working Group Brace en route to their Best Brace in Show win at the Chicago International 1955.

Frasie

14

Double the Fun

While one corgi can be grand, two can be glorious. Even within a breed with the possibility for endless combinations of markings, color and, to some extent, type, several beautifully matched pairs have risen to the top in brace competition. Most have been closely related. It must be doubly satisfying to pilot a sparkling set of Corgis to Best Brace in Show.

A Cote de Neige duo owned, bred and handled by Mrs. Marjorie Butcher, was among the first to gain fame. Ch. Cote de Neige Posy and Cote de Neige Early Glow captured Best Brace in Show at Chicago International in 1955 under breeder judge Mrs. Madeleine Baiter. They also won the Working Group Brace competition at Westminster that year.

In 1956 at Westminster Mrs. Baiter selected Mrs. Donald Duncan's Ch. Lees Symphony and his daughter Ch. Kaydon's Sue's Symphony Best Working Group Brace. They were ably handled by Miss Jane Kamp and Miss Anne Hone Rogers, themselves attired as a brace. What outstanding careers at least three of this team has had in the world of show dogs!

Another early brace to win a Best in Show was Mr. and Mrs. Jack Liecty's litter mates Amer. Mex. Ch. Penricks Most Happy Fella and Amer. Mex. Ch. Penricks Belle A'Ringing. They won Best Brace at the Riverside Kennel Club in Hemet, California, in 1960.

A particularly outstanding father and son combination was owned, bred and handled by Miss Vivien F. Jeffery. They were Ch. Blithe Spirit of Pen-y-Bont, CD, and son Fox Trot of Pen-y-Bont, CD. Miss Jeffery writes:

They were shown seven times, going Group 2nd the first time, and from then on always won the Working Group, and four times went on to Best Brace in Show which included Golden Gate KC in Northern California and KC of Beverly Hills in Southern California, both prestige shows with a touch of theatrics! (thirty-seven braces at the latter show.) Maxwell Riddle gave them one of the Group wins, and told me I was cheating the others on account of the obedience training! But it was not just that, they were just incredibly responsive and the genetic link so apparent . . . I think that Corgi Brace gave me more sheer pleasure than anything I have done with dogs. Perhaps because they seemed to be enjoying themselves so much, eyes ashining and feet tapping before they went on parade or gave an obedience demonstration.

In the Midwest three other red and white braces have had noteworthy success. Mrs. Caroline Bailey's litter mates Ch. Benfro Geoffrey of Gambier and Ch. Benfro Lord Gambier, whelped in 1965, both finished their titles from the puppy classes. The latter went on to multiple Group placements. Among their other wins, these brothers together captured a Best Brace in Show at the Western Reserve KC in 1960 and went on to a Group second at Westminster in 1967.

From Wisconsin Mr. and Mrs. Elwin Leet showed their twins Ch. Leetwood Impersonation and Ch. Leetwood Illustration to a Working Group first at the 1970 Chicago International. Soon after a triplet, Ch. Leetwood Illusion, finished. The dam of the trio, Am. Can. Ch. Welcanis Duplication, was the result of a brother/sister mating which no doubt greatly influenced the uniformity of the litter.

In the 1970s "The Gold Dust Twins," Ch. Cottleston Calico and Ch. Cottleston Cricket, were shown 24 times and won 18 Groups and seven Bests in Show. They were bred by Mrs. Ruth Cooper and Mr. James Mitchell and sold to Mrs. Suzanne Mann of Illinois as her first Corgis. These litter sisters never got along together as house dogs, but they performed magnificently in the show ring under the guidance of handler Denise Kodner.

Not all successful Pembroke braces have been red and white. Two sable look-alike brothers, "Ike" and "Mike," did some nice winning for the Vance G. Moyers of Pennsylvania. Officially named Ch. Moyer's High Storm and Ch. Moyer's High Cloud, they were chosen Best Brace in Show at the Bald Eagle Kennel Club event in 1969 and had other Group placings as well.

One smashing pair of tris, Int. Ch. Ffynondwym Fenella of Llwynog and Ch. Cote de Neige Chance of Fox Run, owned by then Mrs. Robert F. Black, Jr. and handled by Houston Clark, were Best Working Group Brace at Westminster in 1970. This handsome dog and bitch were an exception to the usual rule in that they were totally unrelated and even were bred on different sides of the Atlantic.

The famous Pen-y-Bont brace, Ch. Blithe Spirit of Pen-y-Bont, CD, and his son Fox Trot of Pen-y-Bont, CD.
Ludwig

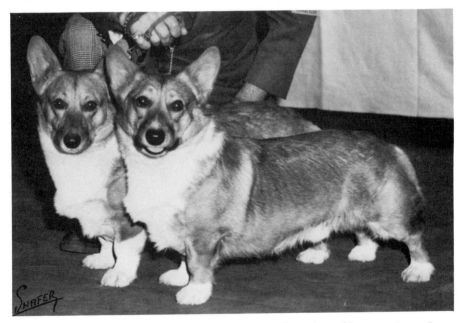

Brothers Ch. Benfro Lord Gambier and Ch. Benfro Geoffrey of Gambier were Brace Group Second at Westminster in 1967.
Shafer

A brace shows a brace: (from left) Anne Rogers Clark handling Ch. Kaydon's Sue's Symphony, judge Mrs. Madeleine Baiter, and Jane Kamp Forsyth handling Ch. Lees Symphony to a Best Working Group Brace win at Westminster in 1956.   *Shafer*

Am. Mex. Ch. Penricks Most Happy Fella and Am. Mex. Ch. Penricks Belle A'Ringing with their breeder-owner Jack Liecty.   *Ludwig*

Ch. Leetwood Impersonation and Ch. Leetwood Illustration with their breeder-owner Mrs. Elwin Leet.

Ch. Moyer's High Storm and Ch. Moyer's High Cloud with breeder-owner Mrs. Vance Moyer.

Shafer

Ch. Cottleston Calico and Ch. Cottleston Cricket, a BIS brace handled by Denise Kodner.

211

If a brace can be three, Mrs. Herman Bohr, Jr.'s red-headed tris and red-headed handler qualify. Ch. Rupertbear of Wey, his daughter, Ch. Rupert's Goody of Robbins Bohr, and Miss Vicki Seiler went to the top to win Best Brace in Show at the Pensacola, Florida show in 1975. Their combined charm could not be denied.

The colorful brace of Ch. Rupertbear of Wey and Ch. Rupert's Goody of Robbins Bohr with handler Vicki Seiler.   *Booth*

Int. Ch. Ffynondwym Fenella of Llwynog and Ch. Cote de Neige Chance of Fox Run with their handler Houston Clark winning Best Working Group Brace at Westminster in 1970.   *Gilbert*

15

Breeding the

Pembroke Welsh Corgi

WITH BEGINNER'S LUCK, you might find you have bred a top-flight puppy in your very first litter. Unfortunately, not all of us are blessed with beginner's luck nor does such luck linger long with those it touches. Undeniably, there is an element of luck in the breeding of dogs, but the ability to breed successive generations of quality dogs depends largely on careful planning and judicious selection of the parents of every litter.

Breeding Principles

Most successful Pembroke breeders, people who have consistently produced quality stock over the years, some for as many as forty years, attribute their success to a program of line-breeding. Line-breeding is the mating of related dogs—such as grandson to grandam, niece to uncle, or cousin to cousin.

In recent years, the term line-breeding has become less rigid in its application. We hear of closely line-bred, loosely line-bred or distantly line-bred animals.

If a dog and bitch being mated together share one or more common ancestors in the first three generations, the resulting puppies are considered to be line-bred. In assessing the strength of a line-breeding, it makes sense that the more times one or two particular dogs appear in the first few generations of a pedigree, the greater the influence of those dogs will be.

Line-breeding is usually the safest course for the novice breeder to follow as opposed to outcrossing or inbreeding.

Outcrossing is the mating of two seemingly unrelated dogs. Outcrossing usually results in a lack of uniformity in the litter, thereby negating any attempt to establish a specific type characteristic of the line.

Inbreeding is the mating of two closely related dogs, such as father to daughter, mother to son or brother to sister. Undertaken by a skillful, truly knowledgeable breeder, inbreeding can be a most effective means of setting type. Misused, the results can be disastrous.

A number of the early Pembroke breeders in America embarked on breeding programs which involved intense inbreeding and line-breeding, the likes of which most breeders today would find quite alarming.

After the war years, though, the nation watched the rapid decline of one of this country's favorite breeds, and the public grew to believe that all "highly bred" show dogs were neurotic or sickly. Influenced by public sentiment and not wanting to be guilty of ruining a fine breed, the majority of present-day Pembroke breeders have studiously avoided close breeding. For a time breeders would boast that all the leading bloodlines in England and America were represented in their kennel. Now, having realized the folly of trying to blend all the winning bloodlines into a single, perfect line, American breeders are beginning to concentrate their efforts on serious line-breeding.

Selection of Breeding Stock

If you have decided you are interested in breeding Pembrokes before purchasing your first bitch, you are in a position to start off in the best possible way. You are not making do with what you have. Instead, you are free to select a nicely bred puppy from an established breeder, a person who can be of great help to you as you go on.

If possible, purchase a quality, line-bred bitch from breeding that is being widely used. You will want to have several alternatives of suitable studs to choose from for your bitch. The purpose of selecting a line-bred bitch to begin with is lost if there are no appropriately related stud dogs available for your use.

Perhaps you have already purchased a Corgi bitch as a pet and have decided you would like to breed her. Before blindly plunging in, give some serious thought to the difficulties you may encounter and be sure you really want to have a go at it.

Even if all goes well, raising a litter of puppies properly involves untold hours of work and a myriad of expenses. Few pet owners who raise a litter of puppies come close to breaking even on the venture, let alone come out ahead.

214

Ch. Cadno Melanie (Eng. Ch. Winrod Peregrine ex Chloe of Cadno), whelped December 13, 1970, breeder: Mrs. B.M. Tulloch, owner: Mrs. Joan L. Maskie. The dam of six champions by Eng. Ch. Kaytop Marshall, Melanie was the top brood bitch for 1976.

Petrulis

Am. Can. Ch. Braxentra Michaelmas (Eng. Ch. Braxentra Barney Two ex Braxentra Stormerbanks Mademoiselle), breeder: Mrs. J.K. Palmer-Cummings, owner: Mrs. Marguerite Nemeth. This promising Midwestern stud dog was a Junior Warrant winner in England at the age of nine months.

Also interesting to note, few people who have bred their pet bitch ever care to repeat the whole performance.

If you are certain you want to breed your bitch, first contact someone with experience in the breed who can tell you if your bitch is suitable for breeding. Identify her best points and possible faults. You will need help in selecting an appropriate stud dog. It would be unwise to mate her to a dog carrying similar faults or to one from a line where one of her faults may be a problem.

The Bitch in Season

A Pembroke bitch can be expected to come in season, or heat, at about eight to nine months of age. An occasional bitch will come in a month or two earlier, and some stall around about it until they are over a year old.

A bitch should not be bred on her first season unless she is over a year old at the time. Even at twelve months, a Corgi bitch is still very much a puppy herself, and should not have to assume family responsibilities quite so soon. Ideally, a bitch should be bred for her first time at her second or third season.

Problems can arise if an older bitch who has never had a litter before is bred. If a bitch is going to be bred at all, it is best that she have at least one litter by the time she is three years old.

There are exceptions to every rule, though, and there have been bitches who have whelped their first litters at six years of age with all going well.

The first indication that a bitch is about to come into season is usually a noticeable swelling of the vulva. If there are male dogs about, they will let you know things are about to happen by showing more than a usual interest in checking the bitch over.

Bitches kennelled together will often come in season close together. If this is about to happen, you may observe the girls being uncommonly sexy, to the point they think it is great fun to ride one another. That's the time to start watching closely for the first signs of the bloody vaginal discharge.

For the first day or so, the discharge will be light pink in color and flow, itself, light. Unless the bitch is under close observation, the actual beginning of the season may be missed.

As the season progresses, the flow increases, and the color of the discharge deepens considerably. Normally, the bitch is not ready for breeding while there is a dark, heavy discharge, and she will not accept the attentions of the male at this time.

A bitch is normally receptive and ready to breed from the tenth to, and including, the fourteenth day. This is not a hard and fast rule, however, as many bitches are successfully bred as early as the seventh day. At the other

Ch. Craythorne's Cassia of Cowfold, whelped January 4, 1955, by New Zealand Ch. Crusader of Cowfold ex Cherryripe of Cowfold (by Stormerbanks Ambrose). Breeder: Miss Murray Wright. Best of Breed at Crufts 1958, she was imported and owned by Mrs. Louise Cleland. Cassia produced eight champions and ties for fourth top producing dam in the United States (1935-1977). *Fall*

Ch. Benfro Eloise (Cote de Neige Going Places ex Ch. Cote de Neige Vineyard Girl), whelped March 26, 1964, breeder-owner: Carolyn C. Bailey. Eloise ties with Benita and Cassia for fourth top producing dam with eight champions from two litters sired by Ch. Benfro Lord Gambier.
Norton of Kent   217

end of the scale, there have been occasional surprise litters from matings which occurred on the eighteenth or nineteenth day. Some successful matings happened even later when the bitch was thought to be well out of season.

As a bitch approaches the receptive period, the vaginal discharge will normally change color from a deep, bright red to a paler, pink or straw color. The discharge seems to be thinner, more watery. If the bitch is kept on newspaper, you will be able to detect the change in the discharge more readily than you can seeing the discharge as it comes from the vulva. The swelling of the vulva also will subside a bit as the discharge lessens.

Exercise a bitch in season on a lead rather than turning her out in a kennel run by herself. In this way you will know how ready for breeding she is by the way she reacts to the sight of a possible male caller. A ready bitch is anxious, and she leaves no doubt about it. When you observe her eagerness, the time has come to let the stud dog have a try at mating her.

The Mating

If the bitch is to go to an outside stud, make arrangements with the owner of the stud dog well in advance of when the bitch is due in season. As soon as the bitch has actually come in season, notify the stud dog owner and set the date that the bitch will be either shipped or brought to the stud for mating. If the bitch is to be shipped, it is best to send her several days ahead of when she will likely be ready for breeding.

Prior to shipping, check the health regulations and requirements. A health certificate and record of a rabies vaccination may have to be sent with the bitch.

If the owner of the stud dog requests that your bitch be tested for brucellosis, this should be done soon after the bitch comes in season. Brucellosis testing of canine breeding stock is becoming more widespread, and it is a wise owner who requests that it be done for both the dog and bitch prior to mating.

In that conception may not take place for several days after the actual mating, it is a good practice to not have the bitch shipped back for four or five days.

Some stud dogs just take charge when put to a bitch who is ready to breed. Such a dog needs little assistance other than to have someone firmly holding the bitch so that she cannot turn on him, pull away or roll over. After the dog penetrates the bitch, the dog's penis will swell tremendously, locking him in the bitch. At this point, both are said to be "tied." The bitch will typically feel discomfort as the dog swells and may turn on the dog or try to pull away. A tie lasts anywhere from a few minutes to a half hour or more. Most often, the dog can be turned after a few minutes so that he is standing next to the bitch rather than having his weight on her for the entire time. If turning a particular dog is known to make him pull away from the bitch prematurely, it is best to hold the dog on the bitch for a short while.

When the tie is completed and the dog pulls away from the bitch, both dogs should be returned to their quarters and rested. The dog, especially, will appreciate a drink of fresh water.

Not all matings are simple events, and how the matings are handled when a young dog is first started on stud work can determine how well the dog is apt to manage subsequent matings.

An occasional Pembroke has sired a litter at seven months of age, but most breeders wait to start their young dogs at ten months or so. And then, they are used sparingly for several months yet. A dog's first ''bride'' ideally should be a bitch who has mated easily before, thus instilling in the dog a confidence in his own ability. Regardless of whether a dog is to service a calm matron bitch or a maiden bitch, a person experienced in handling matings should be on hand. In most cases, it is a mistake for anyone to try handling a mating without help.

Procedures for handling matings differ greatly. Many breeders accustom their stud dogs to mate bitches on a firm table with a non-skid surface. This method allows better control of the dogs and makes it easier to give whatever assistance may be necessary.

If the dog will not work on a table, the alternative would be to simply sit on the ground with the bitch placed across your legs, with your helper holding the bitch's front end steady while you manipulate the bitch's hindquarters to the appropriate height for the dog.

Whatever procedure is used, it is important that the stud dog be conditioned to let you handle him or the bitch as need be, so he is not thrown off if you have to assist.

Occasionally a bitch will be unpleasant about being bred without any obvious reason other than her pride is being hurt. If a bitch is threatening the dog with growls and bared teeth, you can try putting a cut-off nylon stocking over her head. Use the foot end and cut a piece about 18 inches long. This seems to surprise the bitch into behaving. She can see what is happening, she can breathe easily and yet she is not so sure she could open her mouth to bite if she wanted to, making her reluctant to try.

A really tough bitch will try to put an end to the shenanigans despite the stocking, in which case, she should be firmly muzzled with a long, thin strip of cloth.

A bitch can be bred without the dog actually achieving a tie. There are dogs who have sired a number of litters without ever tying a bitch, so do not be alarmed if this is the case when your bitch is mated.

It is a good idea to have the equipment right at hand to artificially inseminate the bitch if the mating does go awry and the dog ejaculates outside the bitch. With necessity being the mother of invention, we found here that a ten cc plastic syringe with a puppy stomach tube attached served very well for inseminating a bitch artificially. The syringe and tube (a #8 French catheter) need not be sterilized, but they must be thoroughly rinsed if they have at any point been cleaned with disinfectant or detergent.

After the semen is collected in the barrel of the syringe (5 to 8 ccs is plenty to do the deed), and you have put the plunger back in the syringe, quickly, but gently, insert the tube into the vagina past the cervix. Slowly press the plunger until all the semen has been injected. If the fluid starts coming out of the vagina as you press the plunger, you do not have the tube inserted past the cervix, so gently try again.

After the tube has been withdrawn, hold the bitch rear-end up in the air, head towards the ground, for a few minutes. This is done to encourage the flow of semen into the uterine cavity rather than letting it immediately drain out of the bitch.

A second mating is unnecessary if all appeared to go well with the first mating. For a young dog just starting stud work, though, a second successful mating may bolster his confidence.

If there is doubt about the success of the first mating, or there is particular pressure that the bitch be successfully mated, a repeat mating about 48 hours following the first mating would be advisable.

An advantage to a single mating is that the date the bitch is due to whelp can be figured more closely. When 63 days pass, the average length of the gestation period, counting the day following the mating as the first day, you are not left wondering whether the bitch is going past her due date from the first mating or is only at her sixty-first day from the second mating.

The Pregnant Bitch

Some bitches will let it be known early on they are in a delicate way, while others will keep you guessing well into their fifth and sixth week.

An observant owner may notice several days after a bitch has been mated that she is urinating more frequently than usual. The increased frequency lasts a day or two at the most and may well be associated with hormonal changes which occur at the time of actual conception.

You can be fairly certain puppies are on the way when, two to three weeks after mating, a high energy, always-on the-go bitch becomes content just to snuggle in your lap, dreamily soaking up all the affection you give her. A bitch who demonstrates a marked personality change is responding to strong hormonal influences. Usually such a bitch will be a super "mum,"

220

Eng. Irish and Am. Ch. Crowleythorn Ladomoorlands, son of Eng. Ch. Crowleythorn Snowman, whelped June 2, 1960, breeder: Mr. R. Duckworth. Imported and owned by August and Isabel Ramm, this dog won 7 C.C.s in England, 7 Green Stars in Ireland and Best of Breed at Crufts 1963.   *Tauskey*

Am. Can. Ch. Rosewood Dark Brandy, West Coast winner strongly line-bred on Ch. Halmor's Hi-Fi and Eng. Ch. Crowleythorn Snowman. Owners: William and Patricia Carter.   *Ludwig*

South African Ch. Drumbeat Wyldingtree of Wey.   *Fall*

being very attentive to her family well past the point when other bitches would have decided the time had come for their puppies to be someone else's responsibility.

It is not uncommon for a bitch to go off her food for several days between the second and third week of pregnancy. Also during the third week, the nipples will become noticeably pinker, this being most obvious in a bitch who has neither been pregnant before nor had a false pregnancy.

If a bitch is carrying a large litter, you may see a rounding of the abdomen during the third week and it will also have a tight drum-like feel. Typically, slight distention of the abdomen will become apparent during the fourth week. The "potty" look will be more noticeable after the bitch has eaten or when she is lying down.

In some cases, a bitch can keep a trim figure throughout the entire gestation period and surprise the unexpecting owners with a puppy or two. If plans are such that it is necessary to know if a bitch is in whelp, a veterinarian can palpate the bitch near the end of the third week and into the fourth week, possibly detecting the presence of little hickory nut-sized embryos. With a positive finding, you know where you stand. Negative results can still fool you. To be absolutely sure a bitch is not in whelp, she can be x-rayed at the end of the eighth week. Otherwise, keep track of when a bitch is due to whelp, and even though she has given no indication of being in whelp, keep an eye on her at that time—just in case.

Little, if any, change should be made in the bitch's diet or routine during the early weeks of pregnancy. A bitch should be at her ideal weight at the time of mating, pregnancy being neither the time for a crash diet nor the time to set right a poorly conditioned bitch.

Starting at the onset of her season and continuing throughout the entire pregnancy, give a bitch raw beef liver once a day. It is an old wives tale that a piece of liver, the size of the palm of your hand, fed daily to pregnant bitches will prevent whelping difficulties. If only it were true! However, liver is an excellent source of valuable nutrients, and feeding it gives the feeling of doing something constructive while you are waiting for the developing family to put in an appearance.

Watch the bitch's weight closely during the pregnancy. If she begins to appear thin over the withers and along the spine, the amount of food given should be increased accordingly. Otherwise, the total amount of food intake should remain close to the usual, but with the percentage of meat and other protein foods, such as cooked eggs and cottage cheese, increased from the fifth week on.

Breeders used to add hefty amounts of vitamin and mineral supplements to the diet of a pregnant bitch, all in an effort to produce big, heavy-boned puppies. Whelping difficulties increase proportionally as the size of the

A Drumbeat son, Int. Ch. Gayelord of Wey, breeder-owner: Mrs. K. Butler.　　　　　*Fall*

A worthy English sire, Sportsman of Wey.　　　　　*Fall*

Pennywise of Wey, a Sportsman son. Breeders on both sides of the Atlantic still turn to lines which go back to Pennywise to bring in good head and expression.　　　*Fall*

puppies whelped increases. How much more sense it makes to encourage the puppies to grow on well after they are on the ground.

If a bitch is fed a good, well-balanced diet and has access to plenty of fresh air and sunshine, she should not need any diet supplements other than, perhaps, a balanced multi-vitamin and mineral tablet. A great many experts insist that even the added vitamin tablet is unnecessary.

Having observed an obvious difference in the condition of adult dogs here, maintained on a vitamin supplement as opposed to when no supplements were given, it would be difficult to believe the added vitamins are without benefit.

However, vitamin and mineral supplements can be as harmful when misused as they can be beneficial when properly used. A crucial balance between vitamins and between minerals is essential to their effectiveness.

Calcium is a popular supplement given to pregnant bitches and is potentially harmful if not judiciously used. For many years, it was thought that in order to have well-boned puppies, the bitches should be given calcium supplement in the form of bone meal or calcium lactate tablets. We now know heavy calcium supplements can destroy the delicate balance of calcium within the body. Breeders also know that genetic influences largely determine the bone and substance of a puppy. A puppy genetically destined to be fine-boned will always be such, regardless of how much calcium is given either to the dam in whelp or later to the puppy.

Generally, the fewer additives given to the pregnant bitch, the better.

As the pregnant bitch increases in size, she will appreciate several small meals a day rather than a single large meal. Two regular feeds plus a bedtime bowl of milk with a few dog biscuits on the side will do nicely.

Nan Butler, who with her husband, Ken, is well-known for their famous Wey Corgis, wrote some years back that she considered the night-time milky feed to be one of the most important meals for helping puppies to grow on well and for bringing youngsters into good bloom. We could not agree with her findings more; likewise we feel the milk feed is every bit as beneficial to the pregnant bitches, who quite relish this end-of-the-day treat.

Plenty of free exercise is essential to the physical and mental well-being of any animal and is especially important in the care of pregnant bitches. Some whelping problems may be eliminated altogether, if the bitch receives adequate exercise. In other instances, the properly conditioned bitch has the stamina and vigor to see her through a difficult whelping situation should it occur.

You can generally let the bitch determine how much exercise she wants to have. Most bitches will look after themselves pretty well, slowing down considerably as their load grows heavier. Despite the increased effort required, bitches accustomed to going on daily walks will want to continue their usual routine until nearly the last minute. Care must be taken if a pregnant bitch is

Ch. Willets Red Jacket, whelped July 13, 1958, breeder: Dr. Matthew Ratchford, owner: Mrs. William B. Long. The all-time top Pembroke Welsh Corgi Best in Show winner, his record of 18 BIS wins include 16 wins under different judges. He also topped 55 Groups from a total of 107 Group placings. *Tauskey*

Ch. Craythorne's Fleetfoot of Wey, owner: Mrs. Ruth Cooper. *Tauskey*

Ch. Cormanby Commotion, breeder-owner: Mrs. Barbara Hedberg. This dog is a Group-winning son of Ch. Craythorne's Fleetfoot of Wey ex Ch. Stormerbanks Saucebox.

exercised with other dogs that she is not run down or jostled about by the group.

Under no circumstances should any jumping be permitted. This rule can be difficult to enforce with house pets and may mean the bitch will have to be confined in an area where she does not have access to inviting furniture.

A large load in combination with a short-legged build makes stairs an impossible obstacle course for a pregnant Corgi. Again, make certain that an in-whelp bitch simply does not have access to stairs lest she should make the decision that one way or another, she can cope with them.

By the last week of a bitch's pregnancy, she should not be allowed outside on her own. As her time approaches, she will begin nosing around for a suitable den in which to have her puppies. Unsupervised, she just might find an unreachable hideout under the garage or an old tool shed.

Whelping Preparations

At least a week prior to the date the puppies are expected, set up the whelping quarters so all is in readiness should the puppies arrive earlier than expected.

Choose a quiet place out of the main stream of activity. It seems nearly all Corgi breeders have their bitches whelp in their own bedroom, a guest bedroom or a bathroom adjacent to either. This makes it possible to have the bitch close at hand during the night so frequent checks on how things are going can be made easily.

A whelping box that is about 30 inches square and 14 inches high is ideal. Such a box is sufficiently large to provide ample room for a large litter, yet not so large that the puppies wander off and cannot find mother. An opening at least 15 inches wide should be cut out in the front of the box. A piece of wood about 5 inches high can be fastened with small latches across the bottom of the opening to keep the puppies in the box while enabling the bitch to go in and out. When the puppies are old enough to toddle out of the box, the bottom piece can be removed.

If two upright pieces of wood are placed directly inside the box, one in each corner on either side of the front opening to form a slot, a 9 inch wide slat of wood can be dropped into place, closing the front side completely. During the first few days after the puppies have arrived, the front should be kept entirely closed to keep heat in the box and to prevent any possibility of even slight drafts on the puppies.

A very satisfactory box can be made out of a good grade, lightweight plywood. Put several coats of a plastic finish, recommended for use on children's furniture, on the inside of the box, sanding with a fine paper between each coat. The resulting hard, smooth surface will protect the box from damp-

Ch. Cormanby Cadenza, whelped March 9, 1966, breeder: Barbara Hedberg, owners: Michael Sauve and Barbara Hedberg. The winner of the Lakeshore PWCC Specialties 1970 through 1972, Cadenza's record includes 4 Group 1sts and 23 Group placings. *Tauskey*

Ch. Kaydon's Anthony (Eng. Am. Ch. Lees Symphony ex Ch. Bonnie Ridge Butter Taffy), breeder: Mrs. J. Donald Duncan. Three BIS and nine Working Group 1sts show on Anthony's record. *Ludwig*

Rover Run Romance, a daughter of Ch. Kaydon's Anthony ex Richochet of Rover Run.

Am. Bda. Ch. Maracas Gale Force of Cleden, whelped November 19, 1955, breeder: Mrs. M.T.S. Thornycroft. A winner of 23 Group placements, his record includes Best of Breed at the 1958 PWCCA Specialty show. A double Knowland Clipper grandson, Gale Force sired 14 champions. Owner: Louise Cleland. *Brown*

Eng. Irish Ch. Zephyr of Brome, third ranking British top ten C.C. winner. By Eng. Ch. Knowland Clipper ex Katrina of Brome. *Fall*

Ch. Cote de Neige Christmas Candy, breeder-owner: Marjorie Butcher, was the sixth ranking all time top ten sire with 22 champions to his credit. Christmas Candy is the sire of Ch. Cote de Neige Penny Wise, which gives Penny lines to Knowland Clipper through Candy as well as through her dam, Gold Coin. *Tauskey*

ness and is easily cleaned. The outside of the box can be painted with a non-toxic enamel paint or can be finished in the same manner as the inside.

If the whelping box is put inside a portable exercise pen the bitch can be free to leave the whelping box to stretch her legs or get a drink of water, but is confined while she is having the discharge that follows whelping.

The floor of the exercise pen is covered with a plastic sheet; shower curtain liners serve the purpose nicely. The whelping box is set on a piece of the rubberized padding that is used under carpets. This keeps the box from sliding on the plastic and if the bottom of the box is at all uneven, the matting prevents the box from rocking. The entire area of the exercise pen is covered with newspaper, as is the bottom of the whelping box. Have stacks of newspaper on hand as you will go through layers of paper during the whelping. As the puppies grow on, it will take bundles of papers to keep the puppy pen clean.

The foam pad made for the #902 Safari crate fits nicely into the whelping box, giving the expectant mother a comfortable bed until labor actually begins, at which time the pad is removed. After the new family has arrived, the box is cleaned and the newspapers are replaced with the foam pad and a piece of carpet. Pad and carpet are then covered with a section of blanket. The edges of the blanket are tucked well under the pad and carpeting so the puppies cannot crawl under the blanket.

Not only do the mothers appreciate the comfort of the foam pad in the whelping box, but newborns like to line up along the side, resting their heads on the pad. The puppies very quickly learn to squirm their way up to mother to nurse, sliding back down to the warmth of the heating pad when they are finished.

Breeders differ in their preference for using a heating pad or a heating lamp for newborn puppies. The preference here is for the heating pad, simply because the amount of heat can be easily regulated, and the bitch can get away from the heat if she is uncomfortable.

The argument in favor of the heating lamp is that a higher ambient temperature can be maintained, and the puppies are not receiving heat just from underneath.

Regardless of method, some form of heat is beneficial during the first few days when the puppy's own mechanism for regulating body temperature is not fully functioning. Care must be taken, though, not to make the bitch and her puppies uncomfortable with too much heat. Puppies who are either too warm or too cold will be restless and continually crying as they move from side to side in the box.

When the puppies are four to five days old, they will usually start avoiding the heated area of the whelping box. Gradually lower the heat, dispensing with the heating pad altogether by the time the puppies are a week to ten days old.

229

By placing the whelping box in a pen that is only slightly wider than the box, it is possible to cover the entire area of the whelping box with a blanket or spread. In a cool room, especially, this is a satisfactory way of keeping the puppies in a warmer environment with less temperature fluctuation. The cover is not only added protection against possible drafts, but it provides the bitch with welcomed den-like privacy.

Whelping

There are a few almost invariable signs to watch for which will indicate the imminent arrival of the new litter.

During the last week or so of pregnancy, the presence of a clear, glassy, odorless vaginal discharge is perfectly normal. Should the discharge become cloudy, discolored or have an odor, consult your veterinarian immediately.

A check on the bitch's temperature will show a drop in temperature as much as five days ahead of whelping. It may hover around 100° to 99.8°, a drop from the normal range of 101° to 102°. The lower temperature seems to be associated with the pre-labor changes taking place within the bitch. A day or so before the pending whelping, the bitch will appear thinner and the hip bones will become more prominent as the weight shifts lower in the body. An internal examination at this time would likely show the dilation of the cervix has begun.

When the temperature takes a sudden nose dive down to the 99° to 98° range, watch for the initial stages of labor to begin. Now is a good time to notify your veterinarian that you may be needing his assistance within the next 24 hours. Thus he will be prepared for your possible middle of night call, or if he is not going to be available, you will have established contact with someone whom you can reach if you need help.

Coinciding with the final temperature drop will be another very obvious change in the bitch's appearance as she becomes what can be best described as "lumped up." The sides of her abdomen will be tense and hard as they seemingly constrict around the laden uterus. The lumps you can feel at this point are the puppies about to be born. Once a bitch has started to lump up, she will most likely refuse any food, no matter how tempting you have made her favorite meal. Should she eat, despite her better judgement, do not expect the food to stay down for long.

Labor begins with shivering, trembling and panting. The bitch, though obviously unsettled and wanting the reassurance of your company, has a far away, withdrawn look about her, as though she had returned to the wilds of her ancestors and was giving birth to her young all on her own. This preliminary stage of labor with the panting, the shivering, the digging and shredding of papers, all interrupted with occasional periods of rest, can continue quite

Ch. Lees Craythorne's Golden Plover is a son of Eng. Ch. Lees Wennam Eagle. Plover, the sire of two BIS winning sons, is the foundation stud dog of Happiharbor Kennels owned by Mr. and Mrs. T. Rutledge Parker.

Ch. Happiharbor Captain Midnite, whelped August 9, 1970, breeder: Gray C. Parker, owners: Mr. and Mrs. C. Still. Cappy is a Golden Plover son out of Gardenshire's Limerick, a daughter of Ch. Cote de Neige Chance of Fox Fun. His record includes one BIS, five Group 1sts, 18 Group placings and 76 BBs. *Twomey*

Ch. Happiharbor Ramblin' Man, whelped June 18, 1973, breeder: Thomas R. Parker, co-owners: Mr. and Mrs. Henry Florsheim and Jeanne Marcovite. He is a BIS and mutliple Group winning son of Ch. Lees Craythorne's Golden Plover out of Ch. Valmayan Happiharbor's Fran. *Graham*

some time before the final stages of labor begin. Some bitches will carry on for ten hours or more before getting down to business. Others will have a puppy out within two hours of tossing up a dinner they really should not have eaten.

When the actual whelping appears to be starting, put a heating pad or hot water bottle wrapped in a towel or piece of blanket in a small cardboard box and cover the carton with a blanket. Place the heated box near the whelping box so the first-born puppies can be put in the box to be kept warm and out of the bitch's way when she is occupied with the delivery of the remainder of the litter. Let the bitch see the puppies being placed in the box, and if she becomes bothered when a puppy in the box squeaks, put the puppy back with her. It is of utmost importance throughout the entire whelping that the bitch feels totally secure, private and not fussed.

Keeping in mind the old adage "a chilled puppy is a dead puppy," remember to take your "incubator" box with you should you have to take your bitch to the veterinarian for assistance with the whelping.

Opinion is divided as to how much assistance should be given to a bitch during whelping. Bitches of some breeds resent any interference to the point where they will prove to be poor mothers unless they are permitted to deliver and care for their young in complete privacy.

Corgi puppies are often slow to start breathing and most breeders, being reluctant to trust to luck that the bitch will get the puppy going in time, will take the puppy away from the bitch as soon as it is born. The puppy is then returned to its dam after it has been dried off and is breathing easily. Fortunately, most Corgi bitches are quite tolerant of any help given during whelping.

When hard labor begins and the contractions become strong and regular, stand by with a towel, an absorbent bath towel is best, ready to lift the puppy away as it emerges from the vulva. If it is an easy birth, and the cord is still attached, you can ease the placenta out immediately after the puppy is born. Quickly break the membrane sac over the puppy's head, cut the cord about two inches from the body with sterilized scissors, open the mouth with your little finger, and dry the puppy briskly with the towel. As soon as the puppy is breathing easily, put him with the bitch so she will realize the newborn is her responsibility.

There are definite pros and cons to letting a bitch eat the afterbirths. Many breeders find the bitches will vomit or have diarrhea if allowed to eat the afterbirths, so they quickly remove each afterbirth when it is passed from the bitch before she can get to it.

Other breeders contend, perhaps rightly so, that Mother Nature is not wasteful in her design and the afterbirths contain nutrients which are beneficial to the bitch after whelping.

232

Ch. Cote de Neige Chance of Fox Run, a Pennysaver son and the top-winning Pembroke Welsh Corgi in 1969 with one BIS and 19 Groups.

Ch. Red Envoy of Brome, CD, breeder: Rose Johnson. Envoy is pictured here at five months.

Ch. Cote de Neige Instant Replay (Ch. Cote de Neige Pennysaver ex Ch. Cote de Neige News Item).

233

Having seen many bitches clean up all the afterbirths from a large litter with no ill effects whatsoever, it would be easy to claim the most natural procedure is best. By the same token, though, bitches who have undergone caesarian sections without having the chance to devour a single placenta seem to do well by their puppies without the added elements stored in the afterbirths. Thus it becomes a matter of your preference and experience as to your procedure here.

The time interval between the delivery of each puppy varies from fifteen or twenty minutes to several hours. If the bitch is resting for most of the time, all is well. Two hours of intermittent, unproductive contractions, though, is a different matter entirely. Hard prolonged labor will wear a bitch down quickly. If labor is allowed to go beyond three hours, the bitch may have a difficult time of it if surgery is required.

Some puppies are presented breech, meaning the hind feet come first. A breech puppy must be freed as quickly as possible as chances are the sac has already broken, and there is danger that the puppy will suffocate. Wrap a piece of towelling around the hindend of the puppy and holding the body with one hand, get a good grasp on the tail with the other. With each contraction pull firmly on the puppy in a downward direction if the puppy is coming tummy down. Pull in an upward direction if the puppy is on his back.

Puppies who have had a difficult birth are often extremely difficult to revive. Their tongue, membranes, and even the pads of their feet may have turned blue. Even though a puppy may appear to be dead, do not give up on it too quickly. Sometimes a puppy will come around after fifteen to twenty minutes of seemingly futile attempts to revive it.

Take the apparent stillborn puppy to another room to work on it so the bitch will not be alarmed by what you are doing to the puppy. If vigorously rubbing the puppy against the hair up the back and neck with a towel does not elicit a response, try briskly swinging the puppy to free the air passages of fluid that may have collected. To do this, use both hands to firmly hold the puppy on its back in a towel. With its head away from you, your arms outstretched, quickly swing the puppy down between your knees. Repeat several times, wiping away any mucous and fluid expelled from the nose. Alternate swinging the puppy with sessions of mouth to mouth rescusitation. Breathe into the puppy's mouth, then press gently on the ribs to force the air back out. Rhythmically repeat the procedure for a minute or two before swinging the puppy again.

If your efforts are successful and the puppy starts to gasp for air, start massaging him with a towel. Rubbing a puppy against the hair up the back of the neck will goad him into crying. Once he has let out with a lusty yell you can take him back to his mother.

One of the most difficult situations to be encountered with a whelping is one where you are able to haul the puppies out of the bitch, but because of the difficult whelping the puppies are stillborn. It is not uncommon for all but maybe one or two puppies of a litter to be lost this way. With the old adage of hindsight being better than foresight proving to be ever so true, you will realize after such a loss that had a caesarian been performed after the first one or two puppies were lost, you may have saved the rest of the litter. If you let the bitch struggle through a rough delivery for a number of puppies, the odds will be that much less in favor of her surviving the surgery. Here is where you are indeed fortunate if you have a veterinarian who is as interested and determined to save the bitch and as many of the puppies as possible as you are. Despite the fact the time taken to perform a caesarian will play havoc with the office schedule, a competent veterinarian will not waste time while you are losing puppies. You can expect to pay good money for the considerable time the veterinarian will give to your whelping bitch. It is well worth it, though, to know if the bitch does not respond to the usual whelping aids, such as intravenous calcium injections or pitocin injections, that surgery will be performed before all is lost.

It is difficult to determine when a bitch has finished delivering a litter. The swollen horns of the uterus can feel hard and lumpy, and consequently are mistaken for being another puppy.

One not altogether reliable indication that the bitch has finished whelping is that the bitch will usually relax and quietly settle down to nurse her new family after the last puppy has been delivered. If you get all the soiled wet papers in the whelping box replaced with fresh dry bedding and the heating pad, only to have yet another puppy arrive, just remember you are far from being the only person who has been fooled this way.

The bitch will do the best by her puppies if she is allowed to have absolute privacy and quiet after she has settled in with her family. This is difficult when there are small, curious children in the family. If the bitch shows no uneasiness about the children coming into the room where her puppies are, no harm will be done by letting the children quietly look at the puppies. Be even more cautious about permitting outsiders to see the puppies, gauging your restrictions on the bitch's reactions.

Care of the Brood Bitch

During the course of the whelping, a bitch will be eager for small drinks of cool fresh water. Some breeders add a bit of honey to the drinking water, making a drink that is rather similar to the glucose in water so many British breeders use. High carbohydrate foods such as honey, sugar, and glucose, or stimulants such as milky tea with glucose will give a short-term energy boost

Eng. Ch. Lees Wennam Eagle (Eng. Ch. Winrod Peregrine ex Wennam Snowbunting), breeder: Mrs. M. New, owner: Miss P.L. Curties. Runner up for the Formakin Stud Dog Cup in 1967, Wennam Eagle was ranked one of England's leading stud dogs from 1966 through 1969.   *Sally Anne Thompson*

that can get a bitch through a single crisis. When a whelping is nearing completion with perhaps one puppy to go, the honey or glucose in water drink may provide a tiring bitch with the necessary energy to finish up.

Feed the new mother lightly for the first day or so after whelping. Small milky feeds, such as milk with cereal can be given three or four times a day with a raw egg yolk added to one of the meals. Small bland meals of rice with cooked chicken can be used to make the transition from the milky feeds to the bitch's regular fare. By the second or third day after whelping most bitches will welcome their usual meals of fresh meat and cereal or biscuit.

Fresh drinking water should be available at all times. This is a must that is all too frequently overlooked.

By the second week after whelping, the demands on the bitch by her rapidly growing family rise quickly, and her food intake has to be increased proportionately. At least three meals a day, preferably four, should be given. Two of the four meals should consist of the bitch's regular food with an ample allotment of fresh meat. The other two meals can be milk and cereal feeds, with or without additional protein supplements such as cottage cheese or a raw egg yolk.

A bitch's milk production is at its absolute peak when the puppies are between three and four weeks old despite the fact that by this time the puppies are beginning to eat from a dish. Although one seldom hears of a Pembroke bitch having eclampsia, be aware that this is the critical time period when eclampsia is most apt to occur if it is going to. Eclampsia, a disorder involving the calcium balance in the body, is characterized by obvious weakness, staggering and possible convulsions. Should a nurisng bitch act at all pecularily, play it safe and give your veterinarian a call.

For the first few days after whelping, the bitch will be reluctant to leave her puppies even for the few minutes necessary to take care of her needs

236

outside. By the end of the first week, she will enjoy going on a few brief walks, letting you know when she thinks she had better hurry back to her family. By the time the puppies are two weeks old, most bitches are eager to join the other dogs on their regular daily walks. The exercise, fresh air, and a chance just to be themselves, provide a welcomed change from the confines of the whelping box.

Few bitches want to stay on around the clock duty after the puppies are four weeks old. Most ask for time off before then. Generally the bitches will stay with their young at night until the puppies are six weeks old. During the seventh week, the bitch may want to visit the puppies occasionally if she still has milk. It is best, though, to start keeping the puppies away from Mum at this point so her milk can dry up completely. Usually by the time the puppies are eight weeks old, the bitch will completely dry, and she can go back with her puppies for playtime. Most bitches love to play with their puppies, and the puppies benefit as well from her discipline as from her love.

Within two months after whelping, the bitch will begin to shed heavily, to the point where she will become as naked as a billiard ball. One cycle has ended, and her system is preparing for a new one to start, with a season due in about two months.

The bitch has put her all into giving you a fine litter. She richly deserves a rest and, except under unusual circumstances, should not be bred at the season immediately following a litter of puppies.

Ch. Stormerbanks Winrod Fergus, imported in 1968 and owned by Marjorie Butcher. Fergus has lines to Ambrose and Supersonic through both his sire, Eng. Ch. Stormerbanks Foxyface, and his dam, Eng. Ch. Winrod Rhapsody. The fifth ranking all time top ten producing sire, Fergus is the sire of 23 American champions and one English champion.   *Harper*

A litter of six-weeks-old puppies born in the early 1950s. The solid red coloring is seldom seen today. Note the difference in type of these puppies from those in the other photographs.

Six-weeks-old bitch puppies.

Spengler

16

Puppies

PUPPIES. A joy to watch whether they are newborns only a few hours old or roly-poly eight-week-old bundles of energy clowning about in a pen.

There is a deep, indescribable satisfaction that comes with rearing a litter of healthy, personable puppies of good quality. The effort, the heartache, the disappointments encountered along the way fade when you see the bright future shining in the eyes of the happy puppies you have bred and raised.

Healthy, newborn puppies are quiet puppies. All that is heard from a contented new litter will be an occasional squeak as a puppy is nudged away from a teat by a tougher litter mate, or when another puppy is frustrated at not being able to locate a teat as quickly as he would like. When not busy nursing, very young puppies will sleep stretched out on their sides. By the time the puppies are a week or so old, they will sleep on their tummies more frequently, often crawling into a heap rather than sleeping all spread out from one another as newborns do.

All is not well if the puppies are restless and crawling from one end of the box to the other while fussing constantly. Puppies will behave in this manner if they are too warm or too cold; if the bitch has insufficient or poor quality milk; or an infection is brewing. A veterinarian should be consulted if the puppies remain fussy and restless for more than eight hours.

Well nourished puppies will feel plump and firm to the touch. Any puppy who is not nursing, or is falling behind his litter mates in size and weight, should be examined for a physical defect such as a cleft palate.

Supplemental Feeding

Newborn puppies will benefit from supplemental feeding if they have been separated from the bitch for any length of time during the whelping, or if the bitch's milk is slow to come in. Also the smaller, weaker puppies can be helped along with several supplemental feedings a day for a few days as can the puppies of a very large litter.

There are prepared canned formulas for puppies available, but a simple homemade formula has proven to be the most satisfactory for supplemental feeding, or for rearing orphan puppies. The formula consists of 1 can condensed goat's milk diluted with ½ to ¾ can of water; 1 raw egg yolk, 1 tablespoonful honey (or white Karo syrup) and ½ teaspoonful limewater.

Fresh goat's milk can be substituted for the diluted condensed milk if available. Condensed cow's milk can be used, but goat's milk, said to be the closest to bitch's milk in composition, is least likely of the substitute milks to produce gas in the puppies. Canned goat's milk is readily available at most health food stores. It would be wise to have a supply on hand before the litter is due. What is not used as formula for the nursing puppies can later be used for weaning the puppies.

The limewater can be made up by your local druggist. It is used to prevent diarrhea. If the puppies become constipated use less limewater.

Be careful when adding the egg yolk not to let any of the egg white slip into the milk mixture. Somehow egg whites in the formula, however small the amount, manage to gravitate to the nipple of the bottle and completely clog the opening.

Warm the formula slightly before feeding. The formula can be fed with a regular baby's bottle and full-sized nipple rather than with the small nipple provided with pet nurser kits. Make sure the milk will flow easily from the nipple without pouring out. To get the puppy to take the bottle, hold him gently by the head, lifting him both up and slightly forward so his front feet are off your lap or the table where you are holding him. With the hand holding the head, gently press the sides of the puppy's mouth open. As the mouth closes on the nipple, pull up and back slightly on the bottle. As the puppy tries to hang on, suction is created.

Tube feeding has become a widely used method of feeding very young puppies. It takes infinitely less time to tube feed an entire litter than it does to feed each puppy with a bottle, a factor which lends appeal to this method of supplemental feeding. For puppies not nursing on their dam, though, tube feeding removes what little form of exercise is left for such puppies. Also with tube feeding, puppies are fed a specific amount of formula regardless of whether or not they are hungry. Surely the very young must benefit from the nursing behavior, or we would hear of busy human mothers tube feeding their infants.

240

While bottle feeding is preferred here for routine supplemental feeding, small puppies who are too weak to nurse either on the dam or the bottle can often be saved with tube feeding. The process of tube feeding may seem scary until you actually try doing it. The instructions that come with the puppy feeding tube kit, available through most animal supply houses, are quite clear, and if you follow closely the amount to feed a puppy, being careful to not overfeed, all should go well.

Orphan Puppies

Rarely are puppies raised by hand truly orphan puppies. Most have been taken away from their dam because she has either developed an infection which can affect the puppies, or she has proven to be one of those unfortunate bitches who will try to kill her puppies.

The puppies to be raised by hand can be kept in a cardboard carton large enough to have a heating pad at one end with sufficient room remaining for the puppies to sleep away from the heat if they are too warm. Place a piece of blanket or towelling over a thick layer of newspapers on the bottom of the box. If the edges of the blanket are tucked in under the newspaper, the puppies will not be able to crawl under the blanket. Cover the box with a towel or light blanket to provide a constant ambient temperature for the puppies.

Experts vary in opinion as to how often the puppies should be fed. Some people believe newborn puppies should be fed every two hours day and night. Others suggest one feeding every eight hours. Puppies here have done well with a feeding every four hours day and night for the first week. Thereafter, the middle of the night feeding is eliminated.

During the first week each puppy will take an average of $\frac{1}{2}$ ounce of formula every four hours. Some puppies are much greedier than others and may have to be limited in the quantity of formula consumed if they show signs of distress after an overly large meal.

If a puppy refuses to take the formula it may need to relieve itself. Young puppies who are not being cared for by their dam need to be massaged in order to urinate and defecate. After every feeding gently stroke the puppy in the pelvic area with cotton moistened with warm water to stimulate urination. Lift the tail (if it has not been docked yet) and gently wipe the anal region with cotton to induce the puppy to empty. If the skin on the abodmen appears red and dry from urine irritation, apply baby oil or a soothing hand cream several times a day. Once you begin to find stools and damp spots on the bedding, you can be sure the puppies are capable of tending to business themselves, making one less chore for you to look after. Constipation can be a chronic problem with orphan puppies. A pinch of Senecot granules added to the formula will serve as a mild laxative. Regulate the amount of Senecot used in accordance with its effect on the puppies after one or two feedings.

241

A hand raised litter is usually introduced to solid foods earlier than is a litter which is nursed by the dam. By the time the puppies' eyes are open, usually around the fourteenth day, the puppies can be given small amounts of solid food. The puppies will greedily suck in small pieces of lean ground beef moistened slightly with warm water. Be careful to not over feed. Baby cereal or meat can be mixed with formula to make a thickened gruel which the puppies can lick from a dish. The puppies are still too wobbly at this age to hold themselves up long enough to eat from a dish, so each puppy will have to be held to the dish for a turn at eating. This is a messy business with the puppies getting more gruel on themselves than in them. Within a few days the puppies will become more adept at eating, and feeding them will become much easier.

Unlike puppies who put considerable energy into nursing on their dam and who benefit from the exercise obtained when competing with litter mates to nurse at the bitch's most productive teats, hand reared puppies get very little exercise. Consequently, as fat, sloppy, pancake-like puppies, they are less well-coordinated for their age than puppies raised under normal circumstances. This difference will gradually diminish as the puppies become old enough to start playing with each other. Heavy puppies will have an easier time getting up on their feet if they are kept on a textured surface (blanketing, indoor-outdoor carpeting) than if they are kept on newspaper.

One last but very important point to be concerned about with hand raised puppies is the matter of distemper–hepatitis immunity. Puppies receive a high concentration of antibodies in the colostrum which is the milk produced by the bitch during the first few days after whelping. Orphan puppies who have not nursed on the dam at all will lack the usual antibody protection. Consult your veterinarian for his recommendations as to what immunization program should be initiated.

Tail Banding

The vast majority of Pembroke Welsh Corgi breeders now remove their puppies' tails with rubber bands rather than having them surgically docked. The advantages of banding over docking are many. The pain and shock caused by surgical amputation is avoided with banding. All the puppy appears to feel is an annoyance at the tingling, pins and needles sensation as the tail becomes numb after the rubber band has been tied in place. The banding method eliminates the worry about possible bleeders and minimizes the concern over removing too much tail.

Over the years the banding method of tail docking has been viewed with considerable skepticism by veterinarians or breeders who have either not seen the tail banding procedure being done, or have not seen it performed

242

Pembroke Welsh Corgi puppies at various ages. The puppies in the top photo are ten weeks old; the tri-color in the center is three months and the puppy at the bottom is four months.

Tail Docking by the Rubber Band Method

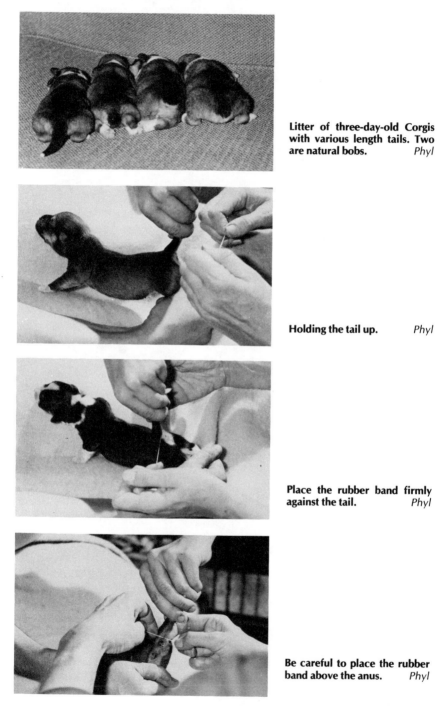

Litter of three-day-old Corgis with various length tails. Two are natural bobs. *Phyl*

Holding the tail up. *Phyl*

Place the rubber band firmly against the tail. *Phyl*

Be careful to place the rubber band above the anus. *Phyl*

Tail Docking by the Rubber Band Method

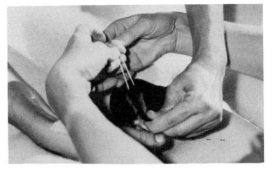

Pull the tail down while holding the ends of the rubber band over the back.   *Phyl*

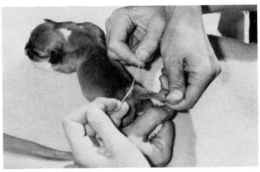

With the rubber band going around the tail only once, tie a tight knot at the top.   *Phyl*

Snip off the ends of the rubber band to ¼ inch.   *Phyl*

Within an hour or so after banding, the tail will go limp, and gradually shrivel (middle puppy), and by the fourth or fifth day will drop off (right puppy). Should seepage occur, the tail area can be swabbed with a mild disinfectant. Check any tail which is slow to come off to make sure it is simply not hanging on by hairs caught up in the band.   *Phyl*

correctly. The main objection these people have had is that banding may cause an infection and, worse yet, gangrene. Apparently infection is commonly associated with the banding of lambs' tails, and the assumption is made it will be likewise with banding puppy tails. Numerous veterinarians who have become acquainted with the banding procedure, as illustrated here, readily concede that it is a simple, efficient method which subjects the puppy to less stress than would be encountered with surgical docking.

No breeder looks forward to the chore of "doing tails and dewclaws," but the sooner done and forgotten about the better. Full term puppies born early in the day usually are sturdy and vigorous enough to have their tails banded and dewclaws removed on the following morning. Puppies born late in the day or at night should not be done until the second morning. Small puppies off to a slow start need not be done until they are three to five days old. If the decision has been made to have the tails surgically docked, make an appointment with the veterinarian for when the puppies will be approximately three days old.

Ideally tail docking, regardless of method, and dewclaw removal should be done early in the day. This permits the puppies to settle in with their dam and forget the whole mean business before your bedtime. Plus it is easier to make frequent checks on the puppies during the daytime.

While most puppies quiet down and are happily nursing on Mum even before the last puppy in the litter has been banded, an occasional litter is encountered in which all of the puppies will fuss and fret at great length. The puppies' crying and constant restless motion around the box is wearing on the puppies and trying on the dam as well as her owner. There is good reason to believe this hypersensitive reaction to tail banding is correlated with a vitamin A deficiency in the puppies. The deficiency results either from a primary deficiency of the vitamin in the dam's diet; from factors in the diet causing rapid oxidation of vitamin A; or through metabolic disturbances resulting from a lack of essential fatty acids in the dam's diet. Any of a number of good vitamin drops prepared for infants can be used at a drop per puppy per day to boost the vitamin A level in affected puppies. The addition of fatty acid—containing supplements (corn oil, safflower oil) and foods rich in vitamin A (liver, carrots and parsley) to the dam's diet during pregnancy and lactation should prevent the deficiency from occurring.

Have a fresh supply of elastic bands on hand. Old rubber bands will snap in two with aggravating frequency just as you are tying the knot. Use a band that is approximately $\frac{1}{16}$ of an inch wide and long enough to handle easily, about two inches. The width of the band is important, as it is the extremely narrow area of pressure on the tail that makes this docking procedure work so well.

246

The tail banding and dewclaw removal operation should be carried out well away from the bitch. If it is a large litter, it works well to take two puppies away from the dam at a time, keeping them warm in a box with a hot water bottle, and exchanging them for two more when they are ready to be returned to Mum. A small litter can be done quickly while Mum is out in the garden, oblivious to your activities.

Surgical Docking

The following explicit description of surgical tail docking was published in the PWCCA *Newsletter* (March, 1967). If your veterinarian has not had considerable experience with the Pembroke breed he may well appreciate having information on the procedure as written by a fellow practitioner.

The unique demands of the fancy for tail docking in the Corgi requires certain special techniques based on these objectives:
1. Painless and bloodless procedure
2. Prompt and uncomplicated healing
3. Total elimination of any tail "stump," with a nice finish to the rump in the mature dog.

Procedure:

Prepare the base of the tail by shaving with a surgical clipper and swabbing with merthiolate or a good antiseptic. Infiltrate above and below the base of the tail with 2% procaine and 1:100,000 epinephrin for anesthetic and hemostatis. Using a sharp, curved scissors, and by placing the tip of each blade at the immediate junction of the tail with the body of the puppy, holding the scissors almost perpendicular to the puppy, make a slightly crescent-shaped cut through the skin on top of the tail. Similarly, make a cut through the skin above the anus to intersect with the original incision and to provide a somewhat shorter and straighter line of incision. Snip the tail between these two incisions flush with the contour of the rump. Secure the skin with two sutures to provide a neat, smooth closure. Gentle digital pressure over the amputation site for two or three minutes will preclude any oozing of blood.

This procedure, done with aseptic technique and a minimum of trauma will provide a painless expedient for tail docking the Corgi, prompt uncomplicated healing and a symmetrical *widow's peak* effect over the anus in the grown dog.

Removal of Dewclaws

While it is not required by the Standard, Corgi breeders, almost without exception, remove all dewclaws on their puppies at the time of tail docking. Check all puppies for dewclaws on their hind legs as well as on the front legs.

Have the following materials ready before you bring in the puppies:

Thin, curved manicure scissors

Sterilized cotton
70% rubbing alcohol
Coagulant powder or liquid (Nail
Clot) or silver nitrate sticks.

Cover the work area with newspapers and have a box of tissues handy in case a puppy urinates or messes during the banding or dewclaw surgery. Disinfect the scissors thoroughly with a piece of cotton saturated with alcohol. Repeat after each puppy has been done.

Using the same type of rubber band as for the banding, make a tourniquet by tying a piece of rubber band around each front leg just below the elbow. Have your assistant who is holding the puppy push with his thumb against one of the puppy's elbows to force the leg out taut, dewclaw facing up. With the curve of the manicure scissors resting on the leg, snip off the dewclaw. Push back the skin to expose the round, white ball of cartilage that lies beneath the dewclaw. Cut this core of cartilage out to prevent the possible return of a stunted dewclaw. Remove the other dewclaw in the same manner. Leave the tourniquets on for about two minutes. Normally at this point there will not be any bleeding where the dewclaws were removed. If bleeding starts again when the tourniquets are removed, reapply the tourniquets, wipe off the excess blood and quickly put coagulant powder on the wound. Give the coagulant a minute to form a seal, and remove the tourniquet. Obviously you do not want to leave the tourniquet on any longer than absolutely necessary at any point in this procedure.

Dewclaws on the hind legs can just be snipped off without benefit of a tourniquet. These dewclaws are more like skin appendages and are much easier to remove than are front dewclaws.

It is a good practice to trim each puppy's nails at this time, and then trim the nails regularly once or twice a week. Keeping puppies' nails short will prevent the bitch from being scratched by busy little feet during nursing. Proper foot care while puppies are young will help achieve the desired neat, tight foot in the adult.

Weaning

If at all possible, postpone any attempts to wean the litter until after the puppies are twenty-eight days old. If the litter is large and the bitch has little milk, of course you must start weaning earlier.

Clarence Pfaffenberger in his excellent work, *The New Knowledge of Dog Behavior* (Howell Book House, New York, N.Y.) emphasizes the necessity of not subjecting a puppy between the ages of twenty-one to twenty-eight days to any abrupt changes, as it is an extremely critical period in a puppy's development when he needs to feel absolute security. Mr. Pfaffenberger writes:

> At twenty-one days of age the puppy not only can start to learn, but will start whether he is taught or not. This change is so abrupt that whereas the puppy does not see (at least very much) or smell or hear at all on his twentieth day of age, within twenty-four hours he does all of these quite well. Naturally, he needs the security of his mother.

Mr. Pfaffenberger continues:

> This period of twenty-one to twenty-eight days is so strange to the puppy that at no other time in a puppy's life can he become so emotionally upset, nor could such an upset have such a lasting effect upon his social attitudes.

To understand how best to care for your puppies during the three to four week period, consider how the young in the wild, raised in the dark silent warmth of their den, become slowly aware of their environment. First there is the warmth and smell of their mother and litter mates; the perception of motion as the dam comes and goes; and the hearing of the quiet, distant woodland sounds. Only when the young are physically, mentally and emotionally ready to cope with their surrounding environment will they cautiously make brief exploratory ventures away from the security of the den. Then contrast this with what a litter of puppies raised in the family kitchen face as their senses spring to life—bright lights, the clatter of pots and pans, a blaring television or radio, a lot of chatter and coming and going of people. The confusion of family life is ideal when it comes to socializing an older puppy, but not a baby. If your puppies have to be moved out of their first accommodations, put them in their new quarters before or after the critical twenty-one to twenty-eight day period.

Four-week-old puppies are physically quite able to stand and eat from a dish which makes them far easier to wean than younger puppies. They will catch on right away to lapping up milky feeds such as milk mixed with baby cereal. By thickening the milk slightly with the cereal, the puppies are less apt to snort the milk up into their nostrils. Ring salad mold pans make excellent puppy feeding dishes. The food is kept close to the outside edges so that the puppies do not crawl through the food to reach it all.

Suggested Diet and Feeding Schedules

Puppies can be fed milky feeds from one dish, or more if it is a large litter, until they are about seven weeks old. At this point, puppies should be fed separately to discourage squabbling over the food. The meat meals should

A natural bob tail at six months. (The subject is the second from the right in the three-day-old litter photograph.) It is usually necessary to remove surgically any length tail stump. Left undocked the heavy, brushy stump will detract from the overall appearance of the adult.

Phyl

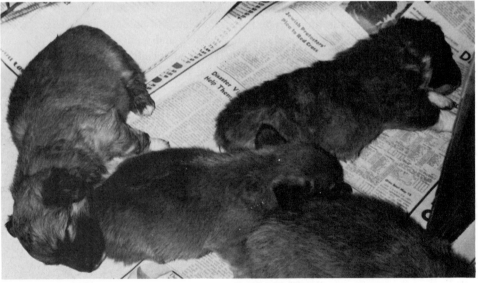

The puppy at the left and the upper right in this four-weeks-old litter already have the overly-long, soft coat of a fluffy. Note the wispy hairs around the ears and on the legs of the fluffy puppies.   *Phyl*

250

always be fed in individual containers to ensure that each puppy gets his full portion.

A suggested feeding schedule is as follows:

4 – 6 weeks: *Morning*—Milk and baby cereal (goat's milk preferred)

Noon—Scraped or minced lean raw beef, 1 to 2 heaping tea-spoonsful

Early evening—Repeat noon feeding

Bedtime—Milky feed.

Start off weaning with one milky feed in the morning and one meat feed later in the day. Build up to the four meal a day schedule by the time the puppies are five weeks old. Reduce the amount of food that is given to the dam and keep her away from the litter for longer periods each day. When the puppies are six weeks old the dam should be visiting them only briefly morning and night. She should be completely dry of milk shortly after and can return to her puppies to get on with her maternal duties of training and disciplining her young.

6 – 8 weeks: *Morning*—Milk and cereal. Cooked oatmeal, Farina, or hard baked (rusked) wholewheat bread can be substituted for baby cereal.

1 raw egg yolk per 4 puppies.

Noon—2–3 oz. lean raw beef cut in small chunks

$\frac{1}{4}$ teaspoonful corn oil

$\frac{1}{2}$ teaspoonful wheat germ

Early evening—Repeat noon meal, omitting the corn oil and wheat germ.

Bedtime—Milky feed.

As the puppies depend less and less on the dam for their supply of essential vitamins and minerals these nutrients must be provided in the basic diet you are feeding. The use of a multi-vitamin–mineral supplement is recommended for all growing puppies. Many breeders are fond of supplementing the diets of puppies with cod liver oil. Not all Corgis can tolerate fish oils in the diet for any period of time. Also because of its high vitamin D content, cod liver oil should be used with caution, especially if used with commercial dog foods which already provide sufficient quantities of the D vitamin.

A vegetable oil high in polyunsaturated fats is used to provide the essential fatty acids which the puppies had been previously obtaining from the bitch's milk. Safflower oil with its high fatty acid concentration is also a good oil to use but a lesser amount should be given than is specified for corn oil. Vitamin E requirements are higher when safflower oil is used, so increase the amount of the daily wheat germ supplement accordingly. Do not substitute hydrogenated oils for the corn or safflower oils.

251

8 – 12 weeks: *Morning*—Milk and cooked cereal. Buttermilk can be substituted for goat's milk.

1 heaping tablespoonful cottage cheese

1 raw egg yolk per 2 puppies 3 or 4 days a week; on alternate days feed $\frac{1}{2}$ to 1 oz. minced raw liver

$\frac{1}{4}$–$\frac{1}{2}$ teaspoonful calcium lactate or calcium gluconate per puppy

Noon—2–3 oz. raw beef chunks. Other meats such as beef heart, tripe or cooked chicken can be gradually introduced.

$\frac{1}{2}$ teaspoonful wheat germ

1 teaspoonful grated raw carrot or chopped parsley. Other vitamin A-rich vegetables such as tomatoes, green beans (cooked) or baked sweet potatoes can be added on occasion.

Early evening—2–3 oz. raw beef chunks. Mix in a small amount of a good quality commercial kibble or dog meal moistened very slightly with warm water. The kibble or meal should not be fed sloppy wet or sticky and pasty.

$\frac{1}{4}$–$\frac{1}{2}$ teaspoonful corn oil

Bedtime—Milk

Unless the puppies are fed a diet entirely composed of commercial dog foods, a calcium supplement should be given to balance the high phosphorus content of the protein supplements. The commercial foods generally contain a high percentage of bone meal and, or calcium additives. If your drinking water has a high calcium content, there is naturally less need to supplement the diet. Otherwise, a supplement of 100 to 200 mgs. of calcium per puppy each day should suffice.

In selecting a commercial food, avoid those which have an unusually high protein and fat level. As a rule Corgis do not tolerate foods which contain large amounts of certain fats or tallow for any length of time.

In following any feeding schedule, allow the puppies some individuality in their eating habits. If ten-week-old puppies toy with their mid-day meal but seem hungry at night, then rearrange the schedule to give a more substantial meal at night while providing a light meal, if any, of milk at noon.

3 – 6 months: *Morning*—Buttermilk and $\frac{1}{2}$ to $\frac{3}{4}$ cup cooked cereal.

Raw egg yolk or 2 oz. liver

Cottage cheese

$\frac{1}{2}$–1 teaspoonful calcium supplement

Noon—Milk

Evening—$\frac{1}{3}$–$\frac{1}{2}$ lb. fresh meat

Approximately $\frac{1}{2}$ cup kibble or meal (measured before soaking in warm water).

$\frac{1}{2}$–1 teaspoonful corn oil

1 teaspoonful wheat germ

Vegetable supplements

Bedtime—Milk feed can be eliminated if desired.

6 – 12 months: Same as for 3–6 months with the elimination of the noon milk feed.

Worming and Vaccination

Virtually all puppies are born with roundworms (ascarids) even though the dam has been checked and cleared just prior to mating. Do not neglect to ask your veterinarian when and how to worm the litter and what immunization program should be followed.

Early Training

The best training a breeder can give a litter of puppies is accomplished by taking the puppies on short, fun walks as soon as the puppies are old enough to go outside, usually at about five weeks of age. At this age the puppies stay close by your feet (usually under them!), as they are too uncertain of themselves to stray off. If you take some older dogs with you their enthusiasm for the walks quickly passes to the puppies and the puppies are soon looking forward to this daily activity. The walks provide excellent opportunities to reinforce a puppy's positive behavior of coming to you. Each time a puppy runs to you either to make sure he has not lost track of you, or because you called him, let him know how pleased you are that he came to you. Show him you love him and that you are enjoying his company. Not only will the puppy never forget that you made him feel extra special for coming to you, but a pattern of rapport and companionship will be established which will remain with the puppy for the rest of his life. To such a dog an open door will signify an invitation to join you, not a temptation to bolt from you.

Another form of early training comes as a matter of course if you start grooming the puppies at an early age. Corgis are independently Welsh! They abhor restraint. Ask any veterinarian who has been the first human being to ever restrain an otherwise docile, well-behaved Corgi when medical attention was required. If a puppy learns to accept physical restraint early, many problems will be avoided later on.

When the puppies are about six weeks old, once or twice a week take each puppy to a room by himself and quietly hold him in your lap or on a table. Gently start combing him with an English fine comb. Keep the first

253

sessions very short, perhaps two minutes or so. Try to stop *before* the puppy starts to squirm to get away. Whatever you do, do not put the puppy down if he struggles to escape. To do so only teaches the puppy forever that all he has to do to get out of any unwanted situation is to scream, growl, bite, flail his legs about, whatever.

If a difficult situation arises, calm the puppy, by rubbing his chest and tummy. At the same time, talk to him as though nothing was wrong, while pretending to still comb him. As soon as the puppy has settled put him down and play a bit with him before returning him to his litter mates. Never let the puppy so much as guess that you did not accomplish exactly what you set out to do. Properly handled, the puppy will soon look forward to. grooming sessions and will even try to cut in on someone else's turn if given a chance. He will have learned there are times when he has to submit to your will, and he will respect you all the more for having that authority.

Evaluating Puppies

From the minute puppies are born the evaluation process begins. It cannot be helped. With each look at a litter, your eyes will gravitate immediately to the particular puppy or puppies who appeal to you the most. As the puppies grow on, you will continue to match the progress of your favorites against the rest of the litter. Many breeders make a point of keeping a puppy whom they find instantly appealing. If you are a lucky gambler, this method of selecting the best puppy will probably work. The best you can do any other way is to make an educated guess, and you still may finish up with a dog whom you dearly love, but who is no show dog. In other words, there are no guarantees.

The first concern in appraising a litter is to determine whether any of the puppies possess shortcomings described in the official Standard (see Chapter 12) as "very serious faults." Puppies with very serious faults are generally sold without registration papers at a considerably lower price than more promising litter mates.

Occasionally the buyer of a puppy with a very serious fault may later decide to enter the dog in obedience or tracking trials. He cannot, however, do so unless the dog is registered with the American Kennel Club. Depending on the nature of the fault, the breeder may agree to provide registration papers upon receipt of proof that the animal has been neutered.

Several very serious faults specified in the Standard involve coat color or coat quality. The color faults, whitelies, mismarks, and usually bluies are obvious at birth. The whitelies (white predominating with red, sable or tricolor markings) and mismarks (more than the acceptable limit of white markings, or white markings in places other than where listed as acceptable by

A normal-coated puppy at five weeks.   *Phyl*

A fluffy puppy at five weeks. Note the long, silky hairs on the forehead and under the forelegs. *Phyl*

Yes, eight-weeks-old fluffies are cute.

Phyl

255

the Standard) are frequently destroyed at birth. If they are part of a large litter, the elimination of the unregistrable puppies alleviates for the bitch some of the strain of raising a big litter. Blues are usually more difficult to detect. A smokey gray cast to the coat accompanied by liver-colored eye rims and nose pigmentation is indicative of the bluie's coloring.

Mature color of the puppies cannot be determined with any certainty at an early age. Tricolors are obviously black, but whether they will be red-headed tris or tris with very pale tan markings may not be apparent for some months. Reds vary tremendously in their development. Some puppies are such a dark brown at birth they appear almost black when they emerge from the sac. These dark puppies can clear to any shade of red or sable, ranging from a pale fawn to a dark, heavily sabled red.

As the puppies grow on, their thick, wooly puppy coats often appear more gray than red. At about three months the adult guard hairs begin to come in, the gray puppy fuzz is shed out and the coat slowly clears to its adult coloring. The color of the new guard hairs growing in at the tip of the docked tail will give a good idea of the puppy's eventual color.

Usually the overly long, soft coat of a fluffy is readily apparent by the time the puppy is five weeks old. By paying close attention to the condition of the hair on newborn puppies, some breeders can detect future fluffies with a fair amount of accuracy. The hair on the skull and back of the neck of a newborn fluffy will appear to be silkier and much shinier than the hair of puppies with acceptable coats. At three to four weeks of age winter puppies or puppies from heavily coated lines will be carrying such heavy coats the entire litter could look as though they were going to be fluffies. If the hair appears stiff rather than soft and silky, and if there is no decided difference in coats between puppies, there is little reason for concern.

Puppies should be checked occasionally for overshot or undershot bites. A grossly overshot bite, sometimes called a "shark mouth," is often apparent at birth. A puppy with a severe, unattractive mouth fault is best put down at birth. This individual would have difficulty nursing, and later eating. He will most likely have serious dental problems as an adult as well.

Before a puppy loses his milk teeth at about five months, he may appear slightly overshot. An allowance of about $\frac{1}{8}$ to $\frac{1}{4}$ of an inch between the inside of the upper baby teeth and the outside of the bottom teeth permits room for the larger permanent teeth to come in with the desired close-fitting scissors bite.

Unfortunately monorchid or cryptorchid puppies cannot be identified early. If both testicles have not fully descended by seven weeks there is reason for concern. Even though missing testicles have shown up in some dogs as late as a year of age, the percentage of puppies who become entire after seven weeks is low. Occasionally a puppy will have a testicle which goes up and

Ch. Cote de Neige Pennysaver celebrated becoming six months old by winning BB at the Longshore-Southport KC under Mrs. Dickie Albin (Hildenmanor). Pennysaver was handled by his breeder-owner, Mrs. Marjorie Butcher. The lower photo shows him as an adult.   *Shafer*

Ch. Cote de Neige Pennysaver, whelped December 13, 1964 (Ch. Stokeplain Fair Chance of Cote de Neige ex Ch. Cote de Neige Penny Wise). The top-winning Pembroke Welsh Corgi in 1966 and 1967, Pennysaver had a total record of five BIS wins, 22 1sts out of 73 Group placings and 118 BBs. He also won two PWCCA Specialties, and is shown winning BIS at the KC of Philadelphia under judge Albert E. Van Court.   *Gilbert*

White head markings are accentuated in young puppies. The wide blaze gradually diminishes as the puppy grows. *Phyl*

At 18 months the marking has narrowed to a pencil-line blaze. *Phyl*

258

down like a yo-yo. This condition usually corrects itself by the time the dog is a year or so old.

Because of the uncertainties involved, a monorchid puppy is usually sold at a reduced price with the understanding that should the second testicle come down, the buyer may have registration papers for the puppy upon payment of the balance of the full purchase price. There need not be any such arrangement for a cryptorchid puppy, as it is not expected that both testicles will descend at a later date.

Ear faults are a problem in that they are generally not apparent until well after a puppy reaches a salable age. If thick, heavy ears are not erect at three months, it may be a good idea to tape them up even though there are doubts as to the actual benefits of taping. Many people believe ears will stand when the physiological conditions are right and not before. This theory is supported with the evidence that very often problem ears will come up on their own after the puppy has completely finished teething at five to six months of age. Favoring early taping, starting at three months, is the concern that the hanging weight of a heavy floppy ear will cause actual structural changes within the ear which make it difficult for the ear to ever stand erect.

There are many ear taping procedures and each breeder seems to have his or her own favorite method. A very simple technique has worked well here in uncomplicated situations. To tape the ears shape each ear into a little devil's horn by gently folding the ear around your index finger and tape into place with a 5 inch long strip of 1½ inch wide Scotch packaging tape or masking tape. Place the tape as far down the ear and close to the head as possible. Free any hairs caught up in the tape that appear to be pulling on the puppy's skin.

Several taping sessions may be necessary. Leave the ears taped for several days. Then remove the tape for a day in between tapings to give the puppy a chance to use his ears on his own, as well as to prevent ear irritations resulting from continual taping.

If it were to come down to selling off every puppy who has some obvious minor faults, you would undoubtedly find yourself with nothing left to run on for showing and breeding.

Instead, select for overall quality. Look for the nicely proportioned puppy with proud, effortless movement, in contrast to the puppy who pounds along, moving as though his legs are wrapped in splints.

Keep in mind the word "moderation" when selecting a puppy. The heaviest-boned puppy is not necessarily the best puppy anymore than is the longest puppy of the lot always a desired length. Refinement in head is essential to maintain the desired foxy look, but neither should a Corgi be so refined that the overall impression is of a toyish dog with a weak, snipey muzzle.

259

Three-weeks-old puppy. The tan markings of the
adult tricolor are light shadings in the young
puppy.   *Phyl*

The same tri male as an adult. The eyebrow markings have become prominent. The black muzzle
markings of the puppy have been replaced by the tan of the typical tricolor pattern.   *Dick Greely*

Miss Anne Biddlecombe has provided some excellent guidelines for selecting the best puppies in a litter in her article, "Champions in Embryo," published in the *1951 Welsh Corgi League Handbook.*

Miss Biddlecombe suggests:

> The mistakes most commonly made by experienced and inexperienced alike, is to hang on to a puppy, hoping against hope, when definitely things have begun to go wrong; and, less often, to discard a puppy unnecessarily when it goes through that awkward age most puppies attain at about four or five months.
>
> Although we generally pick our puppies at three days old, it is really wiser for the novice to wait till they are weaned and wormed, say about eight weeks. The good puppy should by then be beginning to show his points.
>
> He should stand sturdily on thick short legs, with a straight front and his feet forward, a front foot that turns out at this stage nearly always means a bad front later on. Never mind if he is a bit cow-hocked, provided he is not exaggeratedly so, as young puppies seldom stand square behind, and are generally either slightly cow-hocked or slightly barrel-hocked. As the pup grows this should correct itself.
>
> The length of back should be in proportion to height even at this age, and a very short or very long backed puppy can be discarded at once, bearing in mind that a thin puppy will look longer in the back than a fat one.
>
> If the pup's ears are not yet up, a good idea of his future head and expression can be obtained by rolling the puppy over on to his back, the ears will then fall into place.
>
> There should be no tendency to thickness or coarseness in the skull, as this is much more likely to increase rather than decrease as the pup grows older. If, instead of being flat between the ears the skull is slightly domed, this is an advantage, as it will flatten out in time and will ensure plenty of width. A puppy with a domed forehead, i.e. domed immediately above the eyes (apple-headed) can, in general, be discarded, as this will seldom correct itself.
>
> Length of foreface is a bit difficult to judge in a young puppy, one with a long nose can be turned out at once, one with a rather short nose can be kept on till the second dentition, as it may easily grow.

Of eyes and ears, Miss Biddlecombe writes:

> All puppies' eyes are blue when they just open. An eye which is going to be light coloured is a much more clear and intense blue than one which will be darker. The true colour shows first around the pupil and gradually spreads outwards. It should be quite possible by eight or nine weeks to judge the eventual colouring. The size of the ear cannot be judged with safety until later. I prefer a big-eared puppy to a small-eared one, as little triangular cat ears seldom grow enough, and small ears spoil the whole expression.

261

In concluding her article, Miss Biddlecombe writes:

> Generally speaking, in my opinion, the puppies that make into the best dogs in the end are the loose, floppy, slow developers—often unshowable under nine or ten months. There are, of course, exceptions, outstanding ones, but I am convinced that the slow developers are the better in the end.

Selling Puppies

As with other issues, opinion is divided on the best age for selling puppies and sending them off to their new homes. There are now state and interstate regulations which prohibit the sale of puppies under eight weeks of age. Many breeders let puppies leave the kennel at eight weeks of age. Others prefer to hold puppies back until they are at least ten weeks old, preferably twelve weeks. The difference of a few weeks makes a considerable difference in the puppy's emotional development and his ability to cope with new situations. Also, because he is physically more developed, the older puppy has a much easier time complying with the house training rules than he would have had a few weeks earlier.

It is the breeder's responsibility to provide the proper registration papers and an accurate three-generation pedigree when a puppy is sold. Litter registration forms are obtained by sending a request to the American Kennel Club. After the puppies arrive, the litter registration application should be filled out by the owner of the dam and sent to the owner of the stud dog for his or her signature. The completed form is returned to the American Kennel Club with the appropriate fee. The owner of the litter will then receive an individual registration application for each puppy in the litter. It is this blue slip which is transferred to a new owner unless the breeder, himself, applies for the individual registration.

Remember when selling your puppies you are responsible for the fact that your particular puppies even exist. Consequently, you are obligated to see that, to the best of your knowledge, each puppy will go to a home where he will be well loved and well taken care of, and where he will have companionship and security. Never hesitate to refuse a sale if you have any reason to believe a family is not right for the puppy, or vice versa. Families with well-behaved, enjoyable children usually make super Corgi families. However, if the children are ill-mannered and disobedient, you would only be placing a Corgi puppy in jeopardy by subjecting him to the whims of such children. The puppy, too, could become equally unruly and of no credit to the breed if he were to be raised without understanding and discipline.

A little preparation beforehand, on the breeder's part, can make a puppy's transition to a new home ever so much easier for all concerned. Puppies here are crate-trained before they go off with new owners. Thus they are accustomed to spending the night away from their litter mates before they are taken into a totally new environment. Also, because even young puppies are reluctant to mess their sleeping quarters, crate-trained puppies have a head start on their house training.

Starting at eight weeks, our puppies are fed at least one daily meal by themselves in a wire mesh show crate. At night a crate is placed at each end of the puppy pen and, on a rotating basis, two puppies are selected to spend the night in a crate. They can commiserate with their buddies through the wire so do not feel abandoned while becoming accustomed to the crate as their sleeping quarters. As the time nears for the puppies to be leaving, they learn to spend the night quietly in a crate in a room by themselves away from their companions.

We strongly recommend to purchasers of our puppies that they continue to use a show crate (approximately 27″ long x 17″ wide x 22″ high) for the puppy in his new home. The advantages of a crate are many. The presence of a crate will help a puppy feel more secure in his new surroundings and will provide a place to put the puppy when his activity in the house cannot be supervised. In a crate, the puppy does not have to be shut off from the family in the way he would be if he were put in a room with the door closed. The crate is not used just for confining puppies, for crate-trained adult Corgis are a blessing as well. When you entertain or have workmen in the house, it is handy to know your Corgi is in his crate, conveniently out from under foot. There will be no danger of his being let outside by mistake. There are occasions, too, when a dog has to be confined to small quarters to recuperate from perhaps a minor injury or surgery. A crate-trained dog finds this much less of a hardship than does a dog who has not learned to accept confinement.

The Puppy in the New Home

Plan to bring a new puppy into the home when you can concentrate for two or three days on his introductory training. It is far easier to work at establishing desired behavior patterns right at the start than to battle later on to break unpleasant habits.

Obtain a diet schedule from the breeder when you purchase your puppy. If the puppy has been weaned on a food which is not readily available in your locality, ask the breeder to supply you with a small amount of the food to use while making a gradual shift to another brand or type of food.

Also ask the breeder for a list of what vaccines the puppy has had, the dates they were given, the dates of wormings and types of worming medications used. Your veterinarian will want to have this information when you take the puppy in for a routine checkup and any follow-up vaccines he may need.

Give the new puppy a warm welcome to your home and then let him take his time in becoming acquainted with his whole new world. Keep in mind that the new puppy is very much a baby, and like a human infant, he still needs numerous rest periods. Scientific studies have determined that the body produces growth hormones only during sleep periods. This explains why so many times a promising, well-up-to-size puppy will go off so badly when he goes into a busy home where he is kept constantly on the go with little chance to get the sleep a growing puppy requires. Not only is a puppy's growth affected by inadequate rest, but as with the over-tired child, a tired puppy becomes a bratty puppy. Unfortunate behavior, such as nipping and yapping, can become routine if a puppy is encouraged to be a hyperactive play toy.

A Corgi puppy is bright, extremely adaptable and highly impression-able. The personality of your adult Corgi will reflect the care, understanding and training you have given him during his puppyhood. If after meeting your Corgi, friends express a wish to have a dog just like him, you can take satisfaction in knowing that your early training efforts have molded to perfection in your dog the many wonderful personality traits inherent in the Pembroke Welsh Corgi breed.

Am. Can. Ch. Leonine Leprechaun, whelped November 21, 1965, breeder: Mrs. J. Froggatt, owners: Charles Kruger, DVM and Robert Simpson. Peter, a Group winner, is quickly working his way up the listing for top producing sires in this country and has sired 22 champions to date. *Robert*

17

Care of the Adult Corgi

WITH HIS SMALL SIZE and tidy coat, the Corgi is an easy dog to care for and keep in good health.

Feeding

The adult Corgi can do well on the same basic diet he was fed during his puppyhood. The question arises, though, whether it is better to feed one or two meals a day. Many dog owners have found it is easier to maintain a desired weight on both young, active dogs and the older, more sedentary dogs, including spayed bitches, by feeding two meals a day. When a weight gain is desired, the total amount of food fed in a day can be readily increased when split into two meals without causing the intestinal upsets that may occur when just one heavy meal is fed. By feeding the overly ''good-doer'' his total ration for the day in two meals instead of one, the calories contained in a small meal are burned off as usuable energy and are not stored as fat.

With growing information about the interaction between vitamins, minerals and other nutrients in various foods, it makes sense to consider feeding two different types of meals in a day. For example, the phytate found in soy beans is believed to block the absorption of zinc in the small intestine when in the presence of large amounts of calcium. Most of our dry commercial dog foods have a high percentage of calcium, as found in bone meal, and soy products. To counteract the possible interference of zinc absorption in the meal containing a commercial food, the other meal of the day can consist of a cooked cereal and protein supplement. The zinc found in such foods as oatmeal, wheat germ and liver can then be properly absorbed.

265

There are many examples of the interaction between components of foods commonly fed to dogs. The phytate found in wheat bran is known to bind calcium, making the calcium unavailable to the dog's system. Iron interferes with vitamin E utilization. Increased zinc concentrations raise the vitamin A requirement. The list goes on forever and grows as more research is completed.

It becomes apparent if one single food is fed day in and day out, the imbalances within that food, however slight, can have a cumulative effect on the dog. Thus a basic diet providing some variation of protein and vegetable supplements is recommended.

Keep in mind, however, it is totally unwise to jump from one brand of dog food to another. Severe diarrhea usually results from such indiscriminate feeding.

Grooming

The Corgi's grooming requirements are few. A regular once or twice a week combing will usually keep the Corgi's coat in top form. During periods of heavy shedding (and every Corgi seems to have his or her own shedding schedule) more frequent and thorough combings will be needed.

A healthy coat is a naturally clean coat. If a Corgi is receiving a well-balanced diet with sufficient amounts of fatty acids present, his coat will not be at all oily nor too dry. Bathing a Corgi disturbs the natural balance in the skin and only leads to more frequent bathing. If at all possible, complete baths should be avoided. Surface grime can be removed easily by briskly rubbing the dog down with a damp towel. Towelling the dog off after he has been outside on a rainy day will have the same cleansing effect.

The regular grooming sessions should include a quick over-all inspection of the dog for possible problems. Examine the ears for a possible build up of wax and dirt, and teeth should be free of tartar. Check the anal area for a possible skin irritation due to the presence of dried fecal matter. The Corgis' heavy "pants" camouflage any on-going problem in the anal region, and this extremely common problem frequently exists for long periods of time totally unnoticed.

Nail trimming is a must for most Corgis. Corgis exercised on hard pavement may wear their nails down sufficiently and need not have them trimmed. Ideally, nails should be trimmed once a week to keep the quick in the nail well back. Not only are the dogs more comfortable with short nails and their feet more attractive, but inadvertent scratches inflicted by long nails can be avoided. Nails can be trimmed with any of a variety of canine nail clippers, filed with a metal file, or sanded with either a drill with a sanding attachment or with electric clippers outfitted in the same way. If the dog

Eng. Ch. Blands Solomon of Bardrigg, (Eng. Ch. Kathla's Dusky Sparkler of Blands ex Blands Belinda) whelped October 28, 1974, breeder: Mrs. P. Gamble, owners: Mr. and Mrs. W.D. Noall. Solomon won the Leslie Perrins Memorial Trophy in 1976.

Diane Pearce

Can. Ch. Blands Saga (Eng. Ch. Kathla's Dusky Sparkler of Blands ex Kilmarth Christina). Owners: Bill and Joan Kennedy.

Can. Ch. Willoan's Sparticus (Can. Ch. Blands Saga ex Can. Ch. Willoan's Chiquita). Owners: Bill and Joan Kennedy.

proves impossible to cope with during nail trimming sessions, it is better to pay your veterinarian to trim the dog's nails regularly than it is to simply forget the whole business.

Possible Health Problems

The average Corgi is a healthy dog. Relatively few encounter ailments any more serious than a brief intestinal upset resulting from a dietary indiscretion.

There are some conditions which occur in the Corgi with sufficient frequency to warrant being mentioned here, so Corgi owners will be aware of their existence should their dog be having a problem.

The ruptured disc syndrome is perhaps the most common disorder known to occur in Corgis. In this condition, the spongy disc, which acts as a buffer between one bony spinal vertebra and the next, ruptures out of its encasement, so to speak. The pressure of the ruptured disc on the spinal cord causes the animal severe pain, and in extreme cases, the pressure on the spinal cord can cause varying degrees of hindquarter paralysis. Obviously, a veterinarian should be consulted if the dog shows evidence of pain along his back or is walking in a peculiar manner.

Experts used to associate the disc syndrome with long-backed dogs, but since some long-backed breeds have a low incidence of ruptured discs and a number of short-backed breeds are commonly affected, it seems a matter more of individual sensitivity. Most likely there is an inherited bloodline suscepti-bility involved. Ordinary exercise and activities such as climbing stairs or scaling stonewalls will not cause a disc to rupture in a dog who is not already prone to the condition. In a disc-prone dog a disc can rupture when the dog is simply turning around in his crate or rolling over in his sleep. Care should be taken, though, with a dog whose medical history indicates disc problems. He should not be allowed to climb steep stairs or jump over and off furniture, as excess exertion can cause a weakened disc to rupture.

Often, serious complications from a ruptured disc can be avoided if the condition is spotted right away, and in conjunction with veterinary care, the dog is confined to a crate immediately. Knowing that disc syndrome does occur in Corgis, it is wise to be alert to the signs of a possible problem. If a dog shows any reluctance to get up and walk, hangs back on an outing with you, or noticeably hesitates before going up or down stairs (providing he is accustomed to stairs), play it safe and restrict his activity for a few days.

Some Corgis are prone to urinary tract problems. Urine sediment that in more severe cases leads to stone formation can be responsible for recurrent bouts of cystitis or bladder inflamation. Frequent urination, blood in the urine or unsuccessful attempts to urinate call for immediate veterinary attention.

Willoan's Windsong (Can. Ch. Blands Saga ex Willoan's Belinda) was BOS at the 1976 PWCCA Specialty. Note the remarkable similarity of type which Blands Saga passed on to Windsong and her half-brother Sparticus.

Am. Can. Ch. Spartan of Blands of Werwow (Ch. Kathla's Dusky Sparkler ex Swanky Susie of Kyffin), whelped August 27, 1974, breeder: Mrs. Beamish, owner: John Linden. A Junior Warrant holder in England, Ricky has won well on the East Coast with two BIS and multiple Group 1sts.

Most cases of cystitis can be promptly relieved with antibiotic therapy and the administration of urine acidifiers. Dogs who experience recurring bouts of cystitis can generally be maintained on urine acidifiers.

It has been found with some Corgis with a tendency to alkaline urine with accompanying sediment formed in the urine that they respond well to a zinc supplement in the diet. Approximately 5 mg. of elemental zinc a day for an average-sized Corgi will be enough. Vitamin A, approximately 2000 I.U.s daily, has also given good results when used in conjunction with the zinc supplement.

Just at the time of this writing it has been reported to us that a new genetic defect, Von Willebrand's disease, has recently been recognized in Pembroke Welsh Corgis. The disease is an inherited bleeding disorder similar to hemophilia.

Information is not available at this time as to how widespread the condition is, if at all, in the breed. It is mentioned here in order that should breeders encounter any unusual bleeding situations in their stock, they will know to have their dogs tested for Von Willebrand's disease, VWD. Owners of popular stud dogs are urged to have their dogs tested for VWD, as a frequently used, affected stud dog could quickly disseminate the condition throughout the breed.

The Division of Laboratories and Research at the New York State Department of Health in Albany, 12201, is to date the only laboratory in North America doing extensive work with VWD diagnostic assay procedures. W. Jean Dodds, D.V.M., can be contacted at the New York laboratories for additional information about VWD and for special test kits which you or your veterinarian can obtain free of charge.

Routine Health Care

To maintain your Corgi in the best of health, annual visits should be made to the veterinarian to keep your dog up-to-date with his distemper-hepatitis booster vaccines and rabies vaccine where required. In regions where heartworm is known to exist, annual blood checks also should be made to make certain your dog is free of this parasite. At the time of annual boosters, it is advisable to also have a stool sample from the dog checked for the presence of eggs from intestinal parasites. Bitches to be bred should be checked for worms several times before they are due in season. A single negative stool check does not necessarily mean the dog is free of worms, as the worms do not always shed eggs every day. It is important to determine whether or not a bitch has worms. If she does she should be wormed before she is mated.

Exercise

Finally, good care of your Corgi does not consist of feeding a satisfactory diet, periodic grooming, and occasional attention to health care alone. Exercise is paramount to the well-being of any dog. This is an area where a great many dog owners fail badly. Neglect is truly unfortunate, as both dog and owner would benefit not only from the exercise but from the companionship as well.

Am. Mex. Ch. Penrick Most Happy Fella, a sire of four champions and winner of two BIS and five Working Groups 1sts. *Ludwig*

Am. Can. Ch. Mellow de Rover Run, Am. Can. UD, owned by the Douglas Bundocks, pictured at 11 years of age.

Ch. Bundock-Cote de Neige Playboy, a Group winner, owned by the Douglas Bundocks, pictured at 12½ years. *Callea*

18

The Senior Citizen

CORGIS can and often do live to a ripe old age. The average lifespan of the Corgi seems to be between 12 and 13 years. Corgis of 14 and 15 years are not at all uncommon, and occasionally we hear of Corgis still getting about at age 18.

Exercise

Common sense should be your guide in taking care of your aging dog. Exercise should be less strenuous. The length of time an older dog is kept outside in inclement weather, too, should be limited. More care must be taken that an aged dog is thoroughly dried off with a towel after he has been out in the rain or snow.

As your dog begins to lose his sight and his hearing fails, he will need to be accompanied outside for there is a greater risk that he will get in the road or will wander off and not be able to find his way home. Some Corgis really do get quite senile with old age, and these dogs, particularly, need to be supervised outside if they are not enclosed in a fenced yard.

Feeding and Special Supplements

Old dogs generally benefit from several small meals a day rather than one large meal. There is less stress both on the digestive system and on the weakening kidneys with the feeding of small meals. High quality protein foods (chicken, beef, cottage cheese and eggs) in limited amounts with cooked cereals will provide the older dog with essential nutrients while taxing kidney function as little as possible.

Ch. Cote de Neige Derek, bred by Marjorie Butcher and owned in his later years by the Douglas Bundocks. He is shown here at 14½ years of age.   *Phyl*

A young 15-year-old, Ch. Cyclone of Cowfold, one of the foundation dogs of Cappykorns Kennels. He was imported and owned by Margaret Downing.   *Phyl*

Ch. Bowman Benita (Eng. Ch. Bowman Puesedown Passport ex Evancoyd Pride) at 14 years of age, whelped March 21, 1962. Breeder: Mrs. D.J. Cooper, owner: Carolyn C. Bailey. Benita is tied for fourth top producing dam (1935-1977)with eight champions.

Although some experts have questioned the effectiveness of the prescription canned foods available for dogs with kidney problems, many Corgis have benefited from the use of such foods. Your veterinarian can not only supply you with the appropriate prescription diet, but he can also provide you with geriatric vitamin-mineral supplement tablets for your senior citizen. These tablets usually contain some hormones and dessicated thyroid which together will help make up for the diminishing output of an older dog's endocrine glands.

Mild, old age stiffness can be helped considerably with the daily addition of vitamin E to the dog's diet. A 100 I.U. capsule per day will suffice.

Another helpful dietary supplement for aged dogs in the initial stages of nephritis, or loss of kidney function, is sodium ascorbate, the acid-free form of vitamin C. Corgis with early nephritis have responded well to treatment with 200 mgs of sodium ascorbate twice a day. Excessive water drinking and frequent urination, especially during the night, have been markedly reduced in dogs receiving the sodium ascorbate tablets. While the sodium ascorbate seems to slow down the degenerative process in the kidneys, it can in no way be considered a cure. Also, it may not be advisable to give sodium ascorbate to a dog with a heart condition, so check with your veterinarian first.

Morale Boosting

In caring for your aging friend, above all else, do not neglect to spend some time with him just because he no longer makes demands on your time in the way more boisterous young dogs do. A meaningful hug, a quiet pat, a gentle game of ball playing will let your old dog know you still love him every bit as much as you did when you were enjoying his puppyhood antics; the communication will give a boost to his morale and help him stay with you longer still.

Three Counties All-Breed Championship show, 1967, with Mrs. Helen Sheldon (Craythorne) judging. Left: Miss Pat Curties with her Crown Prince daughter, Eng. Ch. Lees Opalsong of Treland. Right: the BB winner, Ch. Hildenmanor Crown Prince with his owner, Mrs. Dickie Albin. Crown Prince won the League's Leslie Perrins Memorial Trophy as Pembroke Welsh Corgi of the Year in 1967.

The winners of the 1969 Welsh Corgi League Championship show: (left to right) Mrs. Kenneth Butler handling Eng. Aust. Ch. Donna Rosa of Rowell of Wey (BB), judge of bitches Mrs. Gladys Rainbow, judge of dogs Miss Patsy Hewan, Mrs. Leila K. Moore handling Eng. Ch. Kaytop Marshall (BOS).   *Lionel Young*

19

Breed Organizations

ALL AROUND THE WORLD, Welsh Corgi fanciers have joined together to form organizations to protect and promote both the Pembroke and the Cardigan. At this point in the Corgi's history, many such organizations exist that actively support all the aspects of Corgi activity covered in the foregoing chapters. Here you will read of many of them and learn how they figure into breed development where they operate.

The Welsh Corgi Club

The first banding together of Corgi enthusiasts was in 1925 when a group of Welshmen in Haverfordwest under the leadership of Capt. J. H. Howell and Capt. Checkland Williams formed the Corgi Club. As described in an earlier chapter, this club, later named the Welsh Corgi Club, was comprised of fanciers of both Cardigan and Pembroke Corgis. The organization, which is active to this day, was the only Corgi club in existence until 1938.

The Welsh Corgi League

Interest in the Corgi soon spread beyond the confines of its Welsh homeland. The breed prospered in England, and gradually Challenge Certificates were offered at many Championship shows. Mrs. Thelma Gray of Rozavel Kennels felt a club should be formed with more accessible headquarters near London, and in June, 1938, the Welsh Corgi League was formed. Over the years it has grown to well over 750 home members. Its world-wide membership, open to all Corgi fanciers, numbered close to 1400 in 1978.

Perhaps the most significant contribution of the League, and one which is appreciated around the globe, is the annual *Welsh Corgi League Handbook*. First published in 1946 with Miss Edith Osborne as the pioneer Editor, the Handbook is distributed free to all members, and it is the model for similar volumes in other countries. It gives pictures and pedigrees of Challenge Certificate winners and overseas titleholders plus numerous kennel ads. The collection of volumes from 1946 on has provided the Corgi world with a permanent record of the breed and its progress.

A major project was the making of the 16 mm, 25-minute color film, *Corgwn Sir Benfro,* said to be the first documentary made by a breed society on either side of the Atlantic. The idea was originated by Miss Anne G. Biddlecombe, Secretary of the League for many years. Miss Biddlecombe thought it would be valuable for people in years to come to see the Corgis of the present day. The well-known BBC personality, Leslie Perrins, then President of the Welsh Corgi League, was instrumental in its preparation.

Each year the League offers a huge number of commemorative cups for wins at Championship and Open shows. The top honor is the Leslie Perrins Memorial Trophy initiated in 1963 for the Pembroke Welsh Corgi of the Year. Two other coveted awards are the Formakin Stud Dog Cup given to the top producing sire of the year, and similarly for the bitches, the Coronet Brood Bitch Cup.

Although the Welsh Corgi Club and the Welsh Corgi League are the main breed organizations in the British Isles, there are smaller groups in existence which usually include both Corgi breeds. A listing of these local clubs is available from the Secretary of the Welsh Corgi League.

The Pembroke Welsh Corgi Club of America, Inc.

It was not long after the arrival of Little Madam with Mrs. Roesler that a group of Pembroke fanciers on this side of the Atlantic were drawn together over their interests in the Corgi. At first, there was a Welsh Corgi Club of both Cardigan and Pembroke fanciers. On February 12, 1936, at the time of the Westminster Kennel Club show, the Pembroke Welsh Corgi Club of America was founded. Although none of those appearing on the original roster are still active in the breed, Derek G. Rayne, now a prominent all-breed judge, joined the PWCCA in 1938 and was listed as a Corgi Club judge in 1939.

A Standard for the breed, only 120 words long, written by the Welsh Corgi Club in 1925, was adopted by the PWCCA and approved by the American Kennel Club in March, 1936. In 1951 the PWCCA went to a slight variation of the 1934 English Standard for the Pembroke Welsh Corgi. For over fifty years this document stood as the official yardstick of the breed. After a careful and thorough revision by the Club, the current Standard for

Eng. Ch. Caswell Duskie Knight, winner of the Welsh Corgi League's Formakin Stud Dog Cup for six successive years, runner-up in 1972, and again winner of the cup in 1973. Sire of 11 English champions and at least six overseas champions. His show record included 38 C.C.s and 21 Reserve C.C.s. He was Pembroke Welsh Corgi of the Year in 1965 and 1970.

Diane Pearce

Eng. Ch. Evancoyd Audacious, heavily line-bred on Duskie Knight, won 18 C.C.s. Sire of Eng. Ch. Dream Girl of Evancoyd, who won 15 C.C.s and was top-winning bitch for 1975 and 1976. Breeder-owner: Mrs. Beryl Thompson.

Fall

279

Pembroke Welsh Corgis in the United States was approved by the AKC on June 13, 1972.

Annual meetings have been held when exhibitors gathered for the Westminster show. Early PWCCA minutes tell of a hiatus of club activities during the war which was ended in 1946 by a meeting ". . . in the center of the Madison Square Garden arena which was practically deserted due to the postpon[e]ment of the show because of the brownout. During the meeting the arena lights were extinguished which caused a hasty adjournment after the last items of business were discussed in semi-darkness."

The PWCCA has several publications. In 1961 Mrs. Gladys Orlowski initiated the quarterly *Pembroke Welsh Corgi Newsletter,* which has grown from a mimeographed news sheet to a professionally printed, well-illustrated magazine. An introductive brochure on the breed was prepared in 1968 for the general public. A handbook, *Pembroke Welsh Corgis in America,* was originally edited by Mr. and Mrs. Ronald Shakely, with yearly supplements now ably compiled by Mrs. Friend Kierstead. In 1975 the booklet, *An Illustrated Study of the Pembroke Welsh Corgi Standard,* was completed and distributed to Corgi fanciers throughout the world as well as to all approved judges of the breed in the United States.

The highlight of the PWCCA year is the Annual Specialty show. Exhibitors gather from all across the country and from Canada to compete and socialize. In 1977 a record 262 dogs were entered. The Sweepstakes, a popular feature for Corgis between six and 18 months of age, has had as many as 101 youngsters exhibited.

PWCCA Affiliate Clubs

Application to the PWCCA is through a sponsorship system. The number of members has always been relatively small, reaching the 250 mark in the mid 1970s. However, representing various parts of the country, there are four affiliate clubs plus a host of forming clubs each with an enthusiastic following.

The Golden Gate Pembroke Welsh Corgi Fanciers, Inc., was founded late in 1956 in the San Francisco area, and has always been a forward moving group. It held the first independent Pembroke Welsh Corgi Specialty in the country in 1963 attracting a large entry of 79 for judge Miss Pat Curties. GGPWCF was also the first Corgi club to issue a newsletter, which was launched by Mrs. Gladys Bundock in 1959. Five years after the club's formation a 148-page handbook became the first American publication of its kind. In 1967 a second, double-sized handbook followed.

By the 1960s there was a sufficient increase in Corgis in Southern California to warrant the formation of a second regional club, and the Pembroke Welsh Corgi Club of Southern California, Inc., came into being.

A highly coveted trophy at the Southern California Specialty is the Pembroke Seal of Excellence given to Best of Winners. This special award by the County Council of Pembrokeshire, Wales, is a plaque with the Pembroke County Coat of Arms, and was arranged for by Mr. Lee Pitt.

Another unique feature of the Southern California Club is a tree with branches of copper on which engraved medallions of the Club's obedience degree winners are hung.

California has not been the only area of burgeoning Corgi activity. In the Midwest, on July 10, 1965, Pembroke fanciers met for dinner and agreed a local club was desirable. The club they formed eventually became known as the Lakeshore Pembroke Welsh Corgi Club, Inc. The first issue of *Corgi Capers*, the LPWCC quarterly newsletter, was published in 1966.

The year 1970 marked the holding of the first Lakeshore Specialty show. This popular event, which boasted an entry of over 100, was topped by Ch. Cormanby Cadenza. Cadenza set an unequalled record by winning the same honor for three straight years.

In the Northwestern corner of the United States the fourth PWCCA Affiliate Club took root during the late 1960s and became the Cascade Pembroke Welsh Corgi Club, Inc. This club has a particularly active number of obedience trainers in its membership. It is the first and only club to date to hold an annual tracking trial exclusively for Pembroke Welsh Corgis.

Although not yet affiliated with the Parent Club, several newer groups deserve mention. The Pembroke Welsh Corgi Club of the Potomac services Corgi fanciers in the Mid-Atlantic states and has already held two successful Specialty shows. The North Texas Pembroke Welsh Corgi Club, a New England aggregate tentatively called the Mayflower Pembroke Welsh Corgi Club, and the Southeast Pembroke Welsh Corgi Club are in various stages of development. Hopefully, these regional clubs will continue to prosper and proliferate as the breed itself gains strength in various sections of the country.

Pembroke Welsh Corgi Association (Canada)

The first Pembroke Welsh Corgis crossed the seas and a great land beyond to find themselves in Sundance, Alberta, in 1932. The breed remained relatively scarce, however, for years despite several enthusiastic exhibitors and a growing number of breeders across Canada. Finally, in November, 1966, the Pembroke Welsh Corgi Association (Canada) was inaugurated in the Vancouver/Victoria area of British Columbia. The PWCA newsletter, now named the *Corgi Courier,* started publication two years later.

Membership in the PWCA increased across Canada until in 1972 the Association was divided into several sections. There are two sections in British Columbia—The B.C. Mainland Section and the Vancouver Islands

A photograph of Mrs. Margery Renner's painting depicting the 1965 PWCCA
Puppy Match held at Willow Farm Kennels with Mrs. Dickie Albin judging.
Courtesy of Mrs. C.W. Van Beynum

Ch. Cote de Neige Rush Hour, winner of the 1965 PWCCA puppy match. Rush
Hour, daughter of Ch. Cote de Neige Christmas Rush (7th Top Producing Dam)
was herself a dam of six champions. Breeder: Mrs. Marjorie Butcher. Owners:
Mr. and Mrs. Neil H. McLain.   *Mrs. Mallory Parker*

and the Islands Section. Moving east, there are the Southern Alberta Section, the Manitoba/Saskatchewan/Northern Ontario Section, the Ontario/Quebec Section and the Maritimes Area. During 1977 three Specialty shows were held.

Australia

On the other side of the world, at about the same time Corgis first appeared in North America, the first Pembrokes reached Australian soil. In 1934 in the state of Victoria a nucleus of Corgi interest grew and eventually pressed north into New South Wales. Presently there are Corgi associations in almost every state. These associations are for both Cardigan and Pembroke fanciers.

The Welsh Corgi Club of New South Wales is the oldest Australian club, as it was founded on May 29, 1950, in Sydney. The great popularity of the breed in this state is reflected in the tremendous number of Corgis at the club's Championship shows. A total of 369 entries (including 88 Cardigans) was reached in 1969.

Other, more regional clubs, are active in New South Wales. These are the Illawarra Welsh Corgi Club, the Newcastle and Northern Welsh Corgi Club, and the Welsh Corgi Club of Canberra. In 1969 the first handbook, *The Welsh Corgi in Australia,* was prepared and underwritten by the Welsh Corgi Club of New South Wales in cooperation with the other Australian clubs.

The Welsh Corgi Club of Victoria was formed in 1953. The number of Corgis in that state soon was sufficient to top the entries at the Royal Melbourne show. Western Australia, South Australia, Queensland and Tasmania all have active Corgi clubs, although Corgi populations are not as large as in New South Wales and Victoria. A complete listing of these clubs appears in the 1974 edition of *The Welsh Corgi,* by Charles Lister-Kaye, edited by Mrs. Dickie Albin (Arco Publishing Company, Inc., New York.)

New Zealand Clubs

Across the Tasman Sea in New Zealand Pembroke Welsh Corgis began to arrive from England in the late 1930s. Pembroke Corgi fanciers in the Auckland vicinity of North Island inaugurated the Dominion Welsh Corgi League in 1951. With the importation of the first Cardigan in 1953, the League embraced both breeds. Now there are three Specialist clubs in New Zealand. The Dominion Welsh Corgi League, Inc., serves North Island and the Auckland area. The South Island Welsh Corgi League, Inc., is self explanatory; and the newest, the Central Welsh Corgi League operates around Wellington. *The New Zealand Welsh Corgi Handbook* is published yearly. All three clubs hold Championship shows.

South African Clubs

The Corgi followed the British Empire to South Africa. There three clubs flourish. Established in the southern section is the Cape Welsh Corgi Club, to the north is the Welsh Corgi Club of the Transvaal, and the Natal Welsh Corgi Club serves its region. The Welsh Corgi Club of Rhodesia is also an active organization.

Clubs in Continental Europe

Considering the relatively short distance from the original source, it is interesting that Welsh Corgis have not been quicker to gain popularity in continental Europe. In Holland, Dutch owners returning from England with their dogs after the war began the influx of Corgis there. In 1950 the Nederlandse Welsh Corgi Club was established.

Corgis were rare in Sweden before 1953. It was not until 1963 that the Swedish Welsh Corgi Club was founded at the suggestion of Per Erik Wallin. The Pembroke Welsh Corgi is still relatively uncommon in Sweden, but the ratio of dogs shown to dogs registered is high, and the Swedish Club now has drawn over 250 members. One special feature is the annual *Corgi Walk* around the parks of Stockholm, where fifty Corgis running loose attract much attention.

Corgis did not appear in Norway until about 1950. Yorken Gallant Knight arrived in 1967 and his spectacular show career helped the breed make strong gains. Corgi popularity has grown steadily stabilizing at 110 to 120 registrations per year. The Norsk Welsh Corgi Klubb was founded in Oslo in 1971. Membership now numbers over 200. Each year a Championship show with approximately fifty entries is judged by an English specialist.

There are other Corgi clubs which have formed or are forming in Europe. The Finnish Welsh Corgi Club is active and holds its own Championship show. A club in Switzerland is thriving. Certainly Pembroke Corgis have been imported into Germany, Italy and elsewhere.

As it is impossible to provide an address for each organization which would not become obsolete quickly, we recommend contacting the national kennel club in each country for direction to their Welsh Corgi club. Most of these associations are for both Pembrokes and Cardigans.

Bibliography of Selected Reading

Books (Some of these books are out of print)

Albin, Dickie, *The Family Welsh Corgi*. A Popular Dogs Handbook. London: Popular Dogs Publishing Co., 1970, 126 pp. (paperback)

Albin, Dickie, Editor, *Corgi Tales*. Margate: Thanet Press, 1976, 113 pp. (paperback)

Chance, Michael, *Our Princesses and Their Dogs*. London: John Murray, 1936, 60 pp.

Elias, Esther, *Profile of Glindy, A Welsh Corgi*. North Quincy, Mass.: The Christopher Publishing House, 1976, 128 pp.

Evans, Thelma, *The Welsh Corgi*. London: Watmoughs, Ltd., 1934, 89 pp. (out of print in 1939, later revised and enlarged by Thelma E. Gray)

Forsyth-Forrest, Evelyn, *Welsh Corgis*. Edited by S. M. Lampson. London: Ernest Benn, Ltd., 1955, 128 pp. (also A. S. Barnes & Co., New York; Wyman & Sons, London)

Gray, Thelma, *The Corgi*. London: W. & R. Chambers, Ltd., 1952, 60 pp.

Gray, Thelma, *The Welsh Corgi*. London: Watmoughs, Ltd., 1936, 226 pp. and 1946, 245 pp. (revision of earlier work by Thelma Evans)

Guillot, Rene, *Little Dog Lost*. New York: Lothrop, Lee & Shepard Co., 1970, 64 pp.

Haight, Mrs. Robert W., Editor, *Welsh Corgies, A Guide to the Training, Care and Breeding of Welsh Corgies*. Jersey City, N.J.: T.F.H. Publications, Inc., 1956, 24 pp. (paperback)

Hubbard, Clifford L. B., *The Pembrokeshire Corgi*. The Dog Lover's Library. London: Nicholson & Watson, 1952, 126 pp.

Johns, Rowland, Editor, *Our Friend the Welsh Corgi, Pembroke and Cardigan*. London: Methues & Co., Ltd., 1948, 1951, 96 pp.; Second edition—1954, 1960, 103 pp.

Lister-Kaye, Charles, *The Popular Welsh Corgi*. London: Popular Dogs Publishing Co., Ltd., 1954, 1956, 1959, 1961, 1965, 224 pp. (In 1968 it was revised and enlarged by Dickie Albin, with a 7th edition in 1970 of 235 pp., and the volume was re-titled *The Welsh Corgi*. An 8th edition was printed in 1974, 237 pp.)

Lister-Kaye, Charles, *Welsh Corgis*. A Foyles handbook. London: W. & G. Foyle, Ltd., 1957, 1958, 1961, 1964, 1966, 87 pp. (Revised by Mario Migliorini, now published by Arco Publishing Co., Inc., New York, 1971, 90 pp.)

Niccoli, Ria, *How to Raise and Train a Pembroke Welsh Corgi*. Jersey City, N.J.: T.F.H. Publications, Inc., 1964, 64 pp. (paperback)

Osborne, Margaret, *Know Your Welsh Corgi*. New York: The Pet Library, Ltd., 1970, 64 pp. (paperback)

Perrins, Leslie, *The Welsh Corgi*. (Also titled *Keeping a Corgi*.) Middleburg, Va.: Denlinger's, 1958, 131 pp. (printed by Wyman & Sons, Ltd., London)

Tudor, Tasha, *Corgiville Fair*. New York: Thomas Y. Crowell Co., 1971, 47 pp.

An Illustrated Study of the Pembroke Welsh Corgi Standard. The Pembroke Welsh Corgi Club of America, Inc., 1975, 32 pp.

Handbooks (available from the clubs which publish them)

The Welsh Corgi League, *The Welsh Corgi League Handbook*. Margate: Thanet Press, 1946 and yearly thereafter.

Pembroke Welsh Corgi Club of America, Inc., *Corgis in America*. Edited by Ronald H. Shakely, 1970, 1971. *Pembroke Welsh Corgis in America*. Edited by Caroline Kierstead, 1972–1978.

New Zealand Welsh Corgi Handbook. Various Editors and years.

The Welsh Corgi Club of New South Wales, *Handbook—The Welsh Corgi in Australia*. Various Editors and years.

Golden Gate Pembroke Welsh Corgi Fanciers, Inc., *Handbook*. Phyllis Young, Editor, 1962, 148 pp.

Golden Gate Pembroke Welsh Corgi Fanciers, Inc., *10th Anniversary Handbook*. Phyllis Young, Editor, 1967, 300 pp.

Newsletters (Information on club publications available through the Secretaries.)

The Welsh Corgi League—England: *Our Corgi World*. (semi-annual, mimeographed, 8–10 pages, articles)

Am. Can. Ch. Halmor Hi-Fi, whelped December 6, 1959, breeder-owner: Mrs. E. Pimlott. He was a Junior Warrant winner in England and Best of Breed at the 1963 PWCA Specialty.

Cammar

Best in Show winner Am. Can. Ch. Suzyque's Southern Snowbear (sitting), with his sire, Mister Showshoes, whelped August 8, 1976, breeders-owners: Henry and Judy Florsheim. *Callea*

Ch. Bear Acres Two for the Road, a Hi-Fi son and sire of Ch. Bear Acres Mister Snowshoes, UD. Owner: Mrs. Stanley Bear. *Henry*

Pembroke Welsh Corgi Club of America, Inc.—U.S.A.: *Pembroke Welsh Corgi Newsletter*. (quarterly offset magazine, 30–60 pages, articles and pictures)

The Pembroke Welsh Corgi Assóciation—Canada: *The Corgi Courier*. (quarterly offset magazine, 20–30 pages, articles and pictures)

Golden Gate Pembroke Welsh Corgi Fanciers, Inc.—Northern California: *Corgi Tracks*. (monthly offset magazine, 20–30 pages, articles and pictures)

Pembroke Welsh Corgi Club of Southern California, Inc.: *The Guardian*. (bi-monthly, mimeographed,8–10 pages, articles, some pictures)

Lakeshore Pembroke Welsh Corgi Club, Inc.—Great Lakes area: *Corgi Capers*. (quarterly offset magazine, 15–20 pages, articles and some pictures)

Cascade Pembroke Welsh Corgi Club, Inc.—Pacific Northwest: *Corgi Clan Tales*. (mimeographed, 6–8 pages, articles)

Pembroke Welsh Corgi Club of the Potomac—Mid-Atlantic states: *The Tide*. (bi-monthly offset magazine, 10–15 pages, articles and some pictures)

North Texas Pembroke Welsh Corgi Fanciers: *The Review*. (monthly offset, 12–16 pages, articles and some pictures)

Many clubs in other countries have similar newsletters. For information, contact the Kennel Club of that country.

Brochures

Golden Gate Pembroke Welsh Corgi Fanciers, Inc., *Pembroke Welsh Corgi Puppy Brochure,* 8 pp. and *The Welsh Corgi,* 4 pp. (both illustrated)

Pembroke Welsh Corgi Club of America, Inc., *An Introduction to the Pembroke Welsh Corgi,* 8 pp. (illustrated)